EMPIRE AND IDENTITY

AN EIGHTEENTH-CENTURY SOURCEBOOK

Edited by
Stephen H. Gregg

First published in 2005 by
PALGRAVE MACMILLAN
Houndmills, Basingstoke, Hampshire RG21 6XS and
175 Fifth Avenue, New York, N.Y. 10010
Companies and representatives throughout the world.

PALGRAVE MACMILLAN is the global academic imprint of the Palgrave
Macmillan division of St. Martin's Press, LLC and of Palgrave Macmillan Ltd.
Macmillan® is a registered trademark in the United States, United Kingdom
and other countries. Palgrave is a registered trademark in the European
Union and other countries.

ISBN-13: 978–1–4039–2140–6 hardback
ISBN-10: 1–4039–2140–7   hardback
ISBN-13: 978–1–4039–2141–3 paperback
ISBN-10: 1–4039–2141–5   paperback

This book is printed on paper suitable for recycling and made from fully
managed and sustained forest sources.

A catalogue record for this book is available from the British Library.

Library of Congress Cataloging-in-Publication Data

Empire and identity : an eighteenth-century sourcebook / edited by Stephen
H. Gregg.
   p. cm.
Includes bibliographical references (p.).
ISBN 1–4039–2140–7 (cloth) – ISBN 1–4039–2141–5 (paper)
   1. Great Britain – Colonies – History – 18th century – Sources. 2. Great
Britain – Foreign relations – 18th century – Sources. 3. Imperialism –
History – 18th century – Sources. I. Gregg, Stephen H., 1960–

DA16.E43 2005
909'.097124107—dc22   2005050396

10 9 8 7 6 5 4 3 2 1
14 13 12 11 10 09 08 07 06 05

Printed in China.

For Nicky

SUFFOLK COUNTY COUNCIL	
06736521	
Bertrams	29.10.05
820.8005	£16.99
641132	

Contents

Contents by Theme

Looking to the Orient

The Pacific

Markers of Difference

The Black Atlantic

Gender and Sexuality

Preface

This anthology was inspired by the reaction of my undergraduate students to a course on the literature of empire and colonialism in the eighteenth century. They were intrigued by the sheer diversity of writings on the colonies and empire of Britain beyond the canonical literary texts (*Robinson Crusoe* or *Oroonoko*, for example) and, importantly, excited by eighteenth-century voices that challenged easy or clear-cut binaries of 'self' and other' and voices that dissented from triumphal imperialism. I soon realised that I needed to make available a diverse range of eighteenth-century texts – including the non-canonical or non-literary – that were otherwise difficult for the student to access in one volume. Of course, such an anthology could only be an introductory resource, but it is hoped that *Empire and Identity* will inspire students to dig deeper in the 'cultures of empire' in the eighteenth century (see 'Further Reading' at the end of this book).[1] In a similar spirit, the introduction sets out the basic terrain of the concepts of 'identity' and 'empire' and offers an overview of the historical-geographical aspects of empire in the eighteenth century. It also briefly exemplifies, with suggestive rather than definitive readings, the critical concerns over cultural difference, gender and the subaltern voice.

The texts chosen to make up this anthology are aimed at introducing to students two related aspects of the British empire in the eighteenth century. The first aim is to allow a glimpse of the huge range of material that touched upon empire and colonialism in the eighteenth century and the differing opinions concerning the character and effect of imperial dominion. The concomitant to imperial expansion in this period was contact with non-European peoples. The second aim of this anthology, therefore, is to reveal how identity in such imperial encounters was debated and represented.

---

[1]   The phrase is Catherine Hall's: 'Introduction: thinking the postcolonial, thinking the empire', *Cultures of Empire: Colonizers in Britain and the Empire in the Nineteenth and Twentieth Centuries*, ed. Catherine Hall (Manchester University Press, 2000), pp. 1–33 (p. 16).

This anthology concerns the languages and culture of empire circulating amongst the people of the British metropolitan centres; therefore, only texts published in Britain were considered (a decision also influenced by concerns of space). To avoid reproducing only the hegemonic ideology of the metropolitan elite this anthology includes voices that cast doubt over the effects of imperial expansion and those that contest the dominant ideologies of empire and nation.

Some notes on terminology. While it is my contention that questions of identity flow from empire, the term 'identity', as we shall see, is used in a way that points up the difference between eighteenth-century assessments of human identity and difference and our own modern notions of individualistic interiority. 'Empire' is, of course, a loose term encompassing a range of very different types of overseas involvement . The texts chosen are representative of the main geographical areas of British overseas interest (the Atlantic, the Mediterranean, the East Indies, the South Seas) and the diversity of these 'imperial' projects. Yet this anthology enables connections to be made across these different projects as well as retaining a sense of their different character.

The focus of this anthology inevitably raises two related aspects of empire in the eighteenth century: first, the forging of 'Great Britain'; second, the slave trade and the debates of abolitionism. The latter has been well served recently, so this anthology does not explicitly address this. As to the former, while the project of empire in the eighteenth century undoubtedly played a significant role in shaping British national identity, it was only one of many constitutive elements. It is not, therefore, the making of British (or English) national identity that primarily concerns this book, but rather the various ways of assessing identity during the encounter with non-European peoples. The texts also testify to the pressures put on the meaning of 'Britishness' and 'Englishness' by the exercise of imperialism. Moreover, 'identity' cannot be subsumed under the term 'national' for, as we shall see, identity in the eighteenth century was assessed according to complex negotiations between multiple reference points.

For the purposes of this anthology 'the eighteenth century' is the period from the Glorious Revolution (1689) to the French Revolution (1789). Choosing the years at which to start and stop the selection has been partly pragmatic: a longer period would have meant a reduction in the diversity of texts on show; a shorter period would have meant omitting some important texts and topics. However, it is also the case that significant cultural, historical and epistemological changes support this periodisation. Arguably, 1689 saw a new constitutional framework for the English government, and a renewed emphasis upon Protestantism and 'liberty' (both of which impacted upon the character of English relations with its colonies and with non-European peoples). The end point reflects the considerable support for the view that there was a paradigm shift inaugurating a more recognisably 'modern' conceptualisation of identity by the closing years of the eighteenth century. Of course, we cannot say such a crucial change took place in this year or that; it was, however, roughly concurrent with major changes to the British empire (crucially, the loss of the American colonies in 1783), the French Revolution (from 1789), and the crucial moments of the British Romantic period (Coleridge and Wordsworth's *Lyrical Ballads* was published in 1798). It made sense, therefore, for the reader to stop at the leading edge of this paradigm shift in thinking about 'empire' and 'identity'.

Acknowledgements

Thanks to the staff at the British Library and at the Brotherton Library, University of Leeds. I am grateful to Edge Hill College of Higher Education, and Gill Davies in particular, for enabling time and funds to be found to help the completion of this book. I warmly thank Julie Proud for some very labour-intensive work, Margaret Forsyth for her painstaking attention to minute detail, and Sonya Barker and Kate Wallis at Palgrave Macmillan for all their help.

The idea for this anthology developed parallel to an undergraduate course entitled 'Imperial Encounters', so my thanks to the students who first attended this course for their ideas. A book like this, which aims to present a vast breadth of material, depends, to a large extent, upon the inheritance of previous scholarship. My own path through the maze of the British empire in the eighteenth century, is indebted to the work of previous academics and editors too numerous to acknowledge individually.

One of the perks of writing a book is to seek and receive help in the form of numerous conversations and small gifts of knowledge: so I thank Elizabeth Bohls, Brycchan Carey, George Haggerty, John McLeod, Robert Sheppard, John Simons and Kathleen Wilson. I am particularly grateful to people who generously read and commented on sections of the anthology in draft form: Srinivas Aravamudan, David Fairer, Felicity Nussbaum, Gurion Taussig, and the anonymous readers.

Finally, this book would have been a vastly inferior creation without the encouragement and support of one person in particular; so my love goes to Nicky Chatten, my most trenchant critic and my loving companion.

Note on Texts

The texts here are a select few from the outpourings of the eighteenth century on the subject of empire. While a number of complete texts are included, to enable a breadth of coverage inevitably many texts are represented by excerpts: I have provided head-notes to focus major issues, enabling each piece to be read in context. Generally, novels or multi-book poems have not been excerpted, since this does no justice to the sense or scope of such texts.

Unless where indicated, first editions have been used as copy texts. To preserve the historical feel of these texts, spelling, punctuation, capitalisation and italicisation have not been modernised. There are a few exceptions: a small number of archaic spellings have been modernised to avoid ambiguity, as has the eighteenth century 'ʃ'; the eighteenth-century practice of using quotation marks at the beginning of every line to indicate speech or quotation has been modernised; the various ways of indicating notes has also been replaced by modern footnote annotation (the authors' original notes are included). A very few silent corrections have been made: this is where they are consistent with the author's own practice in same text; or where they have been collated by using either published errata or later editions; or obvious misprints.

Introduction

Empire and Identity

EMPIRE. *n.f.* [*empire*, French; *imperium*, Latin]
1. Imperial power; supreme dominion; sovereign command.
2. The region over which dominion is extended.

IDENTITY. *n.f.* [*identité*, French; *identitas*, school Latin.]
Sameness; not diversity.

Samuel Johnson, *Dictionary* (1755)

I am no Turk, *but a* Christian.

Joseph Pitts, *A True and Faithful Account
of the Religion and Manners of the Mohammetans* (1704)

I am only a lodger—and hardly that.

Ignatius Sancho, *Letters* (1782)

Imperialism can be defined as 'the extension and expansion of trade and commerce under the protection of political, legal, and military controls'.[1] Yet within Britain's own network of colonies, factories, and outposts of what Burke termed 'this vast, disconnected, infinitely diversified empire', there were different kinds of imperialism.[2] While the plantations of America and the West Indies were formed out of settlement, the displacement of the indigenous population, and the use of imported African slave-labour, the East India Company involved no such colonisation. The Company was scathingly described in 1766 as 'a trading and a fighting Company', revealing its contradictory position as a commercial entity with a private army,

---

[1]   Peter Childs and Patrick Williams, *An Introduction to Post-Colonial Theory* (Harvester Wheatsheaf, 1997), p. 227.

[2]   *A Letter from Edmund Burke, Esq; one of the Representatives in Parliament for the City of Bristol, to John Farr, and John Harris, Esqrs. Sheriffs of that City, on the Affairs of America* (1777), p. 56.

whose increasing belligerence would transform the existing framework of the Mughal Empire.[3] Control over the Mediterranean (involving the outposts of Minorca and Gibraltar) was aimed at the larger strategy of curbing French imperial ambitions. The explorations of the Pacific by James Cook were carried out in the name of science, but he also had orders to annex territory in the name of Britain.

Moreover, the seventeenth century had bequeathed a number of different 'empires' to the eighteenth century. The 'British empire' could mean the aspirations of James I (and his successors) for a sovereign state of England and Scotland, only realised in 1707. Another conceptualisation was of an 'empire of the seas': a loose image of wherever the English Navy was perceived to hold sway. By the eighteenth century, an empire in America was a recognisable concept ('America' often included the English plantations in the Caribbean islands). Only by the second half of the eighteenth century were commentators beginning to conceive of a British empire that encompassed all of the commercial and colonial projects together 'as parts of one whole', in the words of Arthur Young in 1772.[4]

The notion of an 'empire of the seas' was a mytho-poetical (and, as we shall see, ideological) conceptualisation that should alert us to the cultural and representational aspects of the material practices of imperialism. Indeed, the word 'empire' was a historical sedimentation of linguistic meanings, and Samuel Johnson's definitions cited above encompassed two dominant strains of meaning. The first denotes the process of command and the legal authority under which dominion was wielded, a meaning ultimately derived from the *imperium populi Romani* of the Roman Republic. Yet it also connotes a sense of the majesty of sovereignty, deriving from the *Imperium Romanum* under Emperor Augustus (and consecutive emperors). Johnson's second definition encompasses the geographical or territorial extent of this command. The sense of 'empire' handed down to us from the Roman Empire has tended to blend both senses – the geographical area of dominion *and* the authority and rights by which this dominion is carried out. Yet during the eighteenth century – a period of expansion for England's own overseas endeavours – this conceptual obfuscation, exemplified by the phrase 'empire of the seas', was put to the test. The legitimisation of dominion over the regions and outposts of this 'empire' was a fraught ideological battleground.

The British empire in the eighteenth century can easily be taken for granted – an inevitable progression of the rule of Britannia over the seas, a lead-in towards the empire's economic and military supremacy in the

---

3   Jonathan Z. Holwell, *Interesting Historical Events Relative to the Province of Bengal and the Empire of Hindoostan* (1766), quoted in Sudipta Sen, *Distant Sovereignty: National Imperialism and the Origins of British India* (Routledge, 2002), p. xiv.

4   Arthur Young, *Political Essays Concerning the Present State of the British Empire* (1772), quoted in P. J. Marshall, ed., *Oxford History of the British Empire, vol. II*, 'Introduction', p. 4.

nineteenth century and its apogee under the Victorians. What can be forgotten is that, at the time, not everyone viewed Britain's supremacy as at all inevitable. Some were deeply sceptical about the effects or even the desirability of an empire. And more than a few of the most articulate commentators saw, in the encounters between Britons and the peoples they came into contact with, an experience both exhilarating and yet profoundly disturbing. The meanings of 'Britishness' or 'Englishness' were thrown into sharp relief and often transformed by contact with other peoples. As Gayatri Spivak succinctly puts it, 'empire messes with identity'.[5]

'Identity' to many nowadays suggests that sense of an inner self or psychological depth, autonomous individuals whose assessment of their selves is shaped by an identification with categories such as sex, gender, sexuality, nation, ethnicity and perhaps 'race'. But, as Charles Taylor has pointed out, 'it was not always so'.[6] Identity has a history, and ways of conceiving identity or the 'self' have changed over time. In this light, the term 'identity' must be used with an awareness of the difference between our own conceptions of the self and those in the eighteenth century.

In texts that represent or reflect upon the encounter between different cultures, categories such as 'nationalism' or 'race' inevitably come to mind. However, although these concepts of the place and meaning of the individual within larger structures emerged very gradually from the seventeenth to the nineteenth centuries, they gained a dominant momentum only from the closing years of the eighteenth century.[7] These texts, then, address precisely the question of how 'identity' was conceived *before* this point. How is identity imagined before the full flowering of nationalism or race? What questions of identity *flow from* imperial and colonial expansion?

Samuel Johnson's definition of identity, 'sameness, not diversity', suggests a humanistic sense of self that saw people assess themselves as enjoying commonality, as belonging to a community. Certainly, a significant number of the texts in this anthology, written by the intellectual or political elite, seek to construct a homogeneus national community, frequently allied to a sense of national grandeur. In 1740, the son of George II, Prince Frederick, heard the words '*Rule, Britannia, rule the waves;* / Britons *never will be slaves*' for the first time. This brash, confident assertion projected the belief that

---

[5]   Gayatri Chakravorty Spivak, *Outside in the Teaching Machine* (Routledge, 1993), p. 226. Thanks to John McLeod for bringing this quotation to my notice.

[6]   Charles Taylor, *Sources of the Self: The Making of Modernity* (Cambridge University Press, 1989), p. 177. He notes that 'something fundamental changes in the late eighteenth century', p. 390. It is only possible to dismiss the use of identity as anachronistic when applied to the eighteenth century if we limit its sense to a strictly modern conception; see Colin Kidd, *British Identities Before Nationalism: Ethnicity and Nationhood in the Atlantic World, 1600–1800* (Cambridge University Press, 1999), p. 290. For eighteenth-century philosophical debates over the potential instability of 'identity', see also Felicity Nussbaum (1989), Roy Porter and Dror Wahrman in Bibliography.

[7]   See Roxann Wheeler, Dror Wahrman and E.J. Hobsbawm.

liberty and supremacy over the seas were defining characteristics of British identity, and that Britain's national identity was bound up with its empire. Empire was indeed, as Kathleen Wilson notes, 'the means through which national potency could be nurtured and consolidated'.[8] As we shall see, however, such aspirations of national identity were sometimes hedged with doubt or hotly contested.

And how do we think of the individual in relation to these overarching ideas of commonality and community? Social communities are imagined and lived via representations – as in 'Rule Britannia' – so that any communal identity is the 'projection of individual existence into the weft of a collective narrative', as Etienne Balibar has phrased it.[9] However, Raymond Williams makes it clear that the 'personal' should not be conceived as subsumed into the collective or the social: discussions of identity must attempt to analyse 'structures of feeling', the *negotiation* between the individual and emerging collective formations.[10]

Identity as conceived in the eighteenth century was strung between a multiplicity of collective narratives and cultural markers. These cultural coordinates of identity included religion, status, civility and manners, political systems, climate, commerciality, clothing, complexion and gender. Joseph Pitts, a merchant seaman captured by Algerian pirates, offers a vivid sense of one of his own key reference points of identity when he declares to his captors, '*I am no* Turk, *but a* Christian.'

However, such a declaration raises the question: whose collective narrative is this? It points up the limits of identity as commonality and sameness, and emphasises the importance of *difference*. Imperial and colonial expansion in this period generated debates about the nature of the indigenous peoples with whom colonists, merchants, explorers and travellers came into contact or whom they sought to dominate. Constructing and representing 'difference' helped to solidify and reassure certain forms identity by excluding others (as in the case of Christian and 'heathen', or Protestant Britain against Catholic France). It could also authorise imperial dominion by constructing asymmetrical power relations between coloniser and colonised, basing difference upon, for example, differing levels of civility. Identity, then, also relied upon difference and exclusion.

The communal and homogenising narratives of nation, therefore – such as 'Britons', 'Englishness' – need to be set alongside excluded or alternative narratives. In the midst of a letter confidently criticising Britain's handling of the War of American Independence, Ignatius Sancho, born on a slave-ship

---

8   Kathleen Wilson, *The Sense of the People: Politics, Culture and Imperialism in England, 1725–1785* (Cambridge University Press, 1998), pp. 201–2.

9   Etienne Balibar and Immanuel Wallerstein, *Race, Nation, Class: Ambiguous Identities*, trans., Chris Turner (Verso, 1988, 1991), p. 93. See also Benedict Anderson in Bibliography.

10   Raymond Williams, *Marxism and Literature* (Oxford University Press, 1977), pp. 128–35 (p. 132).

and now a shopkeeper in London, suddenly breaks off, 'for my part it's nothing to me—as I am only a lodger—and hardly that'. Whilst Sancho may be deliberately self-deprecating (more of which later), it still bespeaks a sense of exclusion from British civil society. It illustrates the negotiation between lived personal identity and homogenising commonality, and the limits of the claims to a humanistic national or imperial identity based upon 'community'.

Such questions asked of European humanism have been most insistently raised by postcolonial forms of analysis, whose examination of the representation and construction of difference lays bare the workings of imperial and colonial discourse. Postcolonial analyses also pay attention to the *relations* between coloniser and colonised, between metropolitan 'centre' and imperial 'periphery', and suggest that such relations are mutually structuring. Martiniquan psychologist of colonialism, Frantz Fanon, turns on its head the common assumption of imperial dominance when he says 'Europe is literally the creation of the Third World'.[11] Such a perspective can undermine the claims of hegemony made by the imperial centre, whose claims are based upon stability, homogeneity and autonomy. It is this reverberation of mutual dependence between centre and periphery, European and non-European, that underlines a more unstable play of differences and relations. For, if identity is shaped by contact with difference, it can also be transformed by contact.

The effect of travel and migration by the labouring poor, criminals, natural historians, sailors, merchants, military personnel, wives accompanying spouses, travellers, diplomats, visiting indigenous princes, and of course the forced migration of slaves, was to bring eighteenth-century culture face-to-face with questions concerning commonality and difference. It would question the stability and autonomy claimed by a cultural elite attempting to form a homogenous 'national' identity. Such contact took place at the imperial periphery to be sure – America, Africa, the West Indies, India, the Pacific (all represented in this anthology) – but it also took place much nearer home. The 'contact zone', to use Mary Louise Pratt's term, could be extended to include Britain itself – witness Iroquois visiting the Queen; Orientalized nabobs returning to England; Africans, ex-slaves, in London.[12]

Encounters with non-Europeans and the effects of empire at home or abroad were a constant reminder of the *uncertainty* of identity: over the

---

[11] Frantz Fanon, *The Wretched of the Earth*, trans., Constance Farrington, introduction, Jean-Paul Sartre (Penguin, 1967), p. 81. Fanon is speaking in the context of the wealth that has flowed from colonised countries to Europe. In the introduction, Jean-Paul Sartre makes a similar point about the relations of coloniser and colonised and the effect of decolonisation: 'Let us look at ourselves, if we can bear to, and see what is becoming of us. First, we must face that unexpected revelation. The strip-tease of our humanism', p. 21.

[12] Mary Louise Pratt, *Imperial Eyes: Travel Writing and Transculturation* (Routledge, 1992), pp. 6–7.

course of the century, Englishmen captive in Barbary 'Reneg'd' and turned Muslim; American colonists who were encouraged, and indeed often felt themselves, 'to believe *England* their native Soil', by the 1770s had become 'rebels'; British merchants returning home from India were no longer strictly British but 'nabobs', 'tinged by the East'; Englishmen at home were rendered 'effeminate' by imperial consumerism; Britishness and femininity in the West Indies could be altered by the 'effect of climate'; a Tahitian would appear more 'thoroughly *well bred*' than an English gentleman; and a black African living in London could claim a superior sense of 'liberty' than the English around him.[13]

The texts in this anthology reflect upon the enormous transformative pressures put on the cultural coordinates of identity by imperial encounters and by the exercise of imperial governance. Identities such as 'British', 'English' and 'Briton', then, become contestable and unstable. Such mutability of who and what people were, suggests the fragility of identity rather than its solidity: as Stuart Hall comments, 'perhaps instead of thinking of identity as an already accomplished fact ... we should think, instead, of identity as a "production" which is never complete, always in process'.[14]

Ruling the waves

How did Thomson and Mallet come to make such a bold assertion of British identity by 1740? Why were sea-power and liberty so closely connected? Although such connections were made since Oliver Cromwell's 'Western Design' against the Spanish in the 1650s, the Glorious Revolution of 1689 and the accession of William of Orange to the throne signalled a momentous shift in the political and religious foundations of England. The Revolution Settlement ordained that the relationship between Parliament and monarch was to be forever changed: a shift in power meant the beginnings of a constitutional monarchy, for the ministers assumed many powers of executive authority previously exclusive to the monarch, and those ministers, in turn, were dependent upon the Houses of Parliament. In this way, a founding myth of English nationhood was cemented: the nation was an isle peculiarly blessed with political freedom. In the words of political philosopher John Locke, the following year, 'Slavery is so vile and miserable an Estate of Man, ... directly opposite to the generous Temper and Courage of our Nation.'

William's part in the Settlement would be at his coronation to swear on the Bible to protect the nation as a *Protestant* nation (the first time a monarch

---

[13]   See Joseph Pitts; Charles Davenant, and Janet Schaw; Samuel Foote; John Brown; Edward Long; Frances Burney; Ignatius Sancho.

[14]   Stuart Hall, 'Cultural Identity and Diaspora', in Patrick Williams and Laura Chrisman, eds, *Colonial Discourse and Post-Colonial Theory: A Reader* (Harvester Wheatsheaf, 1993), pp. 392–403 (p. 392).

had done so). The ambitions of both government and monarchy were aimed at curbing the perceived dangers of French and Catholic supremacy in Europe; Parliament in particular remembered the links between the English monarchy and Catholicism that had so undermined the English nation under the Stuarts. Ideologically, then, the political elite aspired to bind English national identity with an anti-Catholic Protestantism. This view was given a huge boost by the Union of Scotland and England in 1707 and the creation of Great Britain. It was as if this new nation was Providentially ordained: its topographical separateness, its island-ness, emphasised its unique difference from those across the channel.

If the nation's religious, political and economic character was in flux, the character of the nation's empire was also in process. In particular, it had to face the question of how to square imperial expansion with the preservation of the nation's identification as a 'State, alone, where LIBERTY should live'.[15] The forging of the British empire as a blue-water empire, an 'Empire of the Deep' as James Thomson put it, owed as much to the perceptions of what the empire should *not* be as to what it *should*. Territorial expansion, the conquest of land, had become associated with the ambitions of France and Spain and the quest for a 'Universal Monarchy', perceived by British observers as a tyrannical empire of Catholic and arbitrary monarchical control. Regardless of the fact that all the European empires in the Americas were initially driven by conquest, many traders, colonists and political economists came to mythologise English imperial endeavours in different terms. Indeed, the word 'conquest' would come to be demonised as a marker of other empires: the depredations of the Spanish over the Inca and Aztec civilisations in the Americas serving as an oft-quoted exemplar (Joseph Warton's poem *The Dying Indian* drew upon this idea). The sense of Englishness as enshrining the ideals of freedom dictated that their empire would not be for conquest, land, and gold, but for commerce. And it would be commerce by sea, as Matthew Prior's poem of 1700 on William III makes clear:

> Through various Climes, and to each distant Pole,
> In happy Tides let active Commerce rowl;
> Let *Britain*'s Ships export an Annual Fleece,
> Richer than *Argos* brought to ancient *Greece*,
> Returning Loaden with the shining Stores
> Which lie Profuse on either *India*'s Shores.[16]

The paean to peaceful commerce by sea was an especially literary one: Matthew Prior, Alexander Pope, Edward Young, Richard Glover, James Thomson all waxed lyrical at the seemingly unstoppable success of Britons

---

[15]   James Thomson, *Britannia* (1729) line 195.
[16]   Matthew Prior, *Carmen Seculare for the Year 1700. To the King* (1700), p. 17.

on the 'Ocean of Business'.[17] These poetics of sea-power and liberty would be crystallised most memorably in James Thomson and David Mallet's ode, *Rule Britannia*.

Trade was represented as a mutual interaction of the peoples of the world, uniting to shower their benefits on one another in peaceable transactions. This 'cult of commerce' was bound up with an ideological sleight-of-hand whereby dominion was reconciled with liberty.[18] It would be embodied by such characters as Joseph Addison's 'Sir Andrew Freeport', and George Lillo's 'Thorowgood' who declares that commerce 'promotes Humanity ... by mutual Benefits diffusing mutual Love from Pole to Pole'. This ideology of empire, with small variations, was voiced later in the century by such figures as James Cook, ex-slaves Ignatius Sancho and Ottobah Cugoano, as well as Edmund Burke. In short, Britain came to represent itself and its empire as 'Protestant, commercial, maritime, and free'.[19]

Britain's imperial mission was not only forged in opposition to the French and Spanish, but also to the past. The Roman empire provided an example of an ideal republic, but its decline showed Britons what could go wrong:

> Vain end of human Strength, of human Skill,
> Conquest, and Triumph, and Domain, and Pomp,
> And Ease, and Luxury. O Luxury,
> Bane of elated Life, of affluent States,
> What dreary Change, what Ruin is not thine?

So warned John Dyer in his poem *The Ruins of Rome*, published in the very same year as the confident *Rule Britannia*. The Roman empire had been a beacon of liberty and virtue, then imperial success and economic prosperity was followed by tyranny and luxurious consumerism, then political and moral corruption, and finally decline and ruin. The writings of Charles Davenant and John Brown, and Thomson's *Britannia* all imply that this narrative of empires and nations might apply to Britain. Throughout the eighteenth century, then, the confidence of British nationhood and the virtue of its empire existed alongside a nagging fear that it might repeat the Roman empire's disastrous decline.

The colonists and representatives of the empire in America, the Caribbean and India, especially from the 1760s onwards, were being increasingly perceived to exemplify imperial decline. What happened at the edges of the empire, where cultural margins rubbed against one another, and where the boundaries of identity were tested, did not always bode well.

---

17   Daniel Defoe, *A Plan of the English Commerce* (1728).
18   Linda Colley, *Britons: Forging the Nation 1707–1837* (Pimlico, 1994), p. 56.
19   David Armitage, *The Ideological Origins of the British Empire* (Cambridge University Press, 2000), p. 8.

Atlantic colonies

Could the ideals of Protestantism, commerce and liberty form the basis of an 'imagined political community' – to use Benedict Anderson's term – that encompassed the colonials operating in the thirteen American colonies, or the British islands in the Caribbean?[20] The increasing numbers of people of British descent but born far away from the homeland, posed peculiar problems: were they British? If not, who were they?

The West Indies was an example of both the commercial success that could be had by the empire, and of the luxurious wealth, ignoble manners and barbaric tyranny of the colonist. In 1740, Charles Leslie contrasted the freedom and virtue of Britain with Jamaica, 'A Place not half inhabited, cursed with intestine Broils, where Slavery was established, and the poor toiling Wretches worked in the sultry Heat, and never knew the Sweets of Liberty'.[21] The island itself became a space suffused with the character and (im)morality of slavery, and to many in Britain, the planter-class themselves were infected by their trade. Yet Britons wanted to have their cake of liberty and eat the economic benefits of domination too, so that the inhospitable islands of the Caribbean became a place of disavowal. To some, the Creoles (in this context, descendants of Britons who were both born and living in the West Indies) were degenerate and vaguely un-British, undermining the ideals of British nationhood and empire; to others they exemplified the best spirit of colonialism valiantly maintaining their Britishness in spite of the barbarity all around.[22]

The Creole planter-class were noted for their generosity and vivacity; but even their most vocal supporters, including Edward Long and Janet Schaw, pointed out that this frequently showed itself in extravagance and promiscuity. In an important sense, however, the Creole planters' generosity was, to them, a sign of their civility and, therefore, their proximity to British standards of civilisation. It goes without saying that the planters' supporters also characterised the Creoles' attitude to their slaves as compassionate and humane (in opposition to the perceived barbarity of Africans). Owing to the disproportionately small number of Europeans to blacks in the slave-societies of the Caribbean, Creole identity was intensely bound up with racial difference and was protected by a visual sign: Janet Schaw noticed that Creole women protected their complexions to an extreme; so much so, that she wryly contrasted her 'brown beauty' to their extreme whiteness. The islands also inherited a racial classification from the Spanish which

---

20 Benedict Anderson, *Imagined Communities: Reflections on the Origins and Spread of Nationalism* (Verso, 1983), p. 15. Anderson's phrase is used to indicate the aspirations of transatlantic cultural connections, rather than a full-fledged national identity.

21 Leslie quoted in Kathleen Wilson, *The Island Race: Englishness, Empire and Gender in the Eighteenth Century* (Routledge, 2003), p. 147.

22 'Creole' was a term also used to describe slaves born in the West Indies rather than in Africa.

made minute discriminations between the racial origin and complexion of Negroes, Mulattoes, Quadroons, to name but a few. Citizenship was shaped by race: 'the laws permit all', notes Edward Long, 'that are above three degrees removed in lineal descent from the Negro ancestor, to vote at elections, and enjoy all the privileges and immunities of his majesty's white subjects of the island'. Political freedom, a foundation of Britain's imperial ideal and identity, became inextricably linked to whiteness.

Creole identity, then, was shaped by a performance of civility, humanity and even complexion in opposition to the black slave population, in the hope of maintaining a version of Britishness on the islands. The precarious Britishness of the Creoles suggests a hybrid identity unsure of its foundations; an identity, to borrow Homi Bhabha's phrase, *'almost the same, but not quite'* as those of the imperial homeland.[23]

These questions of identity and imperial ideals erupted in the debates surrounding the War of American Independence (1775–83). The sense of what we might call an 'identity crisis' within the British Atlantic empire was underlined by the repeated reference to the conflict as a 'civil war' (raising the ghost of the national trauma of the seventeenth-century civil war).[24] The other consistent image of the war was of a family torn apart. In John Freeth's lively ballads on the war, countries are imagined as mothers pitted against daughters, and fathers against sons. Janet Schaw, visiting relations in North Carolina, depicted loyalists and revolutionaries locked in fratricide – 'true obedient sons' were being 'insulted by their unlawful brethren'.

To some the colonies were, as the title to Charles Davenant's essay *On the Plantation Trade* hints, more dependent plantations than an empire. As colonies, in the words of George III, they were 'subordinate … to Great Britain', there to be a crucial source of economic and military strength in a larger imperial strategic game to rival the empires of Spain and France.[25] This conception of imperial relations supported some in their views of settlers and American-born colonists as an inferior set of people (confirmed by the disparaged social status of settlers: transported convicts in the late seventeenth and early eighteenth centuries, and the huge emigration of the labouring poor from, for example, Scotland later in the period). From Aphra Behn's portrayal of councillors who have no concept of honour, and Janet Schaw's disdain for lazy planters and vulgar rebels, to Joseph Peart's vicious attack on their transgression of status divisions, this view of imperial relations encouraged representations of American colonists as ill-mannered, dishonourable, fanatical, criminal – in short, as un-British. This

---

23 Homi Bhabha, *The Location of Culture* (Routledge, 1994), p. 89.
24 See Joseph Peart, *A Continuation of Hudibras* (1778).
25 King George III's speech to the opening of Parliament, 26 October 1775. *The Parliamentary Register*, vol. III (1775), p. 1.

subordinate mercantile role for America was pushed to the breaking point when the British government imposed various taxes and duties between 1763 and 1770. These were the catalyst for rioting and war. In the same year America declared independence, Adam Smith radically undercut the ideology of a British empire based on commerce when he argued in his *Wealth of Nations* that, since it brought no profits for Britain, an American empire was merely a 'golden dream'.

Some reached for religion to provide a sense of common identity. The origin of many of the colonies in the emigration of Puritan dissenters in the seventeenth century left them in a peculiar position as regards a community of Protestant identity throughout the Atlantic empire. Both Charles Davenant and Edmund Burke attempted to align religious difference and toleration within an overarching imperial authority, but it was Joseph Peart who voiced the thoughts of many anti-Dissenters. In his pro-government and pro-war satire on the American revolutionaries, they are the direct descendents of the Puritans who fomented the civil war of the seventeenth century against God and King, waiting to again turn the world upside down, to 'throw away the mask' and reveal their true selves.

To some, the settlers and colonists of America were English or British in every political and legal sense. Edmund Burke, for example, sought to emphasise the similarities of English and American identities by appealing to their common inheritance of liberty: 'the people of the Colonies are descendants of Englishmen. ... They are therefore not only devoted to Liberty, but to Liberty according to English ideas, and on English principles.' Liberty, however, proved to be an unstable source of imperial identity. Joseph Peart's poem makes it clear that 'liberty' could be twisted to nefarious ends by the rebellious colonists; it could even undermine order itself: 'Most meaning liberty of using / The name – all order to confuse in'.

Protestantism, commerce and liberty were unable to provide stable foundations of identity to unite the 'imagined political community' of the British Atlantic empire. The colonist was in an ambivalent position, caught in between the realities of imperial dominance (Government over American colonists, or planters over black slaves) and the ideals of British identity, revealing the contradictions within the ideology of empire. The way in which identity in the colonies – the sharp end of empire – was mutated by the project of empire itself was to be repeated in Britain's contact with the East.

Looking to the Orient

Edward Said's *Orientalism* makes it clear that the discourses of the Orient (the array of textual and artistic representations of North Africa and the East, including the fields of scholarship, linguistics, natural sciences, travel writing, philosophy, politics, economics, military history and literature) helped define the West 'as its contrasting image, idea, personality, experience'.[26] The Orient became the imaginary dumping ground for the British empire's unwanted associations; everything that the British empire was not, its *alter ego*.

Britons who had seen at close quarters the Islamic countries of the Turkish empire (for example, Joseph Pitts and Lady Mary Wortley Montagu) and the ethnic groups of India, reproduced a variety of Oriental stereotypes. Jemima Kindersley's *Letters* (1777) includes an account of the Hindus and Muslims in India, including this description of the vizier Sujah Dowlah:

> active, enterprising, deceitful, and unprincipled, bound by no laws divine or human, which can interfere with his interest; supple to the greatest meanness to those he fears; a tyrant in power; in short, a true oriental *Great Man*.

Oriental rulers were stereotypically portrayed as tyrannous despots, given to arbitrary and venal cruelty, in contrast to Britain's emphasis on liberty and peaceful commerce. Indeed, as we shall see, the pervasive tyranny of the Orient was perceived to be reflected in the treatment of women there. Another stereotype constructed the peoples of the East as morally and physically degenerate, in contrast to the supposed moral fibre, virtue and courage of the West's merchants and adventurers. After praising the gentleness and religious devotion of the '*Hindoos*', Kindersley then proceeds to sum up their character as 'superstitious, effeminate, avaritious, and crafty; deceitful and dishonest in their dealings, void of every principle of honor, generosity, or gratitude'. The 'indolent' Shaw Allum's 'chief amusement', Kindersley notes, 'is in smoking his *hooker*, bathing according to the Mahomedan custom, and his *harram* in which he passeth the greatest part of his time'.

Yet while such stereotypes distanced Britain from the Orient, Britons' necessary proximity to the Orient, their very place within these contact zones, produced unsettling disturbances in their identity. When in 1772 Robert Clive (officer in the East India Company army and instrumental in vastly extending British military superiority and influence in India) was charged with corruption, he explained that 'Industan was always an absolute despotic government', implying that his behaviour was perfectly normal in India.[27] This was also worrying for those at home, for it implied that British representatives in India could become 'infected' with local

---

[26]   Edward Said, *Orientalism* (2nd edn, Penguin, 1995), pp. 1–2. Said's book has been criticised in a number of ways, particularly his lack of attention to gender and how stereotypes could be resisted or challenged. As we shall see, Lady Mary Wortley Montagu will be interesting in this light. See also Srinivas Aravamudan, *Tropicopolitans: Colonialism and Agency, 1688–1804* (Duke University Press, 1999).

[27]   Clive's speech in D. B. Horn and Mary Ransome, eds, *English Historical Documents, 1714–1783* (Eyre and Spottiswoode, 1957), p. 809.

customs and morals, that in mimicking the Muslim princes, or nawabs, the British nabobs became un-British. Edmund Burke, addressing the corruption of the East India Company some years later, noted that company officers 'drink the intoxicating draught of authority and dominion' of Indian culture. This is the central premise of Samuel Foote's comedy *The Nabob*, first performed in 1772. Foote's play suggests that the 'contact zone' could include Britain itself: not only is the nabob aping Indian manners, he is importing the tyranny, luxury and degenerate manners of the Orient, corrupting the social and political fabric of Britain. Such scenarios suggested an unsettling fluidity of identity: Sir Mite, the nabob of Foote's play, is 'tinged by the East'.

During the 1770s and 80s, many were smarting over Britain's tarnished imperial image – accusations of tyranny were levelled at West-Indian planters, East India Company officers, and at the government during the American crisis. After the loss of an American empire, the government of the empire in India therefore became crucial. For example, while Edmund Burke acknowledges the plight of the Indian people under such corruption, his insistent concern is with the creation of a lasting monument to the ideals of the British empire, worrying that 'were we to be driven out of India this day, nothing would remain, to tell that it had been possessed, during the inglorious period of our dominion, by any thing better than the ouran-outang or the tiger'.

Another new Eden: the Pacific

Ideals of empire persisted beyond the focus on the American colonies in the eighteenth century, for not only did many turn to India as the next great hope, but the Pacific became a source of fascination too. As Freeth put it: 'The loss of America what can repay? / New colonies seek for at BOTANY BAY'; he even described the South Seas in the very same terms used by the sixteenth-century European discoverers of the Americas: 'This garden of Eden, this new promis'd land'.

Imperial interest in the South Seas did pre-date the loss of America. At the end of the seventeenth and beginning of the eighteenth centuries (especially during the War of Spanish Succession 1702–13), the western coast of the Southern continent of America became the hunting ground of buccaneers, pirates and privateers (who were little more than pirates with a government licence to harry enemy shipping). Figures such as William Dampier and Woodes Rogers mounted expeditions with the backing of the law but were motivated more by a desire for personal fame and the fabled Spanish treasure galleon that plied a route between Acapulco and the Philippines. Their accounts were a soar-away success. Tales of voyage and adventure became a publishing gold-mine, and ensured a readership for fiction such as Daniel Defoe's *Robinson Crusoe* and *Captain Singleton*, and Jonathan Swift's satire *Gulliver's Travels*.

By mid-century, however, thoughts of national pride, commercial utility and scientific knowledge were being voiced. In place of the naked plunder of earlier expeditions, science was the primary impulse of James Cook's expeditions (1768–71; 1772–75; 1776–79). Cook's secret instructions from the Admiralty and the Royal Society emphasised the role of surveying and exploration; developing friendly alliances with the islanders; and the goal of obtaining the consent of the indigenes prior to annexing any territory. While, as Glyndwr Williams comments, 'there was no official master-plan of Pacific discovery', the instructions did, however, note that the discovery of any lands 'will redound greatly to the Honour of this Nation as a Maritime Power, as well as to the Dignity of the Crown of Great Britain, and may tend greatly to the advancement of the Trade and Navigation thereof'.[28] Schemes and projects for Australia, or New South Wales as it was known, had been floated since the 1770s, including its use as a centre for commercial import and export, a military base, the base for a new whaling industry, and as a source of wood and hemp for British fleets. On Joseph Banks' recommendation, Botany Bay became the starting point for the colonisation of Australia.

As we have seen, Britain's imperial identity in particular rested on the ideology of an empire based upon notions of liberty. Cook's exploration was idealised as an extension of British liberty, seen in the closing lines of a popular pantomime entitled *Omai, Or, A Trip round the World*:

> He *came* and he *saw*, not to *conquer*, but save;
> The *Caesar* of Britain was he;
> Who scorn'd the ambition of making a slave
> While Briton's themselves are so free.[29]

Such formulations are an example of what Mary Louise Pratt has termed the rhetoric of 'anti-conquest': 'the strategies of representation whereby European bourgeois subjects seek to secure their innocence in the same moment as they assert European hegemony.'[30] This rhetoric is also found in Anna Seward's *Elegy on Captain Cook*, in which 'HUMANITY' is the presiding spirit of the voyages, and Cook is an 'Orpheus'-like hero exemplifying the highest British values of peaceful exploration and enlightened inter-cultural contact.

However, the extent to which actual contact between the British and the islanders ran according to these ideals, was compromised from the

---

28   Glyndwr Williams, 'The Pacific: Exploration and Exploitation', in Marshall, ed., *Oxford History of the British Empire*, pp. 552–75 (p. 558). 'Instructions' in J. C. Beaglehole, ed., 4 vols, *The Journals of Captain James Cook on his Voyages of Discovery, vol. I, The Voyage of the Endeavour, 1768–71* (Cambridge University Press, 1955), pp. cclxxix–cclxxxiv (cclxxxii).

29   John O'Keeffe and Philippe Jacques de Loutherberg, *A Short Account of the New Pantomime called Omai, Or, A Trip round the World* (1785), p. 24.

30   Pratt, *Imperial Eyes*, p. 7.

beginning by the sheer difference between cultures, cultural misunderstandings, and the limits of the Europeans' benevolence. Cook ignored his instructions when he took possession of Australia in the name of King George without the consent of indigenes, declaring the land *terra nullius* (no person's land).[31] Hawkesworth's tortuous defence, in his 'General Introduction', of violence in the name of knowledge is another example of the limits of enlightened empire. Similarly, in Seward's poem, 'HUMANITY', the muse of Cook's expedition, is unable to save her hero from the 'human fiends' of Hawaii.

Markers of Difference

Seward's comment comes towards the end of a century in which human difference fascinated both the people travelling to the fringes of the British empire and the armchair voyagers who philosophised at home. 'Race' – the sense in which physical attributes are deemed to be primary signs of identity denoting innate characteristics – only became a means of explaining human variety towards the end of the eighteenth century. Certainly, complexion played a significant role in assessing identity: the description of Friday in Defoe's *Robinson Crusoe* (1719) or the puns on skin colour in George Colman's opera *Inkle and Yarico* (1787) attest to the role that complexion played in staging notions of sameness and difference. However, prior to the rise of scientific racism in the closing decades of the century, complexion was only one coordinate of human difference amongst a multiplicity of reference points that also included status, religion, clothes, civility and climate.

Edward Long, in his *History of Jamaica* (1774), reflects how the physical attributes of the white Creole have been affected by the West-Indian climate:

> Although descended from British ancestors, they are stamped with these characteristic deviations. Climate, perhaps, has had some share in producing the variety of feature which we behold among the different societies of mankind, scattered over the globe.

As importantly, this leads into a description of Creole national character (sensual, extravagant, passionate). In climate theory the world was divided into three regions – torrid, temperate and northern. Britain (whether deemed part of the 'Northern' or temperate regions), to most exemplified the highest character of civilisation, home to '*Heroes, Bards*' and '*LIBERTY*'.[32] Italy and Greece became either the fringes of temperate zones (reflecting their decline since ancient times), or part of the demonised 'torrid zones' in the lower latitudes equated with the indolent, sensual, heathen nations

---

31   Williams, 'The Pacific', p. 560.
32   James Thomson, *Britannia*, lines 274–79.

such as Africa or the degenerate Orient. As Long's example shows, that Britons could become something other, or less, than British in its far-flung colonies was a constant fear, and highlights the mutability of identity in the empire's contact zones.

However, for a significant part of the eighteenth century human difference was articulated through cultural markers, or, as Roxann Wheeler terms them, 'proto-racial ideologies'. Until the later eighteenth century,

> older conceptions of Christianity, civility, and rank were *more explicitly* important to Britons' assessment of themselves and other people than physical attributes such as skin color, shape of the nose, or texture of the hair. Embodied in dress, manners, and language, the concepts of Christianity, civility, and rank were not simply abstract categories of difference; they constituted visible distinctions that are difficult for us to recover today.[33]

Cultural difference, then, not *race*, was the dominant model, and religion was one of these powerful markers. As far as Britain's relationship with its immediate rivals was concerned, the primary opposition was structured by the difference between Protestant Britain and the Catholic powers of France and Spain ranged against it in Europe and in outposts around the world (a difference that also reflected different systems of government).[34] However, on the broader canvas of the wider world the fundamental opposition was between Christian and heathen savage (most famously perhaps in Defoe's *Robinson Crusoe*), or Christianity and Islam.

Violent encounters between mariners and Islamic pirates operating out of North Africa were a constant peril. In Joseph Pitts' narrative of his capture, conversion to Islam and escape, it is clear how his sense of himself is powerfully centred on his religious identity. When Pitts describes himself as 'turn'd *Turk*' it is not purely a marker of national identity, for 'Turk' equals heathen; indeed, his father rather pitilessly describes his son's (forced) conversion 'thy horrid Iniquity'. How fluid identity could become is made clear by those Britons around him who, even after rescue, 'Reneg'd' and voluntarily turned towards Islam. It can also be seen in Pitts' admiration of the Muslims' religious devotion in Mecca, and the treatment from his Master, 'which made me sincerely to love him'.

The opposition between clothing and nakedness – anything less than full body clothing – was a recurring trope in the representation of the 'other'. In Defoe's *Captain Singleton*, for example, the strange white man discovered living in the heart of Africa is 'stark naked' – a sign of the dissolution of his European identity. However, what redeems him and guarantees his

---

[33]   Roxann Wheeler, *The Complexion of Race: Categories of Difference in Eighteenth-Century British Culture* (University of Pennsylvania Press, 2000), pp. 8, 7.

[34]   Colley, *Britons*, pp. 11–54.

difference from and superiority over the Africans around him is his display of 'evident Tokens of a mannerly well-bred Person'. In Defoe's vision, civility goes hand-in-hand with commercial society: he has to instruct the Africans around him the value of labour and commerce.

Civility and nobility (and sometimes nobility's concomitant element, high status) were also proto-racial markers. Aphra Behn's heroes in *The Widdow Ranter* (and, similarly, in *Oroonoko*) bond because of their similar marks of noble civility. The love between the colonist Bacon and the Queen of the Native Americans, Semernia, and the respect between him and the King, Cavarnio (note their status and Neoclassical names) is enabled by a shared concept of nobility as high moral character – he crosses what only *seems* a racial divide. Both Behn's play and another tale of cross-cultural desire, Steele's 'Inkle and Yarico', rely upon an important mode of representing the non-European throughout most of the eighteenth century, the 'noble savage'. This highly rhetorical concept functioned as an idealised figure of the human in a state of nature, its nobility reflected in a natural state of happiness uncorrupted by the trappings of a worldly civilisation. This can be seen to good effect in Joseph Warton's poem *The Dying Indian* (the concept was also central to Jean-Jacques Rousseau's influential *A Discourse on Inequality* (1754)).

Encounters with real peoples from around the world came to be seen through the lens of this concept. When four Iroquois sachems visited London in 1711, Jonathan Swift and Joseph Addison saw an opportunity to create a fictional journal, ostensibly written by one of the chiefs, satirising the follies of London. In this, the voice of a supposedly noble and artless non-European unwittingly reveals the corruptions of 'civilization'. Such ideas would find their apogee in the representations of Omai, a prince of the Society Isles brought to London in 1774, and who visited Fanny Burney. In a letter describing the visit she is impressed by the quality of his manners and comparing him to the son of the earl of Chesterfield – supposedly benefiting from the advice of his worldly wise father – she praises Omai's superior civility: 'this shows how much more *nature* can do without *art*, than *art* with all her refinement unassisted by *nature*'.

An alternative schema for human difference was offered in the 'four-stages' theory of human development. Works of the Scottish Enlightenment such as John Millar's *Origin of the Distinction of Ranks* (1771) were highly influential in providing a coherent theory of human civilisation in which the most primitive societies were based upon the nomadic life of hunter-gatherer families, and the highest was exemplified by commercial civilisation. Within this model, primitive societies had the capacity for self-improvement. To many, such improvement would be greatly aided by contact with a superior nation, such as Britain.

However, encounters with the peoples of the Pacific pushed the concepts of the noble savage and the perfectibility of societies to breaking point. Hawkesworth's depiction of the 'natural conscience' and 'artless' emotions of Tahitians was not easily reconciled with the *arrioi* and their sexual rituals and infanticide. Cook was struck with 'horror' (as were the Tahitians) at the demonstration of Maori cannibalism on board his ship. Although he accepts they are civilised 'to a degree', the example of cannibalism is a sign of 'what a savage man is in his natural state'. He adds, 'intercourse with foreigners would reform their manners, and polish their savage minds': in theory, perfectibility comes with the improving effect of imperial contact with civilisations such as Britain. In Anna Seward's elegy to Cook, however, the exportation of 'HUMANITY' has failed – Cook is killed by Hawaiians. Seward's poem is interesting because it betrays a moment when two views of the non-European are uneasily juxtaposed: 'mild Omiah' represents perhaps the last flowering of the concept of the 'noble savage', whereas the 'fiends' of Hawaii come to represent the seemingly unredeemable savagery of non-European nature.

Edward Long's *History of Jamaica* has been viewed as the most infamous example of the ideology of racial difference in the eighteenth century. While his views are extreme even for this period (a product of his defence of slavery and Jamaican planters), his *History* points to an emergent strand of thinking that emphasised the *innate* inferiority of other peoples, in other words, the concept of 'race'. Contradicting his assessment of the effect of climate on white Creole planters, Africans' complexion was judged to be unaffected by changes in climate, so that blackness was more than skin deep and reflected an innate fixity of identity. Underlining this, Long broke with most of his contemporaries by espousing polygenesis (as opposed to monogenesis, or the similitude of divine creation), labelling Africans as a distinct species, and not far removed from apes: Africans are 'the vilest of the human kind, to which they have little more pretension of resemblance than what arises from their exterior form'.

These diverse concepts of human difference are indicative of a wider change wrought over the course the century. At the beginning of the century human identity seemed mutable because it was marked by concepts of difference that allowed fluidity – commerce, civility, religion, clothing, climate. However, by the close of the century conceptions of human difference seemed more fixed, complexion defined inner characteristics, and difference increasingly relied upon skin colour. Further, there was a duality at the heart of the representation of the other. As Hayden White astutely comments: 'Europeans tended to fetishize the native peoples with whom they came into contact by viewing them simultaneously as monstrous forms of humanity and as quintessential objects of desire'.[35] Caught between two fictions of identity, the peoples with whom Britons came into contact on their imperial business found themselves in a strange in-between place.

---

[35]   Hayden White, *The Tropics of Discourse: Essays in Cultural Criticism* (Johns Hopkins University Press, 1978), p. 194.

The Black Atlantic

In his letter discussing the American war, Ignatius Sancho's parting comment, 'for my part it's nothing to me—as I am only a lodger—and hardly that', reveals a sense of alienation that would be shared by many of the black population in London. Brought by force into the centre of the empire, where were they to call 'home'? What place was there for those people who had no place within civil society? By the 1770s there were between ten and fifteen thousand 'black' people living in Britain (comprising Africans, West-Indians, and some South Asians). Though they had been arriving there since the Elizabethan period, the slave trade enormously increased the population of Africans in Britain, the boys often as 'pets' to complete an aristocrat's equipage. Those who escaped or were freed scraped a living as weavers, servants, labourers, artisans, shopkeepers, maids, peddlers, street performers, or sailors, in a land largely hostile to foreigners. To many, the 'Moors', 'Blackamoors', 'Mungos', 'Negurs', or 'people of colour' in England were unalterably alien (such terms also indicates the tendency to homogenise diverse ethnicities). To be black was to be fixed in fictive roles already written: Fridays, Oroonokos, Yaricos, or worse, merely a step above apes.

The disparity between the image of Britain as a land of freedom and the reality of its unforgiving attitude to black Africans is stark in James Albert Ukawsaw Gronniosaw's autobiography. Even more compelling is his encounter with that talisman of civil society, the book: he is unable to make it 'speak', 'because', he thinks, 'I was black'. Conscious of his lack of literacy, alienated from the basis of Western civil society, he is made aware of his identity as a black man through the eyes of those around him. Faced with a similar moment of 'the fact of blackness', twentieth-century psychologist of colonialism Frantz Fanon highlighted how 'on that day, completely dislocated ... I took myself far off from my own presence, far away indeed, and made myself an object'.[36]

The negotiation with the dominant discourses of British identity was not all one way. Protestantism was an avenue that enabled a number of black writers to find a place within the nation – religious awakening is crucial to the accounts of Gronniosaw and Olaudah Equiano, and the poetry of Phillis Wheatley. Indeed, Sancho, Equiano and Cuguano felt that British imperialism allied to humane Christian values had a potentially beneficial role in the world. Yet black identities were not merely hybrids of British and African. The effect of the African diaspora from the seventeenth century onwards was to create peoples whose sense of self was a constant crossing and negotiation between the spaces of empire and diverse coordinates of identity including religion, ethnicity and nation. In the poetry of Phillis Wheatley, her sense of 'liberty' was enabled by imaginative and physical

---

[36] Frantz Fanon, *Black Skin, White Masks*, trans., Charles Lam Markmann (Paladin, 1970), p. 79.

crossings of the Atlantic – between Africa, America, and the dominant arbiter of both those spaces, Britain. Such identities, paradoxically, are able take a position from which to critique, to talk back to the dominant culture.

Srinivas Aravamudan coins the term 'tropicopolitan' to describe such peoples who move between the tropics of the imperial periphery and the metropolitan centre; the tropicopolitan is both 'object of representation *and* agent of resistance'.[37] Gronniosaw's text, for example, reveals the fiction of Briton's virtuous self-image, when he describes England as 'worse than *Sodom*'. Olaudah Equiano appropriated the 'talking book' scenario in his autobiography to insist on his place as a subject (and not an object) within the English literary-political community.[38] Ottobah Cuguano mobilised the language of Christianity and 'the common rights and privileges' of British liberty against the slave trade that upheld the nation's economic success.

The letters of Ignatius Sancho offer a case in point. As a shopkeeper and the only black voter in London, he could recognise himself as a citizen of the British empire, cheering on British forces against the Americans, crying 'We fought like Englishmen'. When anti-Catholic rioters demolished swathes of London in 1780, he satirised their appeal to 'liberty', and described their actions as 'worse than Negro barbarity'. At another time he referred to 'my miserable black brethren' in a letter to the novelist Sterne. His comment, 'I am only a lodger', then, needs to be carefully examined. Sancho's contingent performance of identity reveals that his comment is perhaps the only way to respond; a wry irony at his own expense but also at the expectations of British civil society. The position of slaves and ex-slaves, sometimes moving, most of the time forcibly moved, around the British empire, raises questions concerning commonality, difference, agency and the subject's relation to civil society. These can be seen in the complex negotiations made in these writers' work between their sense of their African ethnic past, the economies of slavery, the importance of literacy, their new sense of Protestant identity, and of their blackness in the culture of the British empire.

'Manly hearts to guard the fair': gender and sexuality

While imperial and national endeavour was associated with men, women – or the 'fair sex' – were deemed symbols of the nation. On the one hand, as Kathleen Wilson has demonstrated, women 'functioned symbolically and literally as the bearers of national values and ideals, just as their alleged "characters" were taken to encapsulate the best and worst features of national manners'.[39] On the other hand, the project of empire and nation

---

[37]   Srinivas Aravamudan, *Tropicopolitans: Colonialism and Agency, 1688–1804* (Duke University Press, 1999), p. 4.

[38]   See Henry Louis Gates, Jr., *The Signifying Monkey: A Theory of African-American Literary Criticism* (Oxford University Press, 1988), pp. 127–69.

[39]   Wilson, *The Island Race*, p. 93.

building was, 'described and glorified as a *manly* occupation'.[40] However, both of these ideals were tested by problems within the conception of empire itself and by imperial encounters. Contact zones were a breeding ground for dangerous mutations of British gender ideals, and contact with different gender and sexual systems could affirm or bring into doubt the belief in the virtue of British patriarchy. Further, the doubtful effects of a powerful British empire undermined the stability of manliness. None of this was helped by the simultaneous idealisation and demonisation of femininity. For example, when, in his hymn to the Royal Exchange (*Spectator*, no. 69, 1711) Joseph Addison details how 'The single Dress of a Woman of Quality is often the Product of an hundred Climates', women function as both a decorative symbol for empire and yet also bear the responsibility for imperial commerce and (over)consumerism.

The most iconographic representation was of course Britannia. In Thomson's 1729 poem of the same name, the figure of Britannia is dejected and dishevelled, reflecting an apathetic nation, its men emasculated by political indolence. In the eighteenth-century mind, ideal masculinity – *manliness* – had as its definitional other the notion of *effeminacy*, which was a corruption of masculinity brought on by excessive contact with women (including sex) or with the feminine sphere. 'Luxury' for example, was demonised because it was associated with the feminine world of sensual and indolent consumerism, and alien to manly virtue. Paradoxically, it was the very success (or over-success) of empire that could lead to luxury, and then effeminacy. Charles Davenant put it this way: 'Extended Dominion, Power atchieved by Arms or Riches flowing in by Trade, beget Effeminacy, Pride, Ambition and Luxuries of all Kinds.' Countless writers – James Thomson, John Dyer, John Brown, Samuel Foote, Janet Schaw included – saw, in the potential corruption of the nation, its empire and its colonists, the spectre of effeminacy.

Britons' demonisation of 'effeminacy' attempted to guarantee that the moral character of the British empire was different to the Spanish, French, and even the Ottoman and Indian Mughal empires. The trouble was, the British empire came increasingly to look as corrupt and effeminate as the Orient. Its culture luxurious and indolent, its people passive to an extreme, the Orient was deemed a feminine space. From Jemima Kindersley's arrival in India she is disparaging about the uxorious 'indolence' of the Muslim princes and the 'effeminate' Hindus. The corruption of imperial governance and East India Company officers' infection by Indian culture is reflected in the nabobs' effeminate tastes (Sir Mite, in Samuel Foote's play, is likened to a 'Macaroni' – a type of effeminate man).

The feminisation of the Orient was part of a powerful coding of the farther reaches of the empire as female. In visual depictions, the continents

---

[40]   Wilson, *Sense of the People*, p. 203.

of Asia, Africa and America were traditionally represented as partially clad women awaiting their discovery by European men, an image idealised by Sir Walter Raleigh who described Guiana as 'a countrey that hath yet her maydenhead' (the same vein of aristocratic courtship reiterated in Aphra Behn's *The Widdow Ranter*).[41] Colonisation and imperialism, then, became a species of romance , reflected in the transracial love plot. John Smith and Pocahantas, the romance of Bacon and Semernia in Aphra Behn's *The Widdow Ranter* and Richard Steele's story of Inkle and Yarico (*Spectator* no. 11), all display the 'ideal of cultural harmony through romance'.[42] The fantasy of transracial romance was maintained by its distance from the imperial metropolis. But only partially: the tragic death of the lovers in Behn's play and the heartless cruelty of the Englishman Inkle in Steel's tale indicate the impossibility of this harmony: romance collapses because the ideology of British imperialism cannot synthesise cultural difference and the realities of economic exploitation.

Of course, the sexualisation of contact reflected Britons' latent fantasies *and* fears of the perceived rampant sexual freedom to be found at the empire's peripheries. Alexander Pope gives us this double vision when he warns Lady Mary Wortley Montagu, travelling to Turkey, that 'you have ... out-traveld the Sin of Fornication, and are happily arrived at the free Region of Adultery'.[43] The obverse of the romance of imperial encounters is the anxiety of sexual and cultural transgression: the East's supposedly degenerate character was encapsulated in the image of Turkish sodomy – witness Joseph Pitts' anxious account of his captors' *'inhumane* and *unnatural'* desires (something the Pacific voyagers suspected the Tahitians of). Cook sought to police his crew's sexual contact with the Pacific women and Janet Schaw lamented, as did many others, that Creole men indulged in 'licentious and even unnatural amours' with black slaves. Yet sexual excess was often displaced upon the innate character of the 'other': African women were considered, in Edward Long's words, 'libidinous and shameless as monkies, or baboons'. The subduing of new lands and its inferior peoples may indeed prove a nation's manly character, but the parallel to the idealisation of a virgin territory was an image of a land of monstrous women who instigated sexual contact on helpless colonists, dangerously undermining their British and manly identity.

The effects of empire on gender identity were not limited to masculinity: British femininity was measured and occasionally transformed by imperial encounters with women from the edges of empire. In the four-stages theory

---

41   Raleigh quoted in Peter Hulme, *Colonial Encounters: Europe and the Native Caribbean, 1492–1797* (Methuen, 1986), p. 159.
42   Hulme, *Colonial Encounters*, p. 141.
43   Pope to Lady Mary Wortley Montagu, 10 November 1716; *The Correspondence of Alexander Pope*, ed. George Sherburn, 3 vols (Clarendon Press, 1956), vol. 1, p. 368.

of civilisation women functioned as markers of human difference and signs of British civilisation, for example, John Millar's *Origin of the Distinction of Ranks* (1771) noted that 'savage nations ... entertain very gross ideas concerning those female virtues which, in a polished nation, are supposed to constitute the honour and dignity of the sex'.[44] The accounts of the Cook expeditions, for example, emphasised that the bodies and manners of the women of New Zealand set them at a lower level of civilisation from the Tahitians. If women were the bearers of civilisation, then to Edward Long it would make sense that the morals of Creole women – who had been frater- nising far too much with black slave women – could be mended by contact with British femininity. Women would 'become better qualified to fill the honourable station of a wife', guaranteeing the morals (and sexual attention) of the men, and securing the future of Jamaica's colonial life.

In opposition to the virtue of females under British society, the Turkish baths, the polygamy of the Ottoman harem (or 'seraglio'), the Indian Muslim zanannah, and the Hindu practice of *sati* (where women burnt themselves upon the funeral pyre of their husband) became the focal points of British fascination because they epitomised the perceived slavery of women under an unnatural domestic tyranny, in contrast to the civilised freedom of women in Britain. Jemima Kindersley, for example, was discon- certed by *sati*, calling it a 'barbarous exertion of virtue'. She also lamented the confinement of women in the zanannah and their exclusion from reli- gion and government, commenting that the women have few talents other than bathing, music and 'smoaking the hooker', and no power 'except the influence of a beautiful face over an ignorant and voluptuous prince'.

While Kindersley implied the superiority of the position of women under British civilisation, Lady Mary Wortley Montagu complicates this view in her letters from Turkey. In her description of the Turkish baths (or 'bagnios'), Lady Mary's description oscillates between an eroticised objecti- fication of Turkish women and a vision of a female-only space of freedom akin to the male coffee-houses of Britain. On the Islamic veil, she com- mented that 'this perpetual masquerade gives them entire liberty of following their inclination without danger of discovery' – Turkish women in her view enjoy an enviable sexual freedom unknown to women in Britain. Lady Mary's view of aristocratic Turkish women was, in Felicity Nussbaum's words, a 'feminotopia' that reversed the common assumption that Britain's women were free in contrast to the domestic tyranny of the Orient.[45] At times masquerading in Turkish clothes, at other times keeping her clothes on (in the baths she only removes her shirt), Lady Mary trod a fine line between 'turning Turk' (in the popular phrase) and maintaining a British femininity.

---

44 Millar quoted in Felicity Nussbuam, *Torrid Zones: Maternity, Sexuality, and Empire in Eighteenth-Century English Narratives* (Johns Hopkins University Press, 1995), p. 10.
45 Nussbaum, *Torrid Zones*, pp. 135–62.

'Manly hearts to guard the fair': in *Rule Britannia* Thomson and Mallet conjured a vision in which women were the icons of civilisation and nation, and men the movers and shakers of empire and national grandeur. However, the contingent and shifting ground of the feminine – at times an ideal, at others a defect – meant that such ideals would be an impossible aspiration. The problems of gender ideals would only be exacerbated by contact with peoples deemed not so 'fair'. Men could become effeminised by the very process of empire, and women such as Lady Mary contested dominant versions of femininity and human difference. Gender identity in the service of nation and empire would never be as stable or problem-free as this iconic ode to the British empire hoped.

Rule Britannia?

By end of the eighteenth and the beginning of the nineteenth centuries conceptions of identity hardened and the crossing of cultural boundaries became more policed.[46] Moreover, doubts and anxieties over Britain's imperial endeavours receded in the successes of the Napoleonic wars, its dominance secured by a huge accession of territories world-wide. At the end of the century, the formation of the London Missionary Society and the Society for the Abolition of the Slave Trade (the slave trade was abolished in 1807, slavery in 1833) underpinned the superior morality that the 'pax Britannica' of the nineteenth century claimed for itself.

It is worth reminding ourselves, then, of what went before:

> I am, and ever have been, deeply sensible, of the difficulty of reconciling the strong presiding power, that is so useful towards the conservation of a vast, disconnected, infinitely diversified empire, with that liberty and safety of the provinces, which they must enjoy ... or they will not be provinces at all.[47]

Edmund Burke's acute observation cuts to the crux of the ideological contradiction within British imperial and national identity. Forging their own identity in opposition to the French, the Spanish, the Ottomans, the Mughals, the dominant sense of British identity rested on an ideal of liberty while simultaneously attempting to 'rule' the rest of the world. It was a precarious identity at best, when accusations of tyranny were levelled from within its own polity against East India Company officers, West-Indian planters, and even the government (over its handling of the American colonies).

As a further mortification, the British empire could not guarantee that Britons 'never shall be slaves'. Or even that they would remain purely

---

[46] See C.A. Bayly, Dror Wahrman and Roxann Wheeler in Bibliography.
[47] *A Letter from Edmund Burke, Esq; ... to John Farr, and John Harris, Esqrs.*, p. 56.

British. When, in 1764, white captives were released by their Ohio Indian captors, William Smith was stunned to see the Native American Indians in tears at having to release their 'captives', and the white captives obviously unwilling to leave their 'captors'. He struggled to reconcile how the Native Americans displayed 'virtues which Christians need not blush to imitate', with the superiority of British civilisation and 'the blessings of improved life and the light of religion'.[48]

Beneath the complacency of British proclamations of imperial superiority and enlightened humanity lay profound fears concerning the impact of its empire on these ideals. Moreover, while Britons' sense of themselves was often vindicated by contact with different peoples, it was just as often made to seem less assured and more mutable by these imperial encounters. In the voices of the not-quite-so-British, in the accounts of ex-slaves, nabobs, Creoles, captives, travellers and colonists of all sorts, we can follow the shifting mood of Britons in the eighteenth century, with their uncertainties of identity and their precarious rule over the seas.

---

[48] William Smith, *Expedition*, (1766).

John Locke, from
Two Treatises of Government
(1690)

John Locke's (1632–1704) position as one of the most influential philosophers of the eighteenth century was a result of his *Essay Concerning Human Understanding* (1690). Before that he was physician to the first Earl of Shaftesbury in 1667, and then held a variety of official posts until he fled to Holland in 1683 in the wake of the Exclusion crisis (parliamentarians sought to exclude Charles II's heir, James, from the throne). Written against this background, Locke's *Two Treatises of Government* theorised the basis of a constitutional state and government by consent. It was often mobilised to support the accession of William III and the Glorious Revolution and influenced the thinking behind the American Declaration of Independence. The *First Treatise* is a demolition of the theory of divine right of kings and absolute monarchy as laid out in Robert Filmer's *Patriarcha* (1680). This extract contains the forceful opening to his whole work which aligns Englishness and liberty; an association that weaves its way throughout the writings on empire and one with which few contemporary Britons would have disagreed. The *Second Treatise* argues the case that people's freedom arises from a civilisation that ensures the protection of property, and then goes on to lay the foundations of government by consent. In the second extract from the *Second Treatise*, Locke justifies the natural rights to property as the fruits of one's own labour, synthesising Biblical precedent and secular reasoning, and thereby providing colonialism with a powerful legitimating ideology.[1]

[From the *First Treatise*, 'The Introduction']

1. Slavery is so vile and miserable an Estate of Man, and so directly opposite to the generous Temper and Courage of our Nation; that 'tis hardly to be conceived, that an *Englishman*, much less a *Gentleman*, should plead for't.

[...]

[From the *Second Treatise*, 'Of Property']

26. God, who hath given the World to Men in common, hath also given them reason to make use of it to the best Advantage of Life, and Convenience. The Earth, and all that is therein, is given to Men for the Support and Comfort of their Being. And though all the Fruits it naturally produces, and Beasts it feeds, belong to Mankind in common, as they are produced by the spontaneous Hand of Nature; and no body has originally

---

[1]   Text from *The Works of John Locke*, 3 vols (1714), vol. 2, pp. 102, 165–6, 167.

a private Dominion, exclusive of the rest of Mankind, in any of them, as they are thus in their natural State: yet being given for the use of Men, there must of necessity *be a means to appropriate* them some way or other, before they can be of any use, or at all beneficial, to any particular Man. The Fruit, or Venison, which nourishes the wild *Indian*, who knows no Inclosure, and is still a Tenant in common, must be his, and so his, *i.e.* a part of him, that another can no longer have any right to it, before it can do him any Good for the Support of his Life.

27. Though the Earth, and all inferior Creatures be common to all Men, yet every Man has a *Property* in his own *Person*. This no Body has any Right to but himself. The *Labour* of his Body, and the *Work* of his Hands, we may say, are properly his. Whatsoever then he removes out of the State that Nature hath provided, and left it in, he hath mixed his Labour with, and joyned to it something that is his own, and thereby makes it his Property. It being by him removed from the common State Nature hath placed it in, it hath by this *Labour* something annexed to it, that excludes the common Right of other Men. For this *Labour* being the unquestionable Property of the Labourer, no Man but he can have a Right to what that is once joyned to, at least where there is enough, and as good left in common for others.

[...]

32. But the *chief Matter of Property* being now not the Fruits of the Earth, and the Beasts that subsist on it, but *the Earth it self*; as that which takes in and carries with it all the rest: I think it is plain, that *Property* in that too is acquir'd as the former. *As much Land* as a Man Tills, Plants, Improves, Cultivates, and can use the Product of, so much is his *Property*. He by his Labour does, as it were, inclose it from the Common. Nor will it invalidate his Right to say, Every body else has an equal Title to it; and therefore he cannot appropriate, he cannot inclose, without the Consent of all his Fellow-Commoners, all Mankind. God, when He gave the World in common to all Mankind, commanded Man also to labour, and the Penury of his Condition required it of him.[2] God and his Reason commanded him to subdue the Earth, *i.e.* improve it for the Benefit of Life, and therein lay out something upon it that was his own, his Labour. He that in Obedience to this Command of God, subdued, tilled and sowed any part of it, thereby annexed to it something that was his *Property*, which another had no Title to, nor could without Injury take from him.

---

[2]   *God ... him*: Genesis, 1: 28, 3: 17–19.

Aphra Behn, from
The Widdow Ranter, or,
The History of Bacon in
Virginia (1690)

Aphra Behn (1640–89) was one of the first women to earn a living entirely from writing, although her successes were dogged by the patriarchal climate of the time: there were slights on her originality and her moral reputation. Her most famous works include the comedy *The Rover* (1677), and the novella *Oroonoko, or, The Royal Slave* (1688), about the African prince Oroonoko and his slavery in the English colony of Surinam in the1670s, inspired by a true event when Behn was there in the 1650s. In her work Behn offers a unique female perspective on honour, nobility, and the sexual power-relations between men and women.

The Widdow Ranter (produced posthumously) is subtitled 'a tragicomedy' which indicates the twin trajectories of its plots. The comic plot is provided by the carnivalesque widow Ranter, and the romances between Hazard and Madam Surelove and between Friendly and Chrisante. The tragic plot concerns the actions of Bacon and the King and Queen of the American Indians. The historical Nathaniel Bacon settled in Virginia in 1674, but in 1676 he rebelled against the Governor (Sir William Berkely) and led a war against local Native American tribes, before dying of a 'flux'. In Behn's play, the social background of the various Governors is the subject of ridicule and bears comparison with the denunciation of dishonourable colonists in *Oroonoko*. The ideology of a new merchant class driven and funded by imperial profit is anathema; to the Tory and Royalist Behn, honour is identified with aristocratic status and 'nobility' equates moral worth and birth. Bacon's war on the American Indians is transcended by a mutual respect between him and the King and Queen of the Native Americans and is a vivid contrast to the upstart Governors. It is this concept of nobility – and the trope of the noble savage – that enables the romance between Bacon and the Queen. However, while the tragic deaths of Bacon and the American Indian nobles reflect a nostalgia for a lost ideal of nobility, the 'antick' dance reminds us how the Native Americans are also made into a spectacle of cultural difference.[1]

In the first scene at Mrs Flirt's inn, Hazard has just arrived in Virgina with a cargo, where he meets Friendly, an old aquaintance who has a Plantation, and they plan to court the local women.

[From ACT I, SCENE I]

Friendly. And thus you'l have an Opportunity to Mannage both our Amours: here you will find Occasion to shew your Courage as well as Express your Love; For at this time the *Indians* by our ill Management of

---

[1]   Text from pp. 3–10, 13–14.

Trade, whom we have Armed against Our selves, Very frequently make War upon us with our own Weapons, Tho' often coming by the Worst are forced to make Peace with us again, but so, as upon every turn they fall to Massacring us wherever we ly exposed to them.

Hazard. I heard the news of this in *England*, which hastens the new Governour's arrival here,[2] who brings you fresh Supplys.

Friendly. Would he were landed, we hear he is a Noble Gentleman.

Hazard. He has all the Qualities of a Gallant Man, besides he is Nobly Born.

Friendly. This Country wants nothing but to be People'd with a well-born Race to make it one of the best Collonies in the World, but for want of a Governour we are Ruled by a Councill, some of which have been perhaps transported Criminals,[3] who having Acquired great Estates are now become your Honour, and Right Worshipfull, and Possess all Places of Authority; there are amongst 'em some honest Gentlemen who now begin to take upon 'em, and Manage Affairs as they ought to be.

Hazard. Bacon I think was one of the Councill.

Friendly. Now you have named a Man indeed above the Common Rank, by Nature Generous; Brave Resolv'd, and Daring; who studying the Lives of the Romans and great Men, that have raised themselves to the most Elevated fortunes, fancies it easy for Ambitious men, to aim at any Pitch of Glory, I've heard him often say, Why cannot I Conquer the Universe as well as *Alexander*? or like another *Romulus*[4] form a new *Rome*, and make my self Ador'd?

Hazard. Why might he not? Great Souls are born in common men, some-times as well as Princes.

Friendly. This Thirst of Glory cherisht by Sullen Melancholly, I believe was the first Motive that made him in Love with the young *Indian*-Queen, fan-cying no *Hero* ought to be without his Princess. And this was the Reason why he so earnestly prest for a Commission, to be made General against the *Indians*, which long was promis'd him, but they fearing his Ambition, still put him off, till the Grievances grew so high, that the whole Country flockt to him, and beg'd he would redress them,— he took the opportunity, and Led them forth to fight, and vanquishing brought the Enemy to fair terms, but now instead of receiving him as a Conquerour, we treat him as a Traytor.

Hazard. Then it seems all the Crime this brave Fellow has committed, is serving his Country without Authority.

---

2   *new Governour*: Lord Culpeper. Governor from 1677 to 1683.

3   *transported Criminals*: by 1700 transportation to America was sometimes used as a lenient alternative to capital punishment. See also Peart, lines 207–10.

4   *Alexander … Romulus*: respectively, the legendary conqueror of lands from the Mediterranean to India and the semi-mythic founder of Rome.

Friendly. 'Tis so, and however I admire the Man, I am resolv'd to be of the Contrary Party, that I may make an Interest in our new Governour; Thus stands affairs, so that after you have seen Madam *Sure-Love*, I'le present you to the Councill for a Commission.

Hazard. But my Kinsman's Character—

Friendly. He was a *Lester-shire* younger Brother, came over hither with a small fortune, which his Industry has increas'd to a thousand pound a year, and he is now Coll. *John Sure-love*, and one of the Councill.

Hazard. Enough.

Friendly. About it then, Madam *Flirt* to direct you.

Hazard. You are full of your Madams here.

Friendly. Oh! 'tis the greatest affront imaginable, to call a woman Mistress, tho' but a retail Brandy-munger.—Adieu!—one thing more, tomorrow is our Country-Court, pray do not fail to be there, for the rarity of the Entertainment: but I shall see you anon at *Sure-loves* where I'le Salute thee as my first meeting, and as an old acquaintance in *England*—here's company, farewell.

[*Exit* Friendly.

Enter Dullman, Timerous, *and* Boozer.[5]
Hazard *sits at a Table and writes.*

Dullman. Here *Nell*—Well Lieutenant *Boozer*, what are you for?

Enter Nell.

Boozer. I am for Cooling *Nants*, Major.[6]

Dullman. Here *Nell*, a quart of *Nants*, and some Pipes and smoak.

Timerous. And do ye hear *Nell*, bid your Mistress come in to Joke a little with us, for adzoors I was damnable drunk last night, and am better at the petticoat than the bottle today.

Dullman. Drunk last night, and sick to day, how comes that about Mr. Justice? you use to bear your Brandy well enough.

Timerous. Ay your shier-Brandy[7] I'le grant you, but I was Drunk at Coll. *Downright's* with your high Burgundy Claret.

Dullman. A Pox of that Paulter[8] Liquor, your *English French* wine, I wonder how the Gentlemen do to drink it.

---

[5]   *Dullman … Boozer*: As described in the *dramatic personae*, Dullman is a 'Captain'; Timerous and Boozer are Justices of the Peace, and each 'a very great Coward'.
[6]   *Nants*: Brandy from Nantes, France.
[7]   *shier-Brandy*: undiluted Brandy.
[8]   *Paulter*: sham.

Timerous. Ay so do I, 'tis for want of a little *Virginia* Breeding: how much more like a Gentleman 'tis, to drink as we do, brave Edifying Punch and Brandy,—but they say the young Noble-men now and Sparks in *England* begin to reform, and take it for their morning's Draught, get Drunk by noon, and despise the Lousy Juice of the Grape.

Enter Mrs Flirt.

Dullman. Come Landlady, come, you are so taken up with Parson *Dunce*, that your old friends can't Drink a Dram with you,—what no smutty Catch now, no Gibe or Joke to make the Punch go down Merrily, and advance Trading? Nay, they say, Gad forgive ye, you never miss going to Church when Mr. *Dunce* Preaches—but here's to you.

> [*drinks.*

Flirt. Lords, your Honours are pleas'd to be merry—but my service to your Honour.

> [*drinks.*

Hazard. Honours, who the Devil have we here? some of the wise Councill at least, I'd sooner took 'em for Hoggerds.[9]

> [*aside.*

Flirt. Say what you please of the Doctor, but I'le swear he's a fine Gentleman, he makes the Prettiest Sonnets, nay, and Sings 'em himself to the rarest Tunes.

Timerous. Nay the man will serve for both Soul and Body, for they say he was a Farrier in *England*, but breaking turn'd Life-guard man,[10] and his Horse dying—he Counterfeited a Deputation from the Bishop, and came over here a Substantiall Orthodox: but come, where stands the Cup?—here, my Service to you Major.

Flirt. Your Honours are pleas'd—but me-thinks Doctor *Dunce* is a very Edifying Person, and a Gentleman, and I pretend to know a Gentleman, —For I my self am a Gentlewoman; my Father was a Barronet, but undone in the late Rebellion[11]—and I am fain to keep an Ordinary now, Heaven help me.[12]

Timerous. Good lack, why see how Virtue may be bely'd—we heard your Father was a Taylor, but trusting for old *Oliver*'s Funerall,[13] Broke, and so came hither to hide his head,—but my Service to you; what, you are never the worse?

---

9   *Hoggerds*: swineherds.
10   *breaking … Life-guard man*: going bankrupt, he became a soldier-bodyguard to the king.
11   *the late Rebellion*: the English Civil War, 1642–46.
12   *fain to keep an Ordinary*: 'glad to keep a tavern'.
13   *old Oliver's Funerall*: Oliver Cromwell (1599–1658), lord protector of England during the Commonwealth period. His funeral was lavish: Flirt's father may have put up money for this but went bankrupt.

Flirt. Your Honours knows this is a Scandalous place, for they say your Honour was but a broken Excise-man, who spent the King's money to buy your Wife fine Petticoats, and at last not worth a Groat, you came over a poor Servant, though now a Justice of Peace, and of the Honourable Council.

Timerous. Adzoors if I knew who 'twas said so, I'd sue him for *Scandalum Magnatum.*[14]

Dullman. Hang 'em Scoundrells, hang 'em, they live upon Scandal, and we are Scandall-Proof,—They say too, that I was a Tinker and running the Country, robb'd a Gentleman's House there, was put into *Newgate,* got a reprieve after Condemnation, and was Transported hither— And that you *Boozer* was a Common Pick-pocket, and being often flogg'd at the Cart's-tale, afterwards turn'd Evidence,[15] and when the times grew Honest was fain to fly.

Boozer. Ay, Ay, Major, if Scandal would have broke our hearts, we had not arriv'd to the Honour of being Privy-Councellors—but come Mrs. *Flirt,* what never a Song to Entertain us?

Flirt. Yes, and a Singer too newly come ashore:

Timerous. Adzoors, let's have it then:

Enter Girl, who sings, they bear the Bob.[16]

Hazard. Here Maid, a Tankard of your Drink;

Flirt. Quickly *Nell,* wait upon the Gentleman;

Dullman. Please you Sir to taste of our Liquor—My service to you: I see you are a Stranger and alone, please you to come to our Table?

[He rises and comes.

Flirt. Come Sir, pray sit down here, these are very Honourable Persons I assure you,—This is Major *Dullman,* Major of his Excellencies own Regiment, when he Arrives, this Mr. *Timorous,* Justice a Peace in *Corum.*[17] This Capt. *Boozer,* all of the Honourable Councill.

Hazard. With your leave, Gentlemen;

[sits.

Timerous. My service to you Sir;

[drinks.

What have you brought over any Cargo Sir, I'le be your Customer.

Boozer. Ay, and cheat him too, I'le warrant him.

[aside.

---

14   *Scandalum Magnatum*: 'The utterance or publication of a malicious report against any person holding a position of dignity' (OED).

15   *turn'd Evidence*: become an informer.

16   *bear the Bob*: sing the chorus.

17   *Corum*: quorum.

Hazard. I was not bred to Merchandizing Sir, nor do intend to follow the Drudgery of Trading.

Dullman. Men of Fortune seldom travel hither Sir to see fashions.

Timerous. Why Brother, it may be the Gentleman has a mind to be a Planter, will you hire your self to make a Crop of Tobacco this year?

Hazard. I was not born to work Sir.

Timerous. Not work Sir, 'zoors your betters have workt Sir, I have workt my self Sir, both set and stript Tobacco, for all I am of the Honourable Councill, not work quotha—I suppose Sir you wear your fortune upon your Back Sir?

Hazard. Is it your Custom here Sir to affront Strangers? I shall expect satisfaction.

> [*Rises.*

Timerous. Why does any body here owe you any thing?

Dullman. No, unless he means to be paid for drinking with us—ha, ha, ha.

Hazard. No Sir, I have money to pay for what I drink: here's my Club—my Guinia,

> [*flings down a Guinia.*

I scorn to be oblig'd to such Scoundrells.

Boozer. Hum—Call Men of Honour Scoundrells.

> [*rise in huff.*

Timerous. Let him alone, let him alone Brother, how should he learn manners, he never was in *Virginia* before.

Dullman. He's some Covent-Garden Bully;[18]

Timerous. Or some broken Citizen turn'd Factor,[19]

Hazard. Sir you lye, and you're a Rascall,

> [*flings the Brandy in's face.*

Timerous. Adzoors he has spill'd all the Brandy.

Timerous *runs behind the door,* Dullman *and* Boozer *strike* Hazard.

Hazard. I understand no Cudgel-Play, but wear a sword to right my self.[20]

> [*draws, they run off.*

Flirt. Good heavens, what quarrelling in my House?

Hazard. Do the Persons of Quallity in this Country treat strangers thus?

---

18 *Covent-Garden Bully*: a pimp of the prostitutes that frequented Covent Garden.
19 *some … Factor*: a satirical phrase for a bankrupt turned merchandiser.
20 *Cudgel-Play … sword*: the cudgel was the weapon of the lower classes. The wearing of a sword traditionally denoted one's status as a gentleman and nobly born.

Flirt. Alas Sir, 'tis a familiar way they have, Sir.

Hazard. I'm glad I known it,—Pray Madam can you inform one how I may be furnisht with a Horse and a guide to Madam *Sure-Love's*?

Flirt. A most Accomplisht Lady, and my very good friend you shall be Immediately—

[*Exeunt*.

SCENE II.

Enter Wellman, Downright, Dunce, Whimsey, Whiff, *and others*.[21]

Wellman. Come Mr. *Dunce*, tho' you are no Councellour, yet your Council may be good in time of necessity, as now.

Dunce. If I may be worthy advice, I do not look upon our danger to be so great from the *Indians*, as from young *Bacon*, whom the People have nick-nam'd *Fright-all*.

Whimsey. Ay, Ay that same *Bacon*, I would he were well hang'd, I am afraid that under pretence of killing all the *Indians* he means to Murder us, Ly with our Wives, and hang up our little Children, and make himself Lord and King.

Whiff. Brother *Whimsey*, not so hot, with leave of the Honourable Board, My Wife is of Opinion, that *Bacon* came seasonably to our Aid, and what he has done was for our defence, the *Indians* came down upon us, and Ravisht us all, Men, Women, and Children.

Wellman. If these Grievances were not redrest we had our reasons for it, it was not that we were insensible Capt. *Whiff*, of what we suffer'd from the Insolence of the *Indians*: But all knew what we must expect from *Bacon* if that by Lawfull Authority he had Arriv'd to so great a Command as Generall, nor would we be huft out of our Commissions.

Downright. 'Tis most certain that *Bacon* did not demand a Commission out of a design of serving us, but to satisfy his Ambition and his Love, it being no secret that he passionately Admires the *Indian Queen*, and under the pre-text of a War, intends to kill the King her Husband, Establish himself in her heart, and on all occasions have himself a more formidable Enemy, than the *Indians* are.

Whimsey. Nay, nay, I ever foresaw he would prove a Villain.

Whiff. Nay, and he be thereabout, my *Nancy* shall have no more to do with him.

21　　*Wellman … Whiff*: as described in the *dramatis personae*, Colonel Wellman is the deputy Governor; Colonel Downright is a 'Loyall Honest Coun.[sellor]'; Parson Dunce was 'for-merly a Farrier fled from England' and is now 'Chaplain to the Governor'; Whimsey is a 'Justice of the Peace, and very great Coward', as is Captain Whiff.

Wellman. But Gentlemen the People dayly flock to him, so that his Army is too Considerable for us to oppose by any thing but Policy.

Downright. We are sensible Gentlemen that our Fortunes, our Honours, and our Lives are at Stake, and therefore you are call'd together to consult what's to be done in this Grand Affair, till our Governour and Forces arrive from *England*; The Truce he made with the *Indians* will be out to Morrow.

Whiff. Ay, and then he intends to have another bout with the *Indians*. Let's have Patience I say till he has thrum'd their Jackets, and then to work with your Politicks as soon as you please.

Downright. Colonel *Wellman* has answer'd that point good Captain *Whiff*, 'tis the Event of this Battle we ought to dread, and if won or lost will be equally fatall for us, either from the *Indians* or from *Bacon*.

Dunce. With the Permission of the Honourable Board I think I have hit upon an Expedient that may prevent this Battle, your Honours shall write a Letter to *Bacon*, where you shall acknowledge his Services, invite him kindly home, and offer him a Commission for General—

Whiff. Just my *Nancy*'s Counsell—Doctor *Dunce* has spoken like a Cherubin, he shall have my voice for General, what say you Brother *Whimsey*?

Whimsey. I say, he is a Noble fellow, and fit for a General.

Dunce. But conceive me right Gentlemen, as soon as he shall have render'd himself, seize him and strike off his Head at the Fort.

Whiff. Hum! his head—Brother

Whimsey. Ay, ay, Doctor *Dunce* speaks like a Cherubin.

Wellman. Mr *Dunce*, your Counsell in extremity I confess is not amiss, but I should be loth to deal dishonourably with any man.

Downright. His Crimes deserve death, his life is forfeited by Law, but shall never be taken by my consent by Trechery: If by any Stratagem we could take him a-live, and either send him for *England* to receive there his Punishment, or keep him Prisoner here till the Governour arrive, I should agree to't, but I question his coming in upon our Invitation.

Dunce. Leave that to me.

Whimsey. Come, I'le warrant him, the Rogue's as stout as Hector,[22] he fears neither Heaven nor Hell.

Downright. He's too Brave and Bold to refuse our summons, and I am for sending him for *England* and leaving him to the King's Mercy.

Dunce. In that you'l find more difficulty Sir, to take him off here will be more quick and sudden: for the people worship him.

---

[22]   *Hector*: hero of Classical Greek legend whose exploits in the Trojan wars meant that he became a byword for fighting strength.

Wellman. I'le never yield to so ungenerous an expedient. The seizing him I am content in the Extremity wherein we are, to follow. What say you Collonell *Downright*? Shall we send him a Letter now while this two day's truce lasts, between him and the *Indians*?

Downright. I approve it.

All. And I, and I, and I.

Dunce. If your Honours please to make me the Messenger, I'le use some arguments of my own to prevail with him.

Wellman. You say well Mr. *Dunce*, and we'l dispatch you presently.

          [*Exit* Wellman. Downright *and all but* Whimsey, Whiff, and Dunce.

Whiff. Ah Doctor, if you could but have persuaded Collonell *Wellman* and Colonel *Downright* to have hang'd him—

Whimsey. Why Brother *Whiff* you were for making him a Generall but now.

Whiff. The Councills of wise States-men Brother *Whimsey* must change as causes do, d'ye see.

Dunce. Your Honours are in the right, and whatever those two leading Councellors say, they would be glad if *Bacon* were dispatcht, but the punctillio[23] of Honour is such a thing.

Whimsey. Honour, a Pox on't, what is that Honour that keeps such a Bustle in the world, yet never did good as I heard of.

Dunce. Why 'tis a Foolish word only, taken up by great men, but rarely practic'd,—but if you would be great men indeed—

Whiff. If we would Doctor, name, name the way.

Dunce. Why, you command each of you a company—when *Bacon* comes from the Camp, as I am sure he will, (and full of this silly thing call'd Honour will come unguarded too,) lay some of your men in Ambush along those Ditches by the *Sevana*[24] about a Mile from the Town, and as he comes by, seize him, and hang him upon the next Tree.

Whiff. Hum—hang him! a rare Plot.

Whimsey. Hang him—we'l do't, we'l do't Sir, and I doubt not but to be made Generall for the Action—I'le take it all upon my self.

                                                              [*aside*.

Dunce. If you resolve upon this, you must about it instantly—Thus I shall at once serve my Country, and revenge my self on the Rascall for affronting my Dignity once at the Councell-Table, by calling me Farrier.

                                                              [*Exit* Doctor.

---

23   *punctillio*: a point of etiquette.
24   *Sevana*: savannah.

Whiff. Do you know Brother what we are to do?

Whimsey. To do, yes, to hang a Generall, Brother, that's all.

Whiff. All, but is it Lawfull to hang any Generall?

Whimsey. Lawfull, yes, that 'tis Lawfull to hang any Generall that fights against Law.

Whiff. But in what he has done, he has serv'd the King and our Country, and preserv'd all our Lives and Fortunes.

Whimsey. That's all one, Brother, if there be but a Quirk in the Law offended in this Case, tho' he fought like *Alexander*, and preserv'd the whole world from perdition, yet if he did it against Law, 'tis Lawfull to hang him; why what Brother, is it fit that every impudent fellow that pretends to a little Honour, Loyalty and Courage, should serve his King and Country against the Law? no, no, Brother, these things are not to be suffer'd in a Civill Government by Law Establish'd,—wherefore let's about it—

[*Exeunt.*

[…]

ACT II, SCENE I. *A Pavilion.*

Discovers the Indian King *and* Queen *sitting in State, with Guards of* Indians, *Men and Women attending: to them* Bacon *richly dress'd, attended by* Daring, Fearless, *and other Officers, he bows to the* King *and* Queen, *who rise to receive him.*[25]

King. I am sorry Sir, we meet upon these terms, we who so often have embrac'd as friends.

Bacon. How charming is the Queen? [*aside.*] War, Sir, is not my bus'ness, nor my pleasure: Nor was I bred in Arms; My Country's good has forc'd me to assume a Soldier's life: And 'tis with much regret that I Employ the first effects of it against my Friends; Yet whilst I may—Whilst this Cessation lasts, I beg we may exchange those Friendships, Sir, we have so often paid in happier Peace.

King. For your part, Sir, you've been so Noble, that I repent the fatall difference that makes us meet in Arms. Yet tho' I'm young I'm sensible of Injuries; And oft have heard my Grandsire say—That we were Monarchs once of all this spacious World; Till you an unknown People landing here, Distress'd and ruin'd by destructive storms, Abusing all our Charitable Hospitality, Usurp'd our Right, and made your friends your slaves.

---

[25]   *Daring, Fearless … King and Queen*: in the *dramatis personae*, Daring and Fearless are both Lieutenant Generals to Bacon. The American Indian King is named Cavarnio, and the Queen is named Semernia.

Bacon. I will not justify the Ingratitude of my fore-fathers, but finding here my Inheritance, I am resolv'd still to maintain it so, And by my sword which first cut out my Portion, Defend each inch of Land with my last drop of Bloud.

Queen. Ev'n his threats have charms that please the heart:

[*aside.*

King. Come Sir, let this ungrateful Theme alone, which is better disputed in the Field.

Queen. Is it impossible there might be wrought an understanding betwixt my Lord and you? 'Twas to that end I first desired this truce, My self pro-posing to be Mediator, To which my Lord *Cavarnio* shall agree, Could you but Condescend—I know you're Noble: And I have heard you say our tender Sex could never plead in vain.

Bacon. Alas! I dare not trust your pleading Madam! A few soft words from such a Charming mouth would make me lay the Conqueror at your feet as a Sacrifice for all the ills he has done you.

Queen. How strangely am I pleas'd to hear him talk

[*aside.*

King. Semernia see—the Dancers do appear; Sir will you take your seat?

[*to* Bacon:

[*He leads the* Queen *to a seat, they sit and talk.*]

Bacon. Curse on his sports that interrupted me, My very soul was hovering at my Lip, ready to have discover'd all its secrets. But oh! I dread to tell her of my pain, And when I wou'd, an Awfull trembling seizes me, And she can only from my dying eyes, read all the Sentiments of my Captive heart.

[*sits down, the rest wait.*

Enter Indians *that dance Anticks;*[26] *After the Dance the* King *seems in discourse with* Bacon, *the* Queen *rises, and comes forth.*

Queen. The more I gaze upon this English Stranger, the more Confusion struggles in my Soul, Oft I have heard of Love, and oft this Gallant Man (When Peace had made him pay his idle Visits) has told a thousand tales of dying Maids. And ever when he spoke, my panting heart, with a Prophetick fear in sigh reply'd, I shall fall such a Victim to his Eyes.

---

[26]   *dance Anticks*: grotesque and bizarre dancing.

Charles Davenant, from
Discourse on the
Plantation Trade (1698)

Charles Davenant (1656–1714) was the eldest son of the dramatist William D'Avenant. He was the commissioner of excise under James II, and, although not employed under William III, was appointed inspector-general under Queen Anne from 1705 until his death. Davenant was a prolific analyst of political economy, writing works such as *A Discourse on the Publick Revenues and of the Trade of England* (1698) and *Essays on the Balance of Power* (1701). His collected works were published in 1771 by Charles Whitworth MP.

In the first half of the eighteenth century, Davenant's *Discourse* was the foremost analysis of the government of colonies, and it drew out a number of key concerns. First, that the extent of liberty and religious toleration needed to be carefully judged. Davenant also felt that colonies ought to exist for the common good, so that private interests should be discouraged. Finally, he also wanted to avoid the problems associated with an over-extended or even over-successful empire – luxurious wealth, political corruption, moral decline and even effeminacy. The reprinting of his works in 1771 and this essay in 1775 gives an indication of the relevance of Davenant's thinking in the run-up to the War of American Independence. Indeed, he noted that these thoughts 'may be thought needless at present, and rather useful for posterity'. In all of these issues was the insistent question of the relationship of colonial identity to English identity.[1]

The Welfare of all Countries whatsoever depends upon good Government; and, without Doubt, these Colonies will flourish, if they are intrusted to honest, discreet, and skilful Hands, who will let them perceive they enjoy the Rights and Liberties of *Englishmen*, though not in *England*.

Industry has its first Foundation in Liberty: They who either are Slaves, or who believe their Freedoms precarious, can neither succeed in Trade nor meliorate a Country. We shall not pretend to determine whether the People in the Plantations have a Right to all the Privileges of *English* Subjects; but the contrary Notion is perhaps too much entertained and practised in Places which happen to be distant from St. *Stephen's* Chapel.[2] Upon which Account it will peradventure be a great Security and

---

[1] Text from *Select Dissertations on Colonies and Plantations. By Those Celebrated Authors, Sir Josiah Child, Charles D'avenant, LL.D. and Mr. William Wood* (London, 1775), pp. 53, 58–59, 63–65, 68–69. The 'posterity' quotation is from p. 84.

[2] *St. Stephen's Chapel*: Either St. Stephen's, Westminster, near the Houses of Parliament; or, St. Stephen's, Walbrook, which was on the door-step of the financial and commercial institutions that were the powerhouse of the British empire: the Bank of England and the Royal Exchange.

Encouragement to these industrious People, if a declaratory Law were made that *Englishmen* have Right to all the Laws of *England*, while they remain in Countries subject to the Dominion of this Kingdom. But as the arbitrary Proceedings and Mal-administration of Governors should be severely animadverted upon, so frivolous and wrong Complaints should be as much discouraged.

[...]

The Welfare of all Countries in the World depends upon the Morals of their People.

For though a Nation may gather Riches by Trade, Thrift, Industry, and from the Benefit of its Soil and Situation; and though a People may attain to great Wealth and Power, either by Force of Arms, or by the Sagacity of their Councils; yet, when their Manners are depraved, they will decline insensibly, and at last come to utter Destruction.

When a Country is grown vicious, Industry decays, the People become effeminate and unfit for Labour. To maintain Luxury, the great Ones must oppress the meaner Sort; and to avoid this Oppression, the meaner Sort are often compelled to seditious Tumults, or open Rebellion.

Such therefore who have modelled Governments for any Duration have endeavoured to propose Methods by which the Riotous Appetites, the Lusts, Avarice, Revenge, Ambition, and other disorderly Passions of the People, might be bounded.

And to preserve Societies of Men from that perpetual War with which the State of Nature must be attended, and to restrain that Discord which must for ever embroil those who only follow the wild Dictates of ungoverned Nature, the Founders of Cities, States, and Empires, have set a-foot Forms of religious Worship to awe their Minds, and devised wholesome Laws to keep within Bounds the Persons of the People.[3]

It has been set forth in the Series of this Discourse, of what Profit the *American* Plantations have been to *England*; and it may not be improper before we conclude, to add something concerning their future Polity and Government, and to shew what methods, in all Likelihood may preserve their Being in that remote Region, give them Stability and a firm Existence, and so render them a lasting Mine of Riches, and a perpetual Advantage to this Kingdom.

And as a Foundation, we think it necessary to lay down, that those Countries cannot subsist long in a flourishing Condition, and in their Obedience to this Crown, unless Care be taken to cultivate Morality and

---

[3]   *And ... People*: that humankind in a 'state of nature' exists in a state of 'perpetual war' echoes the thoughts of Thomas Hobbes in *The Leviathan, or, The Matter, Form, and Power of a Commonwealth, Ecclesiastical and Civil* (1651), part one, ch. 8.

Virtue among them, to promote Religion, and to establish sound Laws, by which they may be well and wisely governed.

But here it may be objected, 1st, What Form of Religion shall be set up among a People, who, many of them, have left their Native Soil, chiefly to enjoy a more ample Liberty in religious Matters? 2dly, How can virtuous Principles be instilled into Men, the Badness of whose Lives and Manners have compelled most of them to seek another Habitation?

To the First Objection we answer, That the same Liberty of Conscience ought to be permitted there as here; but that the Governors and Magistrates should take Care to keep the People to the Observation of some Religion or other; and now more especially, since the Laws have in a Manner allowed every Man to chuse which Sect he pleases.

To the Second Objection we say, That the *Roman* Nation was first composed of Thieves, Vagabonds, fugitive Slaves, indebted Persons, and Outlaws; and yet, by a good Constitution and wholesome Laws, they became and continued for some Ages, the most virtuous People that was ever known; so that as loose Administration corrupts any Society of Men, so a wise, steady, and strict Government, will in Time reform a Country, let its Manners have been never so depraved.

[...]

In order to Protection, they ought to believe *England* their native Soil; and in order to preserve them in their Obedience, we ought to imprint this Notion in their Minds as much as possible.

Few Crimes, either private or relating to the Public, can be committed by those whose Minds are early seasoned with the Principle of loving and promoting the Welfare of their native Country. For, generally speaking, all our Vices whatsoever turn to her Prejudice; and if we were convinced of this betimes, and if from our very Youth we were seasoned with this Notion, we should of Course be virtuous, and our Country would prosper and flourish, in Proportion to this Amendment of our Manners.

Wherever private Men can be brought to make all their Actions and Counsels, Thoughts and Designments, to center in the common Good, that Nation will soon gather such Strength as shall resist any home-bred Mischief or outward Accident.

No great Thing was ever done, but by such as have preferred the Love of their Country to all other Considerations; and wherever this Public Spirit reigns, and where this Zeal for the Common Good governs in the Minds of Men, that State will flourish and encrease in Riches and Power; and wherever it declines, or is set at nought, Weakness, Disorder, and Poverty, must be expected.

This Love to their Native Soil, where it has been deeply rooted, and where it could be preserved, has made little Cities famous and invincible, as

Sparta, Corinth, Thebes and *Athens*, and from thence all the *Roman* Greatness took its Rise.[4] But where they are wretchedly contriving their own Ends, without any Care of their Country's Profit, or trafficking its Wealth and Liberties for Rewards, Preferments and Titles; where every One is snatching all he can from the Prince; and where there is a general Neglect of national Interest, they grow luxurious, proud, false and effeminate; and a People so depraved, is commonly the Prey of some Neighbour seasoned with more Wise and better Principles.

In a Kingdom but too near us, we may see all Sorts of Men labouring the Public Welfare, and every one as vigilant in his Post, as if the Success of the whole Empire depended on his single Care and Diligence; so that to the Shame of another Place, they seem more intent upon the Prosperity and Honour of their Country, under a hard and oppressive Tyranny, than they are in some free Nations, where the People have a Interest in the Laws, and are a Part of the Constitution.

Homer in his two Poems seems to intend but two Morals. In the *Illiads* to set out how fatal Discord among the great Ones is to States and Armies. And in his *Odysseys* to shew, that the Love of our own Country ought to be stronger than any other Passion; for he makes *Ulysses* quit the Nymph *Calypso* with all her Pleasures, and the Immortality she had promised him, to return to *Ithica*, a rocky and barren Island.[5]

The Affairs of a Country relating either to Civil Government, War, the Revenues, or Trade, can never be well and prosperously conducted, unless the Men of principal Rank and Figure divest themselves of their Passions, Self-interest, overweening Opinion of their own Merits, their Flattery, false Arts, mean Ambition, and irregular Appetites and Pursuits, after Wealth and Greatness.

No People did ever become famous and powerful but by Temperance, Fortitude, Justice, Reverence to the Laws, and Piety to their Country; and when any Empire is destined to be undone, or to lose its Freedom, the Seeds of this Ruin are to be first seen in the Corruption of its Manners. In vicious Governments all Care of the Public is laid aside, and every one is plundering for himself, as if the Commonwealth were adrift, or had suffered Shipwreck; and where a People is thus depraved, their National Assemblies have the first open Marks of the Infection upon them, from whence spring all Disorders in the State whatsoever. For then, such as have most Eloquence, Valour, Skill in Business, and most Interest in their Country, throw off the Mask of Popularity which they had put on for a Time, and in the Face of the World desire Wealth, Honours, and Greatness upon any Terms; and this Ambition leads them to corrupt others, that their

---

[4]   *Sparta ... Athens*: all cities that were central to ancient Greek greatness.
[5]   *Homer*: classical author of the epic poems *The Iliad* (about the hero Achilles and the war against Troy) and *The Odyssey* (on the adventures of Odysseus returning from the Trojan war).

own natural Vices may be the less observed; so that in a Constitution ripe for Change, those who are best esteemed and most trusted begin to buy the People's Voices, and afterwards expose to Sale their own Suffrages; which Practice is always attended with utter Destruction, or the Loss of Liberty.

This Error in the first Concoction does presently deprave the whole Mass; for then the Dignities of the Commonwealth are made the Reward of Fraud and Vice, and not the Recompence of Merit. All is bought and sold, and the worst Men who can afford to bid highest, are accepted; and where the Management is once got into such Hands, Factions are suffered to grow, rash Counsels are embraced, and wholesome Advices rejected; every one is busy for himself, and careless of the Common Interest; Treachery is winked at, and private Persons are allowed to become wealthy by the public Spoils: All which is followed with the Loss of Reputation Abroad, and Poverty at Home.

[...]

That Government is happy where the Bounds between the chief Power and the People are so wisely laid out and fixed, that no Encroachments can be easily apprehended; for the Disputes and Quarrels concerning these Bounds and Limits have always been the chief Gain and Harvest of bad and designing Men, and the Field in which they exercise those Wicked Arts that so often embroil a Country.

To make this National Assembly a lasting Benefit to the Colonies, such as are sent to govern those Parts should take all possible Care to cure the present Vices, and prevent the future Corruption of the People.

The Natural Steps to Ruin in Politic Institutions, that have a Mixture in them of Popular Government, seem to be in this Manner: 1st, Extended Dominion, Power atchieved by Arms or Riches flowing in by Trade, beget Effeminacy, Pride, Ambition and Luxuries of all Kinds; these Vices, as they obtain Strength and Growth, produce quickly private Poverty, and then public Want; private Poverty puts ill Men upon wicked Arts to get Wealth, and public Want but too often makes those ill Men necessary in a corrupted State.

Thus the *Roman* Gentry were so debauched by their Luxuries, and pressed with their Wants, that they assisted *Cinna, Sylla, Marius, Cataline* and *Cæsar* to invade the Commonwealth; till, at last, *Cæsar*'s Tyranny became all the Refuge which the Public had in its Disorders and Calamities.[6]

---

6   *Cinna ... Cæsar*: all examples of Roman politicians who rebelled against Rome. Marius: Gaius Marius (b. *c.* 157BC) consul and general who led an army against Sulla and, together with Cornelius Cinna, was proclaimed consul of Rome (86BC). Sylla: Cornelius Sulla Felix (*c.* 138–70BC), senator and general who rebelled in 88BC, and again in 84BC when he was appointed dictator, though he eventually restored democracy. Cataline: Sergius Catalina, organised a conspiracy against senator Cicero in 62BC. Julius Caesar (100–44BC), general and commander of Gaul, invaded Italy in 49BC, and eventually declared himself dictator in perpetuity in 44BC.

When the Gentry for some Time have been set loose in their Principles, the Common People begin to lay aside their Worth and Integrity, and the whole Mass of Blood in the Body Politic grows so corrupted, as not to be capable of those Remedies which good Lawgivers and wise Statesmen would offer; so *Augustus* saw the *Romans*, in that Age, not fit for Freedom, which, probably, hindered him from restoring Liberty, and made him chuse rather to continue the Empire in the Hands of a single Person, and transmit it to *Tiberius*.[7]

These National Assemblies, the Use of which are here recommended for our Northern Colonies, will be of little Benefit, unless the People, by whose Voices they must be chosen, can be kept from being corrupted in their Elections; for, otherwise, they will prove but a false Appearance of Freedom, which is the worst Kind of Slavery.

Joseph Pitts, from
A True and Faithful Account of the Religion and Manners of the Mohammetans ... With an Account of the Author's being taken Captive, and of his Escape (1704)

Joseph Pitts (1663–?1735) was a merchant seaman from Topsham, Devon. In 1678 he was captured off the coast of Spain by corsairs from the Regency of Algiers, and was in captivity until 1693. The Barbary states, on the north coast of Africa, were part of the Islamic Ottoman empire and posed a threat to British aspirations to wrest control from France and Spain in the strategically vital Mediterranean. However, the British empire's outposts in Gibraltar and Minorca were also dependent upon

---

[7]　*Augustus ... Tiberius*: after the rule of Julius Caesar, Augustus (63BC–AD14) was the first emperor of Rome (43BC–AD13). Tiberius (42BC–AD19) was emperor (AD14–19) after Augustus.

the Barbary states for supplies: as a result, the British were reluctant to go to war and instead ransomed and bargained (sometimes offering weapons) for the return of Barbary captives. Barbary corsairs plagued merchant shipping, stealing cargoes and enslaving the crews, and were a potent symbol, reminding all that Britons could indeed be slaves.

In *A True and Faithful Account*, Pitts wavers between horror and fascination as he reflects on his experience of 15 years in Islamic north Africa. On the one hand he reproduces Oriental stereotypes (of Turkish sodomy, for instance). Moreover, after a graphic account of the tortures he had received under his first *patroon* to convert him to Islam, his sense of religious identity comes under considerable pressure as can be seen in the painful correspondence with his father. On the other hand, Pitts frequently stresses the religious devotion of the Muslims, especially in his extraordinary account of the pilgrimage to Mecca, the *hajj*; he even feels he loves his final *patroon* 'like a Father'. Pitts finally escaped and returned home, and his final words praise God's providential hand in his life and hopes for the conversion of heathens. Pitts's remarkable account of his captivity and conversion reveals both the importance of the Christian/heathen dichotomy to English identity, and yet how mutable that identity could be.[1]

When I was about Fourteen or Fifteen years of Age, my *Genius*[2] led me to be a Sailor, and to see Foreign Countries: (much contrary to my Mother's mind, tho' my Father seem'd to yield to my humour) and after having made two or three short Voyages, my Fancy was to range further abroad, for which I sufficiently suffered, as in the sequel of the Story will appear.

Having Ship'd my self *Easter-Tuesday*, *Anno* 1678, with one Mr. *George Taylor*, Master of the *Speedwell of Lymson* near *Exeter*, (Mr. Alderman *George Tuthill of Exon* Owner) bound to the Western Islands from thence to *Newfoundland*, from thence to *Bilboa*, from thence to the *Canaries*, and so Home, had God permitted. We got safe to *Newfoundland*; and our Business being ended there, with a fair Wind we put out for *Bilboa*, and after we had been out about 40 days from *Newfoundland*; coming near the Coast of *Spain* (which we knew was the Place where the *Algerines* us'd to haunt for poor Ships that come from the Westward) we look'd out sharp for Ships, avoiding all we saw, but especially did we look out in the Morning at Sun-rising, and in the Evening at Sun-setting. The day in which we were Taken, our Mate, Mr. *John Milton*, was early at Top-mast-head, and cried out, *Asail!* The Master ask'd him *Where? At Leeward*, replied the Mate, *about five or six Leagues*. And so, *to be brief in my Relation*, about Mid-day, being almost overtaken by them, (the Enemy being but about a Mile distance from us) our Master said, it will be in vain for us to make our Flight any longer, seeing it will be but an Hour or two e'er we shall be Taken, and then probably fare the worse if we continue our Flight. I may leave any Person to judge what

---

1   Text from, pp. 1–3, 18, 81– 2, 142–9, 170–2, 182–3.

2   *Genius*: in this case, either a person's disposition or the fateful influence over a person's life.

an heartless Condition we were in, but yet still we could not forbear kenning the Ship, that unwelcome Object, who Devil-like was eager in the pursuit of us. All hope now failing, and there being no place for refuge, we hawled up our Sails and waited for them. As soon as the Pyrate came up with us, the Captain being a *Dutch* Renegade, and able to speak *English*, bid us hoist out our Boat; which we could not do without much Trouble and Time, by reason that a few Days before, one of our Men in a great Storm was wash'd over-board, and I myself was Scalded and so disabled for Working, so that we had but Four Men that were able: And therefore, before we could make half ready to hoist out our Boat, they came a-board us in *theirs*. I being but Young the Enemy seem'd to me as monstrous ravenous Creatures, which made me cry out, *O Master! I am afraid they will kill us, and eat us. No, no, Child*, said my Master, *they will carry us to* Algier, *and sell us*.

The very first words they spake, and the first thing they did, was Beating us with Ropes, saying, *Into Boat you English Dogs!* And without the least Opposition, with Fear, we tumbled into their Boat, we scarce knew how. They having loaden their Boat, carried us aboard their Ship, and diligent Search was made about us for Money, but they found none. We were the first Prize they had taken for that Voyage, and they had been out at Sea about Six Weeks. As for our Vessel, after they had taken out of her what they thought fit and necessary for their use, they sunk her; for she being laden with Fish, they thought it not worth while to carry or send her Home to *Algier*.

[...]

When their Camp is setting forth, (of which in the next Chapter) then especially they are apt to drink, (*i.e.* the Soldiery) and are abominably Rude, insomuch that it is very dangerous for any Woman to walk in any By-place, but more dangerous for *Boys*, for they are extremely given to *Sodomy*; and therefore Care is taken that it be cried about the Town, *That all People take care of their Wives and Children*. And yet this horrible Sin of *Sodomy* is so far from being punish'd amongst them, that it is part of their ordinary Discourse to boast and brag of their detestable Actions of that kind. Tis common for Men to fall in Love with Boys, as tis here in *England* to be in Love with Women: And I have seen many when they have been drunk, that have given themselves deep Gashes on their Arms with a Knife, saying, *'Tis for the Love they bear to such a Boy*. There are many so addicted to this prodigious Sin, that they *loath the Natural Use of the Woman*; (such the Apostle inveighs against, *Rom*.I.27.) And I *assure* you, That I have seen many that have had their Arms *full* of great Cuts, as so many Tokens of their Love (or rather worse than *Bestial Lust*) to such their *Catamites*. But this being so *inhumane* and *unnatural* a thing, I profess I am asham'd to enlarge further upon it, as I could. But what I could say on this Subject, must needs be *disgustful* to every modest and christian Reader; and therefore, I think, I am obliged to forbear: Only I crave leave to make this *Reflection*, viz. *That* Intemperance *in Drinking hurries Men on to the worst of Vices; and tho'* the Inclination of these hot People, and the Countenance *that is given to such* Crimes, are too great Incentives; yet, avoiding Intemperance, *they would be* less *liable to them.*

[…]

As soon as we come to the Town of *Mecca*, the *Dilleel*, or Guide, carries us into the great Street, which is in the midst of the Town, and to which the Temple joyns; and after the Camelsare laid down, he first directs us to the *Fountains*, there to take *abdes*;[3] which being done, he brings us to the *Temple*; into which (having left our Shoes with one who constantly attends to receive them) we enter at the Door called *Bab-el-Salem, i.e.* the *Welcome Gate*; after a few Paces entrance, the *Dilleel* makes a stand, and holds up his Hands towards the *Beat-olloh*[4] (it being in the middle of the *Temple* or *Mosque*) the *Hagges* imitating him, and speaking after him the same Words. At the very first sight of the *Beat-olloh* the *Hagges* melt into Tears; then we are led up to it, still speaking after the *Dilleel*; then we are led *round* the *Beat-olloh* seven times, and then make two *erkaets*.[5] This being done, we are led out into the Street again, where we are sometimes to run, and sometimes to walk very quick with the *Dilleel*, from one place of the Street to the other, about a Bow-shoot.[6] And I profess, I could not chuse but admire to see those poor Creatures so extraordinary *Devout* and *Affectionate* when they were about these *Superstitions*, and with what *Awe* and *Trembling* they were possess'd. Insomuch, that I could scarce forbear shedding of *Tears* to see their Zeal, tho' *blind* and *Idolatrous*. After all this is done, we return to the place in the Street where we left our Camels with our Provision and Necessaries, and then look out for *Lodgings*; where, when we come, we *Disrobe* and take off our *Hirrawems*,[7] and put on our ordinary Cloths again.

[…]

I was very much concern'd for one of our Countrymen who had endur'd many Years of Slavery, and after he was Ransomed, and went home to his own Country, came again to *Algeir* and voluntarily, without the least Force used towards him, became a *Mohammetan*.

---

3   *abdes*: ritual ablutions. 'Note, that before they'l provide for themselves they serve God in their way' [Pitts's note].

4   *Beat-olloh*: the Ka'bah, the large cubic stone structure in the centre of the Grand Mosque. The 'Black Stone' set in the corner of the Ka'bah is also venerated.

5   *erkaets*: the recitation of a prayer of two *raka'āt*.

6   *some times to run … Bow-shoot*: the ritual walking between the hills of Safā and Marwah.

7   *Hirrawems*: or *ihrām*, the pilgrim's sacred robes of two seamless wrappers.

Another *English-man* I knew, who was bred to the Trade of a *Gun-Smith*, who after he was Ransomed, and only waited for his Passage, Reneg'd, and chose rather to be a *Mohammetan* than to return to his own Country.

About two or three Months, as near as I can guess, after I was taken a Slave, I writ a Letter to my Father, giving him an Account of my Misfortune; to which Letter I did receive from my Father a kind and affectionate Answer. A Copy of the Letter I have not by me, but I well remember that therein he gave me very good Counsel, *viz. To have a care and keep close to God, and to be sure never, by any Methods of Cruelty that could be used towards me, to deny my blessed Saviour: And that he had rather hear of my Death, than of my being a* Mohammetan. But this first Letter from my Father came not to my Hands 'till some Days after I had, through my *Patroon's* Barbarity to me, turn'd from my Religion. Which after, through extreme Torture, and out of Love to a *Temporal Life*, I had done, I became very sad and melancholy, considering the Danger my poor Soul was in. The said Letter was taken up in *Algier* by my Master *George Taylor* of *Lymson*, who sent it to the Camp, and directed to an *English* Lad, one of the *Bey's*, or General's Slaves; who being afraid to deliver me the Letter openly, slid it into my Hand as he past by me. As soon as I cast my Eye upon the Superscription, I knew it to be my Father's Hand, and in a great deal of Sorrow, made what haste I could out of the Camp, as pretending to go to ease my self, to read the Letter; but when I had open'd it, could scarce read a Word for weeping. And I am apt to think, that if the Letter had come to my Hands before I had turn'd *Turk*, that my *Patroon* would rather have accepted of the promis'd Ransom for me, than that I should become a *Mohammetan*. After I had read some part of the Letter (for I could not read it through at once, for fear my *Patroon* should find me wanting) I was ready to sink. I put up the Letter therefore, intending to read the whole another time, and return'd to our Tent, with a more dejected Heart and Countenance than before; insomuch, that my *Patroon* perceiving it, ask'd me whether I had been weeping. I reply'd, *Sir, you don't see me weep*. Many other angry Words he had with me; and at length truly my Heart was so big, that I could not contain any longer, but fell into Tears; and at the same time produc'd him the Letter which I received from my Father, and told him that my Father would ransom me; *And, said I, I am no* Turk, *but a* Christian. My *Patroon* answered me with, *Hold your Tongue, you Dog, for if you speak such a Word again, I'll have a great Fire made, and therein burn thee immediately.* At which I was forc'd to be silent.

In two or three Days after this, I writ my Father a second Letter, which I was forc'd to do by piece-meals, in a great deal of Danger and Fear, in which I gave him a perfect Account of the whole matter, and told him the naked Truth, least he should have thought that what I did, I did voluntarily and without any Coercion. And in order thereunto, I privately desired the aforesaid *English* Lad, a Servant to the *Bey*, to lend me Pen, Ink, and Paper; and took an occasion to go outside the Camp, and there in Fear writ two or three Lines at a time, as I could, without discovery, 'till I had finish'd my Epistle.

The substance of my Letter, was, that tho' I was forc'd by that cruelty that was exercis'd upon me, to turn *Turk*, yet I was really a Christian in my Heart; (some may term me *Hypocrite* for so doing, but I'll not reply any more, than this, That I speak it not to extenuate my Sin, but to set the Matter in a true Light, how I turn'd, & the *Reasons* of my so doing.) And withal, I assur'd my Father and Mother that I would, as soon as ever I could find an opportunity, endeavour to make my escape: and therefore intreated them to be as contented as they could under their great Trouble and Affliction, and expect what time would produce.

Sometime after my Father receiv'd this my Second Letter, he sent me another, which was directed (as the former) to my Master *Taylor* in *Algier*, and he sent it forward, and directed it to an *Englishman* at *Bleda*, where I then lived, of whom I receiv'd it; and I look upon it as a signal Providence, for there was but that one *Englishman* then living in the Town. The Substance of the Letter is as followeth, *viz.*

Yet I cannot chuse but call thee dear and loving Son, altho' thou hast denied thy Redeemer that bought thee; especially, considering the Tenderness of thy Age, the Cruelty of thy Usage, and the Strength of thy Temptations. I confess, when I first heard of it, I thought it would have overwhelm'd my Spirits: And had it not been for divine Supports, it had been a Burden too too unsupportable for my weak Shoulders to have crippled under; especially considering the loss of thy Soul.

But withal, my Father in his Letter comforted me, with telling me, That he had been with several Ministers, who unanimously concurred in their Opinion, that I had not sinned the *Unpardonable Sin*. And therefore he goes on to comfort me:

Truly Child, I do believe, that what thou hast done with thy Mouth, was not with thy Heart; and that it was contrary to thy Conscience. Take heed of being hardned in thine Iniquity; give not way to Despondency, nor to Desperation. Remember that Peter *had not so many Temptations to deny his* Lord and Master, *as thou hast had; and yet he obtain'd Mercy, and so may'st thou. Yet the Door of Grace and Mercy is open for thee. I can hardly write to thee for weeping, and my time is but short; and what shall I say to thee more, my poor Child? I will pawn the loss of my Soul, upon the salvation of thine, that if thou dost but duly and daily repent of this thy horrid Iniquity, that the Blood of that Jesus whom thou hast denied, there is sufficient Satisfaction in him to save thee to the utmost, or otherwise let me perish. I will promise thee as welcome to me upon thy Return and Repentance, as though thou hadst never done it. And if there be such Bowels of Pity in an earthly Parent, which is but drops to the Ocean, what dost thou think of the boundless Mercies of GOD, whose Compassions are like to himself, Infinite? I confess, It's something difficult for thee to make thy Escape, but yet*

I am confident, that if thou dost keep close to GOD, notwithstanding this thy Miscarriage, that infinite Wisdom and Power will be set at work to find out Ways, in such untrodden Paths, that I cannot imagine, for thy Relief. Which is the daily Prayers of thy

Affectionate Father, John Pitts.

It pleased GOD that this my Father's second Letter, though cause of many sorrowful Reflections in me, did yet administer great Support and Comfort to me; and I would often go into some By-corner, or under some Hedge of a Garden, to read it.

The Reader may easily think, that one under my Circumstances could have but very few Opportunities of writing home to his Parents and Friends, which was the reason why I writ no oftner.

In my Return from *Mecca* to *Algier*, at *Alexandria* I accidentally met with *John Cleak* of *Lymson*, who belong'd to Captain *Bear's* Ship of *Topsham* (as I related to you before, p. 113.) in whom, being my old Acquaintance, I could put Confidence, and so desired him to carry a Letter for me, which he readily granted me. But since I came home to *Exon*, he the said *Cleak* told me, that he was under great Fear and Concern, least the *Turks* Officers on Board (who are much like our Tidesmen) should, when searching their Chests etc. find the Letter in his Custody; to prevent which, he hung it inside the Ceiling of the Ship. The Reader will excuse my not dating the Letter, when I tell him, that truly then I forgot the Month and the Year; because the *Turks* reckon after a different manner from us; and therefore I did not only omit the Date of the Letter, but sent it also unsealed; as the manner of sending Letters is there: For indeed they are very Illiterate, not One in an Hundred being able to Read; and therefore they run no great Risque in sending their Letters unsealed.

Honoured and dear Father and Mother,

It is not the want of Duty or Love, which makes me negligent of Writing to you; but 'tis chiefly the Consideration of the little Comfort you can take in hearing from me, having been a great Grief and Heart-breaking to you.

Dear Father and Mother, *How often have I wished that I had departed the World when I hung upon your Breasts, that I might not have been the bringer of your grey Hairs with Sorrow to the Ground. Therefore, if you would be an Ease to my Grief, I desire you to wait GOD's Leisure.*

Your Grief, tho' great, is but little, in comparison of mine. Put it to the worst, you have lost but a Son; but I for my part have lost both a dear Father and Mother, Brothers, Relations, Friends, Acquaintance, and all! But my greatest Sorrow is, that GOD hath deprived me of his Holy Scriptures, of any good Counsel or Discourse; for I see nothing but Wickedness before mine Eyes.

The Lord of Heaven reward you for your Endeavours to bring me up in the Ways of Jesus Christ; for the bad Improvement of which Priviledge, I now here-find and suffer the want of it. I am in great Fears, and great Hazards do I run, in writing these few Lines. About fourteen Months I have been wanting from Algier, *for I have been with my* Patroon *to* Mecca; *where is, they say, the House of GOD; and after they have been to pay their Devotions thither, they do account that all their Sins are forgiven.*

Mecca *is about forty days Travel beyond* Grand Cairo; *being now therefore in my way back again to* Algier *(as far as* Alexandria*) I embrace this Opportunity of sending to you from hence. With my kind Love to all my Brothers, Relations, Friends and Neighbours, desiring yours, and the Prayers of all good People to GOD for me, I rest,*

> Your dutiful Son 'till Death,
> Joseph Pitts.

[...]

All this while no *English* or *Dutch* Ships came to *Smyrna*; the Consul[8] and Mr. *Elliot* therefore consulted which was my best way to take; to tarry in *Smyrna* after all the *Algerines* were gone, would look suspiciously; and therefore they advised me not to tarry in *Smyrna*, but either to go to *Scio* with the *Algerines*, which is part of our way back to *Rhodes*, or else to go up to the *Constantinople*; and when I were there, to write to the said Mr. *Elliot*, to acquaint him where I was; and to stay there 'till I had Directions from them to return to *Smyrna*, or what else to do.

I pursued their Advice, and went with some of the *Algerines* to *Scio*, and there I made a stop 'till all the *Algerines* were gone from thence, and writ Mr. *Elliot* where I was. A short time after, he writ me, that he was very glad that I was where I was; but withal, gave a damp to my Spirits, with the bad News, that our *Smyrna* Fleet were said to be intercepted by the *French*; with the cold reserve of Comfort, that it wanted Confirmation, and that they hop'd it was not true.

Now the Devil was very busy with me, tempting me to lay aside all thoughts of Escaping, and to return to *Algier*, and continue a *Mussulman*. What with the Temptation, and what with the Disappointment, I was very melancholy. But here the Goodness of God was manifested to me in such a measure, that I at last surmounted all the Temptations and Fears that so furiously beset me, which were indeed very great: For it was suggested to me, first, That it was a very difficult, if not a desperate Attempt, to endeav-our to make my Escape; and that if I were discovered in it, I should be put to death after the most cruel and exemplary manner. And also, in the next place, the Loss that I should sustain thereby, in several respects, *viz.* The loss

---

8   *Consul*: the English Consul at Smyrna was William Raye.

of the profitable Returns which I might make of what Money I had to *Algier*; and the Loss of receiving eight Months Pay due to me in *Algier*; and the frustrating my Hopes and Expectation which I had from my *Patroon*, who made me large Promises of leaving me considerable Substance at his Death; and I believe he meant as he promised; for I must acknowledge he was like a Father to me.

After I had my Liberty to go from him, or live with him, I chose to live with him; and he was so willing of it, that he gave me my Meat, Coffee, Washing, Lodging and Cloths, freely; and in short, lov'd me as if I had been his own Child; which made me sincerely to love him, I do acknowledge. This was also a great Temptation for me to return to *Algier*.

In the midst of all, I would pray to God for his Assistance, and found it. For I bless God, that after all my Acquaintance were gone from *Scio* to *Rhodes*, I grew daily better and better satisfied; though my Fears were still very great, you must imagine; and I was indeed afraid every-body I met did suspect my Design. And I can truly say, that I would not go through such a Labyrinth of Sorrows and Troubles again, might I gain a Kingdom. For at this very Hour, when I reflect upon my Danger, my Concern revives, and my very Flesh trembles.

[...]

Thus have I briefly given the World an Account of my Travels and Misfortunes; and of the good Providences of Almighty God towards me; which if it may do any manner of Good, in any Respect, to any individual Person, I shall reckon it a great Happiness.

And as to my own part, I hope I shall never forget the Wonderful Goodness of the Lord towards me; whose blessed Name I desire to Glorify *in the fight of all Men*.

To Him therefore, Father, Son and Holy Ghost, be all Worship, Honour, and Thanksgiving, for ever and ever! *Amen*.

'O Merciful GOD, who hast made all *Men*, and hatest nothing that thou hast made; nor wouldest the Death of a Sinner, but rather that he should be Converted & Live; have Mercy upon all *Jews*, *Turks*, *Infidels*, and *Hereticks*; and take from them all Ignorance, Hardness of Heart, and Contempt of thy Word; and so fetch them home, Blessed Lord, to thy Flock, that they may be saved among the Remnant of the True *Israelites*, and be made one Fold, under one Shepherd, Jesus Christ our Lord, who Liveth and Reigneth with Thee and the Holy Spirit, One God, World without end.'
Amen.

Richard Steele,
The Spectator, no. 11
(13 March 1711)

The Spectator

This periodical was written largely by Richard Steele (1672–1729), MP, dramatist and author of *The Christian Hero* (1701) and Joseph Addison (1672–1719), MP, poet, and author of the tragedy *Cato* (1713). *The Spectator* appeared daily from March 1711 to December 1712 and was one of the most influential periodicals of the eighteenth century – it was said that if one owned only two books one would be the Bible, the other the *Spectator* papers. It represented a fictional 'club' of gentlemen from different walks of life, and addressed the moral and cultural issues of the day, with 'Mr. Spectator' typically depicting himself as an impartial observer of urban life. Its fictional club members – from the country JP Sir Roger, through a lawyer, a merchant, a captain, a 'gallant', to a clergyman – suggests a socially inclusive concept of rank and status. However, the *Spectator* resolutely articulated what we might now call a middle-class ideology, in which ostensibly differing ranks shared a similar set of moral, commercial and aesthetic concerns, and which was an attempt to transform the values of 'nobility' for use by an urban professional class.

[Inkle and Yarico]

The source of Steele's tale in this issue is Richard Ligon's short account in *A True and Exact History of the Island of Barbadoes* (1657) of a Carib Indian slave being made pregnant by a Christian servant. Later she saves the life of a young man from a ship and they fall in love, the story ending with the youth selling her in Barbados as a slave, 'and so poor *Yarico* for her love, lost her liberty'.[1] Steele gave the tale its definitive shape and that is the one that endured in the memory of the eighteenth century. He also set the tale within a frame narrative concerning male inconstancy, calculated to appeal to a middle-class desire for the improvement of manners. However, the fable of Inkle and Yarico was to have lasting resonance throughout the eighteenth century, transformed into numerous poems (such as Stephen Duck's *Avora and Amanda*, 1736), plaintive epistles written from the point of view of Yarico (like Edward Jerningham's *Yarico to Inkle: An Epistle*, 1766), and a comic opera by George Colman in 1787. It sparked a diverse range of responses, but only later in the century did it become marked by a clear anti-slavery tone. This early incarnation, then, raises some intriguing questions concerning commerce, cross-cultural desire, manliness and femininity, and the representation of Native American women.

---

[1]   From Ligon, *A True and Exact History*, in Frank Felsenstein, ed., *English Trader, Indian Maid: Representing Gender, Race, and Slavery in the New World. An Inkle and Yarico Reader* (Johns Hopkins University Press, 1999), pp. 55–80 (p. 74).

Dat veniam corvis, vexat censura columbas. Juv.[2]

Arietta is visited by all Persons of both Sexes, who have any Pretence to Wit and Gallantry. She is in that time of Life which is neither affected with the Follies of Youth, or Infirmities of Age; and her Conversation is so mixed with Gaiety and Prudence, that she is agreeable both to the Young and the Old. Her Behaviour is very frank, without being in the least blameable; and as she is out of the Tract of any amorous or ambitious Pursuits of her own, her Visitants entertain her with Accounts of themselves very freely, whether they concern their Passions or their Interests. I made her a Visit this Afternoon, having been formerly introduced to the Honour of her Acquaintance, by my Friend *Will. Honeycomb*, who has prevailed upon her to admit me sometimes into her Assembly, as a civil, inoffensive Man. I found her accompanied with one Person only, a Common-Place Talker, who, upon my Entrance, rose, and after a very slight Civility sat down again; then turning to *Arietta*, pursued his Discourse, which I found was upon the old Topick, of Constancy in Love. He went on with great Facility in repeating what he talks every Day of his Life; and, with the Ornaments of insignificant Laughs and Gestures, enforced his Arguments by Quotations out of Plays and Songs, which allude to the Perjuries of the Fair, and the general Levity of Women. Methought he strove to shine more than ordinarily in his Talkative Way, that he might insult my Silence, and distinguish himself before a Woman of *Arietta*'s Taste and Understanding. She had often an Inclination to interrupt him, but could find no Opportunity, 'till the Larum ceased of its self; which it did not 'till he had repeated and murdered the celebrated Story of the *Ephesian* Matron.[3]

Arietta seem'd to regard this Piece of Raillery as an Outrage done to her Sex, as indeed I have always observed that Women, whether out of a nicer Regard to their Honour, or what other Reason I cannot tell, are more sensibly touched with those general Aspersions, which are cast upon their Sex, than Men are by what is said of theirs.

When she had a little recovered her self from the serious Anger she was in, she replied in the following manner.

Sir, When I consider, how perfectly new all you have said on this Subject is, and that the Story you have given us is not quite two thousand Years

---

2   *Dat ... columbas*: From Juvenal (*c*.55–*c*.140) *Satires*, II: 'The crows are absolved, while the doves are censured.' Steele has chosen this epigraph from a satire on masculinity.

3   *the Ephesian matron*: a story from Petronius (d. 66). In his *Satyricon*, a matron goes into the catacomb with the body of her husband, intending to die of weeping. After fasting for five days, a soldier, who is guarding several crucified corpses nearby, invites her to share his supper, and they are immediately sexually attracted to each other. For three days and nights they make love within the tomb. The soldier then discovers one of the corpses is missing for which the penalty is death. However, the woman urges him to replace that body with the body of her husband, asking why she should lose two good men in a less than a week.

Old, I cannot but think it a Piece of Presumption to dispute with you: But your Quotations put me in Mind of the Fable of the Lion and the Man.[4] The Man walking with that noble Animal, showed him, in the Ostentation of Human Superiority, a Sign of a Man killing the Lion. Upon which the Lion said very justly, *We Lions are none of us Painters, else we could show a hundred Men killed by Lions, for one Lion killed by a Man.* You Men are Writers, and can represent us Women as Unbecoming as you please in your Works, while we are unable to return the Injury. You have twice or thrice observed in your Discourse, that Hypocrisy is the very Foundation of our Education; and that an Ability to dissemble our Affections, is a professed Part of our Breeding. These, and other such Reflections, are sprinkled up and down the Writings of all Ages, by Authors, who leave behind them Memorials of their Resentment against the Scorn of particular Women, in Invectives against the whole Sex. Such a Writer, I doubt not, was the celebrated *Petronius*, who invented the pleasant Aggravations of the Frailty of the *Ephesian* Lady; but when we consider this Question between the Sexes, which has been either a Point of Dispute or Raillery ever since there were Men and Women, let us take Facts from plain People, and from such as have not either Ambition or Capacity to embellish their Narrations with any Beauties of Imagination. I was the other Day amusing my self with *Ligon's* Account of *Barbadoes*; and, in Answer to your well-wrought Tale, I will give you (as it dwells upon my Memory) out of that honest Traveller, in his fifty fifth Page, the History of *Inkle* and *Yarico*.

Mr. *Thomas Inkle* of *London*, aged 20 Years, embarked in the *Downs* on the good Ship called the *Achilles,* bound for the *West-Indies*, on the 16th of *June* 1647, in order to improve his Fortune by Trade and Merchandize. Our Adventurer was the third Son of an eminent Citizen, who had taken particular Care to instill into his Mind an early Love of Gain, by making him a perfect Master of Numbers, and consequently giving him a quick View of Loss and Advantage, and preventing the natural Impulses of his Passions, by Prepossession towards his Interests. With a Mind thus turned, young *Inkle* had a Person every way agreeable, a ruddy Vigour in his Countenance, Strength in his Limbs, with Ringlets of fair Hair loosely flowing in his Shoulders. It happened, in the Course of the Voyage, that the *Achilles*, in some Distress, put into a Creek on the Main of *America*, in Search of Provisions: The Youth, who is the Hero of my Story, among others, went ashore on this Occasion. From their first Landing they were observed by a Party of *Indians*, who hid themselves in the Woods for that Purpose. The *English* unadvisedly marched a great distance from the Shore into the Country, and were intercepted by the Natives, who slew the greatest Number of them. Our Adventurer escaped among others, by flying into a Forest. Upon his coming into a remote and pathless Part of the Wood, he

---

4   *Fable ... Man*: Aesop's Fables, no. 219.

threw himself breathless on a little Hillock, when an *Indian* Maid rushed from a Thicket behind him: After the first Surprize, they appeared mutually agreeable to each other. If the *European* was highly Charmed with the Limbs, Features and wild Graces of the Naked *American*; the *American* was no less taken with the Dress, Complexion and Shape of an *European*, covered from Head to Foot. The *Indian* grew immediately enamoured of him, and consequently sollicitous for his Preservation: She therefore conveyed him to a Cave, where she gave him a Delicious Repast of Fruits, and led him to a Stream to slake his Thirst. In the midst of these good Offices, she would sometimes play with his Hair, and delight in the Opposition of its Colour, to that of her Fingers: Then open his Bosome, then laugh at him for covering it. She was, it seems, a Person of Distinction, for she every day came to him in a different Dress, of the most beautiful Shells, Bugles and Bredes.[5] She likewise brought him a great many Spoils, which her other Lovers had presented to her; so that his Cave was richly adorned with all the spotted Skins of Beasts, and most Party-coloured Feathers of Fowls, which that World afforded. To make his Confinement more tolerable, she would carry him in the Dusk of the Evening, or by the favour of Moon-light, to unfrequented Groves and Solitudes, and show him where to lye down in Safety, and sleep amidst the Falls of Waters, and Melody of Nightingales. Her Part was to watch and hold him in her Arms, for fear of her Country-men, and wake on Occasions to consult his Safety. In this manner did the Lovers pass away their Time, till they had learn'd a Language of their own, in which the Voyager communicated to his Mistress, how happy he should be to have her in his Country, where she should be Cloathed in such Silks as his Wastecoat was made of, and be carried in Houses drawn by Horses, without being exposed to Wind and Weather. All this he promised her the Enjoyment of, without such Fears and Alarms as they were there Tormented with. In this tender Correspondence these Lovers lived for several Months, when *Yarico*, instructed by her Lover, discovered a Vessel on the Coast, to which she made Signals, and in the Night, with the utmost Joy and Satisfaction accompanied him to a Ship's-crew of his Country-Men, bound for *Barbadoes*. When a Vessel from the Main arrives in that Island, it seems the Planters come down to the Shoar, where there is an immediate Market of the *Indians* and other Slaves, as with us of Horses and Oxen.[6]

To be short, Mr. *Thomas Inkle*, now coming into *English* Territories, began seriously to reflect upon his loss of Time, and to weigh with himself how many Days Interest of his Mony he had lost during his Stay with *Yarico*. This Thought made the Young Man very pensive, and careful what Account he

---

5　　*bugles, and bredes*: tubular glass beads and braids.

6　　*an immediate market*: the proportion of American Indians transported as slaves to the West-Indies was relatively small compared to the trade from Africa. While by 1711 it had been sold, Steel had inherited a sugar plantation in Barbados, so was well aware of the realities of the slave trade.

should be able to give his Friends of his Voyage. Upon which Considerations, the prudent and frugal young Man sold *Yarico* to a *Barbadian* Merchant; notwithstanding that the poor Girl, to incline him to commiserate her Condition, told him that she was with Child by him: But he only made use of that Information, to rise in his Demands upon the Purchaser.[7]

I was so touch'd with this Story (which I think should be always a Counterpart to the *Ephesian* Matron) that I left the Room with Tears in my Eyes; which a Woman of *Arietta*'s good Sense, did, I am sure, take for greater Applause, than any Compliments I could make her.

Jonathan Swift and Joseph Addison, *The Spectator*, no. 50 (27 April 1711)

[The Indian Kings]

In 1710 four Iroquois *sachem* from the Confederacy of the Five Nations came to London, staying for five weeks. This was at the height of the War of Spanish Succession with France (1702–13), and American colonial leaders had hoped to form a bond between the Iroquois and England, seeking Queen's Anne's aid for a joint invasion of French-held Canada (Native American tribes would be pawns in the power struggles between France and Britain in America until after the War of American Independence). The visit was very much a public performance planned by diplomats, they were given invented royal titles, displayed in their indigenous dress, supplied with English finery and invited to a bewildering array of social functions. At a number of times, their attendance at plays was advertised on the playbill, suggesting that this exotic spectacle was part of the evening's entertainment. Their public presence was often accompanied by crowds, and they were the subject of much social commentary. The idea of a fictional account that would be in the voice of one of the sachems was originally Jonathan Swift's, and bears comparison with his other satirical writings. By ventriloquising the voice of a noble savage from beyond the shores of 'civilisation', Swift and Addison created a satirical distinction between the uncorrupted nature of the American natives, and the follies and hypocrisies of contemporary society.

---

[7]   *rise in his demands*: Inkle is aware that he can raise the price because the purchaser is getting two slaves: Yarico and her child.

Nunquam aliud Natura, aliud Sapientia dixit. Juv.[1]

When the four *Indian* Kings were in this Country about a Twelve-month ago, I often mix'd with the Rabble and followed them a whole Day together, being wonderfully struck with the Sight of every thing that is new or uncommon. I have, since their Departure, employed a Friend to make many Enquiries of their Landlord the Upholsterer relating to their Manners and Conversation, as also concerning the Remarks which they made in this Country: For next to the forming a right Notion of such Strangers, I should be desirous of learning what Ideas they have conceived of us.

The Upholsterer finding my Friend very inquisitive about these his Lodgers, brought him some time since a little Bundle of Papers, which he assured him were written by King *Sa Ga Yean Qua Rash Tow*, and, as he supposes, left behind by some Mistake. These Papers are now translated, and contain abundance of very odd Observations, which I find this little Fraternity of Kings made during their Stay in the Isle of *Great Britain*. I shall present my Reader with a short Specimen of them in this Paper, and may perhaps communicate more to him hereafter.[2] In the Article of *London* are the following Words, which without Doubt are meant of the Church of St *Paul*.

'On the most rising Part of the Town there stands a huge House, big enough to contain the whole Nation of which I am King. Our good Brother *E Tow O Koam* King of the *Rivers*, is of Opinion it was made by the Hands of that great God to whom it is consecrated. The Kings of *Granajah* and of the *Six Nations* believe that it was created with the Earth, and produced on the same Day with the Sun and Moon. But for my own Part, by the best Information that I could get of this Matter, I am apt to think that this prodigious Pile was fashioned into the Shape it now bears by several Tools and Instruments, of which they have a wonderful Variety in this Country. It was probably at first an huge mis-shapen Rock that grew upon the Top of the Hill, which the Natives of the Country (after having cut it into a kind of regular Figure) bored and hollowed with incredible Pains and Industry, till they had wrought in it all those beautiful Vaults and Caverns into which it is divided at this Day. As soon as this Rock was thus curiously scooped to their Liking, a prodigious Number of Hands must have been employed in chipping the Outside of it, which is now as smooth as polished Marble; and is in several Places hewn out into Pillars that stand like the Trunks of so many Trees bound about the Top with Garlands of Leaves. It is probable that when this great Work was begun, which must have been many Hundred Years ago, there was some Religion among this People; for they

---

[1]   *Nunquam ... dixit*: Juvenal, *Satires*, XIV. 'Never does Nature say one thing and Wisdom another.'

[2]   *hereafter*: in *Spectator* no. 56, 4 May 1711; they had also appeared earlier in *Tatler*, no. 171, 3 May 1710.

give it the Name of a Temple, and have a Tradition that it was designed for Men to pay their Devotions in. And indeed, there are several Reasons which make us think, that the Natives of this Country had formerly among them some sort of Worship; for they set apart every seventh Day as sacred: But upon my going into one of those holy Houses on that Day, I could not observe any Circumstance of Devotion in their Behaviour: There was indeed a Man in Black who was mounted above the rest, and seemed to utter something with a great deal of Vehemence; but as for those underneath him, instead of paying their Worship to the Deity of the Place, they were most of them bowing and curtisying to one another, and a considerable Number of them fast asleep.

'The Queen of the Country appointed two Men to attend us, that had enough of our Language to make themselves understood in some few Particulars. But we soon perceived these two were great Enemies to one another, and did not always agree in the same Story. We could make a Shift to gather out of one of them, that this Island was very much infested with a monstrous Kind of Animal, in the Shape of Men, called *Whigs*; and he often told us, that he hoped we should meet with none of them in our Way, for that if we did, they would apt to knock us down for being Kings.

'Our other Interpreter used to talk very much of a kind of Animal called a *Tory*, that was as great a Monster as the *Whig*, and would treat us as ill for being Foreigners. These two Creatures, it seems, are born with a secret Antipathy to one another, and engage when they meet as naturally as the Elephant and the Rhinoceros. But as we saw none of either of these Species, we are apt to think that our Guides deceived us with Misrepresentations and Fictions, and amused us with an Account of such Monsters as are not really in their Country.

'These Particulars we made a Shift to pick out from the Discourse of our Interpreters; which we put together as well as we could, being able to understand but here and there a Word of what they said, and afterwards making up the Meaning of it among our selves. The Men of the Country are very cunning and ingenious in handicraft Works; but withal so very idle, that we often saw young lusty raw-boned Fellows carried up and down the Streets in little covered Rooms by a Couple of Porters who are hired for that Service. Their Dress is likewise very barbarous, for they almost strangle themselves about the Neck, and bind their Bodies with many Ligatures, that we are apt to think are the Occasion of several Distempers among them which our Country is entirely free from. Instead of those beautiful Feathers with which we adorn our Heads, they often buy up a monstrous Bush of Hair, which covers their Heads, and falls down in a large Fleece below the Middle of their Backs; with which they walk up and down the Streets, and are as proud of it as if it was of their own Growth.

'We were invited to one of their publick Diversions, where we hoped to have seen the great Men of their Country running down a Stag or pitching a Bar, that we might have discover'd who were the Men of the greatest

Perfections in their Country; but instead of that, they conveyed us into an huge Room lighted up with abundance of Candles, where this lazy People sat still above three Hours to see several Feats of Ingenuity performed by others, who it seems were paid for it.

'As for the Women of the Country, not being able to talk with them, we could only make our Remarks upon them at a Distance. They let the Hair of their Heads grow to a great Length; but as the Men make a great Show with Heads of Hair that are none of their own, the Women, who they say have very fine Heads of Hair, tie it up in a Knot and cover it from being seen. The Women look like Angels, and would be more beautiful than the Sun, were it not for little black Spots that are apt to break out in their Faces, and sometimes rise in very odd Figures.[3] I have observed that those little Blemishes wear off very soon; but when they disappear in one Part of the Face, they are very apt to break out in another, insomuch that I have seen a Spot upon the Forehead in the Afternoon, which was upon the Chin in the Morning.'

The Author then proceeds to shew the Absurdity of Breeches and Petticoats, with many other curious Observations, which I shall reserve for another Occasion. I cannot however conclude this Paper without taking Notice, That amidst these wild Remarks there now and then appears something very reasonable. I can't likewise forebear observing, That we are all guilty in some Measure of the same narrow Way of Thinking which we meet with in this Abstract of the *Indian* Journal; when we fancy the Customs, Dresses, and Manners of other Countries are ridiculous and extravagant, if they do not resemble those of our own.[4]

Joseph Addison, *The Spectator*, no. 69 (19 May 1711)

[The Royal Exchange]

The *Spectator*'s spokesperson for trade was the character 'Sir Andrew Freeport', whose values echo the dominant ideology of the British empire as one based upon

---

[3]   *little black Spots*: patches for the face, sometimes made out of silk, were fashionable. They also covered up skin blemishes.

[4]   *I cannot ... own*: this echoes Michael Montaigne (1533–92) 'Of Cannibals' in his *Essays* (1580, trans. 1603).

peace: 'His Notions of Trade are noble and generous, and ... he calls the Sea the *British Common*. He is acquainted with Commerce in all its Parts, and will tell you that it is a stupid and barbarous Way to extend Dominion by Arms; for true Power is to be got by Arts and Industry.'[1] In this issue, Addison's paean to the hub of Britain's commercial networks, the Royal Exchange, was part of a wider vindication of the new urban commercial class to sceptics who looked to land as the traditional foundations of Britain's wealth. Addison's paper in this issue naturalises the spread of goods around the globe but, more importantly, naturalises Britain's role as the centre of this worldwide commerce.

> *Hic segetes, illic veniunt felicius uvæ:*
> *Arborei fætus alibi, atque injussa virescunt*
> *Gramina. Nonne vides, croceos ut Tmolus odores,*
> *India mittit ebur, molles sua thura Sabæi?*
> *At Chalybes nudi ferrum, virosaqua Pontus*
> *Castorea, Eliadum palmas Epirus equarum?*
> *Continuo has leges æternaque fædera certis*
> *Imposuit Natura locis—*   *Vir.*[2]

There is no Place in the Town which I so much love to frequent as the *Royal-Exchange*.[3] It gives me a secret Satisfaction, and, in some measure, gratifies my Vanity, as I am an *Englishman*, to see so rich an Assembly of Country-men and Foreigners consulting together upon the private Business of Mankind, and making this Metropolis a kind of *Emporium* for the whole Earth. I must confess I look upon High-Change to be a great Council, in which all considerable Nations have their Representatives. Factors[4] in the Trading World are what Ambassadors are in the Politick World; they nego-tiate Affairs, conclude Treaties, and maintain a good Correspondence between those wealthy Societies of Men that are divided from one another by Seas and Oceans, or live on the different Extremities of a Continent. I have often been pleased to hear Disputes adjusted between an Inhabitant of *Japan* and an Alderman of *London*, or to see a Subject of the *Great Mogul* entering into a League with one of the *Czar* of *Muscovy*. I am infinitely delighted in mixing with these several Ministers of Commerce, as they are

---

[1] See *Spectator* no. 2, 2 March 1711.

[2] *Hic ... locis*: Virgil (70–19 BC), *Georgics*, 1: 54–61, 'Here corn, there grapes spring luxuriantly; elsewhere fruitful trees shoot up, and grasses unbidden. See you not, how Tmolus sends us saffron fragrance, India her ivory, the soft Sabaeans their frankincense; but the naked Chalybes give us iron, Pontus the strong-smelling beaver's oil, and Epirus prize-winning mares for the Olympics? From the first, Nature laid these laws and eternal covenants on certain lands.'

[3] *Royal Exchange*: a large two-story building built in 1669 around a great courtyard, located on Cornhill, London, and ornamented with statues of English monarchs. It was the centre of Britain's commercial dealings.

[4] *Factors*: merchants and agents.

distinguished by their different Walks and different Languages: Sometimes I am justled among a Body of *Armenians*: Sometimes I am lost in a Crowd of *Jews*, and sometimes make one in a Group of *Dutch-men*. I am a *Dane, Sweed*, or *French-Man* at different times, or rather fancy my self like the old Philosopher,[5] who upon being asked what Country-man he was, replied, That he was a Citizen of the World.

Though I very frequently visit this busie Multitude of People, I am known to no Body there but my Friend, Sir ANDREW, who often smiles upon me as he sees me bustling in the Croud, but at the same time connives at my Presence without taking any further notice of me. There is indeed a Merchant of *Egypt*, who just knows me by sight, having formerly remitted me some Mony to *Grand Cairo*; but as I am not versed in the Modern *Coptick*, our Conferences go no further than a Bow and a Grimace.[6]

This grand Scene of Business gives me an infinite Variety of solid and substantial Entertainments. As I am a great Lover of Mankind, my Heart naturally overflows with Pleasure at the sight of a prosperous and happy Multitude, insomuch that at many publick Solemnities I cannot forbear expressing my Joy with Tears that have stolen down my Cheeks. For this reason I am wonderfully delighted to see such a Body of Men thriving in their own private Fortunes, and at the same time promoting the Publick Stock; or in other Words, raising Estates for their own Families, by bringing into their Country whatever is wanting, and carrying out of it whatever is superfluous.

Nature seems to have taken a particular Care to disseminate her Blessings among the different Regions of the World, with an Eye to this mutual Intercourse and Traffick among Mankind, that the Natives of the several Parts of the Globe might have a kind of Dependence upon one another, and be united together by their common Interest. Almost every Degree[7] produces something peculiar to it. The Food often grows in one Country, and the Sauce in another. The Fruits of *Portugal* are corrected by the Products of *Barbadoes*: The Infusion of a *China* Plant sweetned with the Pith of an *Indian* Cane: The *Philippick* Islands give a Flavour to our *European* Bowls. The single Dress of a Woman of Quality is often the Product of an hundred Climates. The Muff and the Fan come together from the different Ends of the Earth. The Scarf is sent from the Torrid Zone, and the Tippet from beneath the Pole. The Brocade Petticoat rises out of the Mines of *Peru*, and the Diamond Necklace out of the Bowels of *Industan*.

If we consider our own Country in its natural Prospect, without any of the Benefits and Advantages of Commerce, what a barren uncomfortable

---

[5]   *Philosopher*: either Diogenes the Cynic or Socrates.

[6]   *modern Coptick … grimace*: unfamiliar with modern Egyptian, he merely exchanges a facial expression to indicate recognition: a 'grimace' was not necessarily pejorative at this time.

[7]   *Degree*: degree of latitude.

Spot of Earth falls to our Share! Natural Historians tell us, that no Fruit grows originally among us, besides Hips and Haws, Acorns and Pig-Nutts, with other Delicacies of the like Nature; That our Climate of it self can make no further Advances towards a Plumb than to a Sloe, and carries an Apple to no greater a Perfection than a Crab: That these Fruits, in their present State, as well as our Melons, our Peaches, our Figs, our Apricots, and Cherries, are Strangers among us, imported in different Ages, and natural-ized in our *English* Gardens; and that they would all degenerate and fall away into the Trash of our own Country, if they were wholly neglected by the Planter, and left to the Mercy of our Sun and Soil. Nor has Traffick more enriched our Vegetable World, than it has improved the whole Face of Nature among us. Our Ships are loaden with the Harvest of every Climate: Our Tables are stored with Spices, and Oils, and Wines: Our Rooms are filled with Pyramids of *China*, and adorned with the Workmanship of *Japan*: Our Morning's-Draught comes to us from the remotest Corners of the Earth: We repair our Bodies by the Drugs of *America*, and repose our selves under *Indian* Canopies. My friend Sir ANDREW calls the Vineyards of *France* our Gardens; the Spice-Islands our Hot-Beds; the *Persians* our Silk-Weavers, and the *Chinese* our Potters. Nature indeed furnishes us with the bare Necessaries of Life, but Traffick gives us a great Variety of what is Useful, and at the same time supplies us with every thing that is Convenient and Ornamental. Nor is it the least part of this our Happiness, that whilst we enjoy the remotest Products of the North and South, we are free from those Extremities of Weather that give them Birth; That our Eyes are refreshed with the green Fields of *Britain*, at the same time that our Palates are feasted with Fruits that rise between the Tropicks.

For these Reasons there are not more useful Members in a Commonwealth than Merchants. They knit Mankind together in a mutual Intercourse of good Offices, distribute the Gifts of Nature, find Work for the Poor, add Wealth to the Rich, and Magnificence to the Great. Our *English* Merchant converts the Tin of his own Country into Gold, and exchanges his Wooll for Rubies. The *Mahometans* are cloathed in our *British* Manufacture, and the Inhabitants of the Frozen Zone warmed with the Fleeces of our Sheep.

When I have been upon the '*Change*, I have often fancied one of our old Kings standing in Person, where he is represented in Effigy, and looking down upon that wealthy Concourse of People with which that Place is every Day filled. In this Case, how would he be surprized to hear all the Languages of *Europe* spoken in this little Spot of his former Dominions, and to see so many private Men, who in his Time would have been the Vassals of some powerful Baron, Negotiating like Princes for greater Sums of Mony than were formerly to be met with in the Royal Treasury! Trade, without enlarging the *British* Territories, has given us a kind of additional Empire: It has multiplied the Number of the Rich, made our Landed Estates infinitely more Valuable than they were formerly, and added to them an Accession of other Estates as Valuable as the Lands themselves.

Alexander Pope, from
Windsor-Forest (1713)

Although marginalised by his Roman Catholic faith (and severe disability) from the society of his day, Alexander Pope's (1688–1744) intellectual brilliance and satirical wit placed him at the centre of the literary circles that included Addison, Steele, John Gay and Jonathan Swift. He was the first poet to raise a fortune solely on his poetry, and his most famous works include *An Essay on Criticism* (1711), *An Essay on Man* (1733–34), *The Rape of the Lock* (1714), his series of moral *Epistles* (1731–35), and *The Dunciad* (1728, but revised until 1743), as well adaptations of Horace and an extremely successful translation of Homer.

Windsor-Forest is a complex and allusive poem praising the British nation at peace under Queen Anne, and its catalyst was the Treaty of Utrecht which signaled the end of the War of Spanish Succession (1701–13). The poem's dominant generic model is Virgil's *Georgics*, which is reflected in the poem's depiction of the hunt in the royal forest and the opening hymn to the fertility and beauty of an edenic British landscape. The opening is contrasted by a section detailing the effect on the country of the tyrannical William the Conqueror (and by implication the Dutch William III who came to power in 1689). This reading of English history indicates a Tory, possibly even Jacobite, stance. After praising the pantheon of past kings which Windsor Castle represents, Pope laments the turmoil of seventeenth-century England. The extract below follows. The poem's imperial imaginings may seem triumphalist: the mindset of an empire grounded in peace is central to British self-imagining. Yet the references to slavery and the details of the *Asiento des negros* should alert the reader: the complexities of *Windsor-Forest*'s imperialism, therefore, have to be carefully negotiated.[1]

> Hail, sacred Peace![2] hail long-expected days,
> That *Thames*'s glory to the stars shall raise!
> Tho' *Tyber*'s streams immortal *Rome* behold,   355
> Tho' foaming *Hermus* swells with tydes of gold,[3]
> From heav'n itself tho' sev'n-fold *Nilus* flows,
> And harvests on a hundred realms bestows;
> These now no more shall be the Muse's themes,
> Lost in my fame, as in the sea their streams.   360
> Let *Volga*'s banks[4] with Iron squadrons shine,

---

[1]   Text from *The Works of Alexander Pope* (1717), pp. 64–7.

[2]   *Peace*: the preliminaries to the Treaty of Utrecht were signed in London in 1711, signalling the end of the War of Spanish Succession. The Treaty secured substantial colonial territories (Newfoundland, Nova Scotia, St. Kitts and Hudson Bay from France, Minorca and Gibraltar from Spain). It also secured the *Asiento des negros*, whereby Britain was granted the monopoly contract for the slave trade to the Spanish colonies.

[3]   *Tyber's … Hermus*: rivers in Italy.

[4]   *Volga's banks*: a river in Russia, where Charles XII of Sweden (1682–1718) had been at war.

And groves of Lances glitter on the *Rhine*,[5]
Let barb'rous *Ganges*[6] arm a servile train;
Be mine the blessings of a peaceful reign.
No more my sons shall dye with *British* blood   365
Red *Iber's* sands, or *Ister's* foaming flood;[7]
Safe on my shore each unmolested swain
Shall tend the flocks, or reap the bearded grain;
The shady empire shall retain no trace
Of war or blood, but in the sylvan chace,   370
The trumpet sleep, while chearful horns are blown,
And arms employ'd on birds and beasts alone.
Behold! th'ascending *Villa's* on my side,
Project long shadows o'er the crystal tyde.
Behold! *Augusta's*[8] glitt'ring spires increase,   375
And Temples rise, the beauteous works of Peace.
I see, I see where two fair Cities[9] bend
Their ample bow, a new *White-Hall* ascend!
There mighty nations shall enquire their doom,
The world's great Oracle in times to come;   380
There Kings shall sue, and suppliant states be seen
Once more to bend before a *British* Queen.
　　　Thy Trees, fair *Windsor*! now shall leave their woods,
And half thy forests rush into my floods,
Bear *Britain's* thunder, and her Cross display,[10]   385
To the bright regions of the rising day;
Tempt icy seas, where scarce the waters roll,
Where clearer flames glow round the frozen Pole;
Or under Southern skies exalt their sails,
Led by new stars, and borne by spicy gales!   390
For me the balm shall bleed, and amber flow,
The coral redden, and the ruby glow,
The pearly shell its lucid globe infold,
And *Phoebus* warm the ripening ore to gold.
The time shall come, when free as seas or wind   395

5　　*Rhine*: in 1704 John Churchill, First Duke of Marlborough (1650–1722) had commanded
　　　forces that won a significant victory at Blenheim. They had marched through the Rhine
　　　valley.
6　　*Ganges*: an allusion to the wars of the Moghul emperor of India, Aurangzeb (1618–1707).
7　　*Iber … Ister*: references to the Allies' campaign in Europe. Iber is in Spain, Ister is the river
　　　Danube.
8　　*Augusta*: London.
9　　*two fair cities*: London and Westminster, still at that time two distinct towns.
10　 *Cross*: the red cross of St George, patron saint of England.

Unbounded *Thames* shall flow for all mankind,
Whole nations enter with each swelling tyde,
And Seas but join the regions they divide;
Earth's distant ends our glory shall behold,
And the new world launch forth to seek the old.   400
Then ships of uncouth form shall stem the tyde,
And feather'd people[11] crowd my wealthy side,
Whose naked youth and painted chiefs admire
Our speech, our colour, and our strange attire!
Oh stretch thy reign, fair Peace! from shore to shore,   405
Till Conquest cease, and slav'ry be no more:
Till the freed *Indians*[12] in their native groves
Reap their own fruits, and wooe their sable Loves,
Peru once more a race of Kings behold,
And other *Mexico's* be roof'd with gold.   410
Exil'd by thee from earth to deepest hell,
In brazen bonds shall barb'rous Discord dwell:
Gigantic Pride, pale Terror, gloomy Care,
And mad Ambition, shall attend her there.
There purple Vengeance bath'd in gore retires,   415
Her weapons blunted, and extinct her fires:
There hateful Envy her own snakes shall feel,
And Persecution mourn her broken wheel:
There Faction roars, Rebellion bites her chain,
And gasping Furies[13] thirst for blood in vain.   420
      Here cease thy flight, nor with unhallow'd lays
Touch the fair fame of *Albion's* golden days.
The thoughts of Gods let *Granville's* verse recite,[14]
And bring the scenes of opening fate to light.
My humble Muse, in unambitious strains,   425
Paints the green forests and the flow'ry plains,
Where Peace descending bids her olives spring,
And scatters blessings from her dove-like wing.
Ev'n I more sweetly pass my careless days,
Pleas'd in the silent shade with empty praise;   430
Enough for me, that to the list'ning swains
First in these fields I sung the sylvan strains.

---

[11]   *feather'd people*: referring to the visit, in 1710, of four Iroquois chiefs (see *Spectator*, no. 50).
[12]   *Indians*: the American Indians under Spanish colonial rule.
[13]   *Furies*: in Greek legend, these are the goddesses of vengeance.
[14]   *Granville's verse*: Lord Lansdowne, George Granville, the Secretary-at-War who signed the Treaty and who was the poem's dedicatee. His poetry had praised James II as possessing god-like qualities.

[Jocelyn], from
An Essay on Money and Bullion (1718)

The central tenet of British mercantile economic theory at this point in the eighteenth century is attested by this pamphlet's emphasis on the 'circulation' of gold and silver (and money and goods). 'Circulation' was also a metaphor for the nature of trade, reflected in the images of blood and water. Here, it was also used to point up the perceived contrast between the stasis of the Spanish empire and nation and the British empire of circulation and prosperity.[1]

The Riches of a Nation consist in the Plenty of those Commodities, which are most useful in Human Life, whose Air is Healthy, whose Soil is Fruitful, whose People are Diligent and Ingenious, and busied in Manufactures; whose Ports are open and free for Commerce with Nations about it. This Nation is Rich, tho' it has not in it an Ounce of Gold and Silver; whereas that Nation may be very Poor, wherein are Mines of Gold and Silver, and the People Freeze and Starve for want of Bread to Eat, and Cloaths to Cover them. How naturally do *England* and *Spain* present themselves to our View, the former abounding in Riches, tho' she has scarce a Mine of Gold or Silver in all her Dominions; the latter in Poverty, possessed of the greatest Mines in the World, and drinking continually from those Fountains of Treasures;[2] for the Country is Barren, and the People so very lazy, that they will not work their own Wool, from their Affluence of Gold and Silver imagining themselves to be Rich, whereas they are Poor and Naked, and have need of all Things.

[...]

'Tis a common but vain Imagination, to think we shall grow rich by the great Quantity of Gold or Silver we heap up, and keep in the Nation. They will serve us neither for Food nor Raiment; nor will they generate, increase or multiply in any Soil. All Prohibitions upon the Exportations of them are a Hindrance to our Increase in Wealth, and a Stop to the Commerce of the World. A Merchant may as well expect to grow rich by locking up all his Money in his House, and never letting it go out, as a Nation by keeping its Bullion within its self.

---

1   Text from pp. 11–12, 13–14. Nothing is known of the ostensible author.
2   *Fountains of Treasures*: Spain was renowned for its mines in South America.

You often hear of the Circulation of Money: As that ought to circulate in a Nation, so ought Bullion to circulate in the World; and our Coin, as long as it keeps a Proportion of Value with it. You may as well expect to keep Life in the Body, by stopping up the Arteries, and leaving the Veins open, and so filling the Heart with Blood, as to keep Life in Trade, by leaving those Ports open at which Bullion enters, and stopping up those at which it goes out. As the Blood by running preserves Life in the Body, and conveys a proper Increase to every Part, though it self be neither; so Bullion, by running about the World, preserves the Life of Trade, and brings Riches wherever it comes, tho' in it self it be neither. Those nations who prohibit the Exportation of it, seem to me like that Clown, who observing the Overflowing of the River made his Meadow fruitful; the next Flood damm'd the Water all in, and so turned it into a Bogg, which for a long time after bore nothing but Sedge: Whereas it was not the Water it self that enriched his Soil; but those Particles of Earth it brought, and left behind it.

Daniel Defoe

Daniel Defoe (1660–1731), famous for *Robinson Crusoe* (1719), was an entrepreneur, spy, journalist, poet, and writer of fictions who has hundreds of works to his name. His enormous output covered economics, politics, religion, trade, history, superstition, marriage and sex, family conduct, piracy, servants, gentlemanliness and royal education. His writing fame was ensured by the satirical poem *The True-Born Englishman* (1701), but his most outstanding publication was the thrice-weekly *Review*, for which he was the sole writer and which ran from 1704 to 1713. He turned to fiction late in life beginning with *Robinson Crusoe* (and the sequels *The Farther Adventures of Robinson Cruso*e in 1719 and *The Serious Reflections ... of Robinson Crusoe* in 1720). Other fictions include *Moll Flanders, A Journal of the Plague Year, Colonel Jack* (all in 1722) and *Roxana* (1724). Born into a Presbyterian family, Defoe's politics are harder to pin down; indeed his contemporaries accused him of being a hack for hire, but he was certainly anti-Jacobite. If he had one defining interest, it was trade, and throughout his prolific writing career he was fascinated with the changing and charged atmosphere of the economic success story that was England in the late seventeenth and early eighteenth centuries.

From *Captain Singleton* (1720)

One of Defoe's less well-known novels, *Captain Singleton* is a rambling tale that concerns the adventures of Bob Singleton from his sea-faring as a boy, his capture by Algerian pirates, his trek across Africa, his piracy as an adult, and his eventual reformation while returning to England disguised as a Persian. The extract below is from the African section of the narrative. After being delivered by Portuguese sailors from the pirates, he is stranded on Madagascar. His escape with a group of men results in them trekking across the continent of Africa, heading for the West coast, during which they battle with 'savages' and take some prisoners to use as servants (effectively slaves). What happens next is an encounter with a fellow Englishman in the heart of Africa, and his tale registers Defoe's concern that more support should be given to the Royal Africa Company's merchants and commercial activities. The extract also reveals that complexion was not the sole basis for conceiving human difference in the eighteenth century. In this encounter, difference is registered in the signs of civilisation: civility, clothing and commerce.[1]

As we went forward our whole Carravan being in a Body, our Negroes, who were in the Front, cry'd out, that they saw a *White Man*; we were not much surprized at first, it being, as we thought, a Mistake of the Fellows, and asked them what they meant; when one of them stept to me, and pointing to a Hutt on the other Side of the Hill, I was astonished to see a White Man indeed, but stark naked, very busy near the Door of his Hutt, and stooping down to the Ground with something in his Hand, as if he had been at some Work, and his back being towards us, he did not see us.

I gave Notice to our Negroes to make no Noise, and waited till some more of our Men were come up, to shew the Sight to them, that they might be sure I was not mistaken, and we were soon satisfied of the Truth; for the Man having heard some Noise, started up, and looked full at us, as much surprized, to be sure, as we were, but whether with Fear or Hope, we then knew not.

As he discovered us, so did the rest of the Inhabitants belonging to the Hutts about him, and all crouded together, looking at us at a Distance: A little Bottom, in which the Brook ran, lying between us, the white Man, and all the rest, as he told us afterwards, not knowing well whether they should stay, or run away: However, it presently came into my Thoughts, that if there were white Men among them, it would be much easier for us to make them understand what we meant, as to Peace or War, than we found it with others; so tying a Piece of white Rag to the End of a Stick, we sent two Negroes with it to the Bank of the Water, carrying the Pole up as high as they could; it was presently understood, and two of their Men, and the white Man, came to the Shore on the other Side.

However, as the white Man spoke no *Portuguese*, they could understand nothing of one another, but by Signs; but our Men made the white Man understand, that they had white Men with them too, at which they said the white Man laught. However, to be short, our Men came back, and told us they were all good Friends, and in about an Hour four of our Men, two Negroes, and the Black Prince went to the River Side, where the white Man came to them.

---

[1]   Text from *The Life, Adventures, and Pyracies of the Famous Captain Singleton* (1720), pp. 156–62, 164–6.

They had not been half a Quarter of an Hour, but a Negro came running to me, and told me the white Man was *Inglese*, as he called him; upon which I run back, eagerly enough you may be sure with him, and found as he said, that he was an *Englishman*; upon which he embraced me very passionately, the Tears running down his Face. The first Surprize of his seeing us was over before we came, but any one may conceive of it, by the brief Account he gave us afterwards of his very unhappy Circumstance; and of so unexpected a Deliverance, such as perhaps never happened to any Man in the World; for it was a Million to one odds, that ever he could have been relieved; nothing but an Adventure that never was heard or read of before, could have suited his Case, unless Heaven by some Miracle that never was to be expected, had acted for him.

He appeared to be a Gentleman, not an ordinary bred Fellow, Seaman, or labouring Man; this shewed it self in his Behaviour, in the first Moment of our conversing with him, and in spight of all the Disadvantages of his miserable Circumstance.

He was a middle-aged Man, not above 37 or 38, tho' his Beard was grown exceeding long, and the Hair of his Head and face strangely covered him to the Middle of his Back and Breast, he was white, and his Skin very fine, tho' discoloured, and in some Places blistered and covered with a brown black-ish Substance, scurfy, scaly, and hard which was the Effect of the scorching Heat of the Sun; he was stark naked, and had been so, as he told us, upwards of two Years.

He was so exceedingly transported at our meeting with him, that he could scarce enter into any Discourse at all with us for that Day, and when he could get away from us for a little, we saw him walking alone, and shew-ing all the most extravagant Tokens of an ungovernable Joy; and even after-wards he was never without Tears in his Eyes for several Days, upon the least Word spoken by us of his Circumstances, or by him of his Deliverance.

We found his Behaviour the most courteous and endearing I ever saw in any Man whatever, and most evident Tokens of a mannerly well-bred Person, appeared in all things he did or said; and our People were exceed-ingly taken with him. He was a Scholar, and a Mathematician; he could not speek *Portuguese* indeed, but he spoke *Latin* to our Surgeon, *French* to another of our Men, and *Italian* to a Third.

He had no Leisure in his Thoughts to ask us whence we came, whither we were going, or who we were; but would have it always as an Answer to himself, that to be sure wherever we were a-going, we came from Heaven, and were sent on purpose to save him from the most wretched Condition that ever Man was reduced to.

Our Men pitching their Camp on the Bank of a little River opposite to him, he began to enquire what Store of Provision we had, and how we pro-posed to be supplied; when he found that our Store was but small, he said he would talk with the Natives, and we should have Provisions enough; for he said they were the most courteous, good natured Part of the Inhabitants in all that Part of the Country, as, we might suppose by his living so safe among them.

The first things this Gentleman did for us were indeed of the greatest Consequence to us; for first he perfectly informed us where we were, and which was the properest Course for us to steer: secondly, he put us in a Way how to furnish our selves effectually with Provisions; and Thirdly, he was our compleat Interpreter and Peace-maker with all the Natives, who now began to be very numerous about us; and who were a more fierce and politick People than those we had met with before; not so easily terrified with our Arms as those, and not so ignorant, as to give their Provisions and Corn for our little Toys, such as I said before our Artificer made; but as they had frequently traded and conversed with the *Europeans* on the Coast, or with other Negro Nations that had traded and been concerned with them, they were the less ignorant, and the less fearful, and consequently nothing was to be had from them but by Exchange for such things as they liked.

This I say of the Negro Natives, which we soon came among; but as to these poor People that he lived among, they were not much acquainted with Things, being at the Distance of above 300 Miles from the Coast, only that they found Elephants Teeth upon the Hills to the North, which they took and carried about sixty or seventy Miles South, where other trading Negroes usually met them, and gave them Beads Glass, Shels, and Cowries[2] for them, such as the *English* and *Dutch* and other Traders, furnish them with from *Europe*.

We now began to be more familiar with our new Acquaintance; and first, tho' we made but a sorry Figure as to Clothes our selves, having neither Shoe, or Stocking, or Glove or Hat among us, and but very few Shirts, yet as well as we could we clothed him; and first our Surgeon having Scissers and Razors, shaved him, and cut his Hair; a Hat, as I say, we had not in all our Stores, but he supply'd himself by making himself a Cap of a Piece of a Leopard Skin, most artificially. As for Shoes or Stockings, he had gone so long without them, that he cared not even for the Buskins and Foot-Gloves we wore, which I described above.

As he had been curious to hear the whole Story of our Travels, and was exceedingly delighted with the Relation; so we were no less to know, and pleased with the Account of his Circumstance, and the History of his coming to that strange Place alone, and in that Condition, which we found him in, as above.

This Account of his would indeed be in it self the Subject of an agreeable History, and would be as long and as diverting as our own, having in it many strange and extraordinary Incidents, but we cannot have Room here to launch out into so long a Digression; the Sum of his History was this.

---

[2]   *Cowries*: another kind of shell, often used as a kind of currency in Africa at this point.

He had been a Factor for the *English Guiney* Company at *Siera Leon*,[3] or some other of their Settlements which had been taken by the *French*, where he had been plundered of all his own Effects, as well as of what was intrusted to him by the Company. Whether it was, that the Company did not do him Justice in restoring his Circumstances, or in further employing him, he quitted their Service, and was employed by those they called Separate Traders; and being afterwards out of Employ there also, traded on his own Account; when passing unwarily into one of the Company's Settlements, he was either betray'd into the Hands of some of the Natives, or some how or other was surprized by them. However, as they did not kill him, he found Means to escape from them at that time, and fled to another Nation of the Natives, who being Enemies to the other, entertained him friendly, and with them he lived some time; but not liking his Quarters, or his Company, he fled again, and several times changed his Landlords; sometimes was carry'd by Force, sometimes hurried by Fear, as Circumstances altered with him (the Variety of which deserves a History by it self) till at last he had wandred beyond all Possibility of Return, and had taken up his Abode where we found him, where he was well received by the petty King of the Tribe he lived with; and he, in Return, instructed them how to value the Product of their Labour, and on what Terms to trade with those Negroes who came up to them for Teeth.

[...]

The next Morning he came to us again, and being all met in Council, as we may call it, he began to talk very seriously with us, that since we were now come after a long Journey to a View of the End of our Troubles, and had been so obliging to him, as to offer Carrying him with us, he had been all Night revolving in his Mind what he and we all might do to make our selves some Amends for all our Sorrows; and first he said, he was to let me know, that we were just then in one of the richest Parts of the World, tho' it was really otherwise, but a desolate, disconsolate Wilderness; for says he, there's not a River here but runs Gold, not a Desart but without Plowing bears a Crop of Ivory. What Mines of Gold, what immense Stores of Gold those Mountains may contain, from whence these Rivers come, or the Shores which these Waters run by, we know not, but may imagine that they must be inconceivably rich, seeing so much is washed down the Stream by the Water washing the Sides of the Land, that the Quantity suffices all the Traders which the *European* World send thither. We ask'd him how far they went for it, seeing the Ships only trade upon the Coast. He told us, that the Negroes on the Coast search the Rivers up for the Length of 150 or

---

3   *Siera Leon*: Sierra Leone was a major source of slaves from the sixteenth century onwards.

200 Miles, and would be out a Month or two or three at a Time, and always come Home sufficiently rewarded; but, says he, they never come thus far, and yet hereabouts is as much Gold as there. Upon this he told us, that he believed he might have gotten a Hundred Pound Weight of Gold, since he came thither, if he had employed himself to look and work for it, but as he knew not what to do with it, and had long since despaired of being ever delivered from the Misery he was in, he had entirely omitted it. For what Advantage had it been to me, said he, or what richer had I been, if I had a Ton of Gold Dust, and lay and wallowed in it; the Richness of it, *said he*, would not give me one Moment's Felicity, or relieve me in the present Exigency. Nay, says he, as you all see, it would not buy me Clothes to cover me, or a Drop of Drink to save me from perishing. 'Tis of no Value here, says he; there are several People among these Hutts that would weigh Gold against a few Glass Beads, or a Cockle-Shell, and give you a Handful of Gold Dust for a Handful of Cowries.

From *A Plan of the English Commerce* (1728)

One of his last major works on trade, *A Plan of the English Commerce* reflects Defoe's life-long belief in – obsession with, even – the potential of British commerce to dominate the world. In this extract, taken from the introduction, he sets out the patriotic case for the expansion of colonisation to provide overseas markets. Such a move would circumvent the blockage or competition in goods and markets by countries such as France and Germany and create a self-sustaining imperial commerce. Allied to this is his praise of the adventurer-explorer from earlier centuries: for Defoe, the modern merchant is the new adventurer; indeed the very word 'adventure' carries associations with both individual heroism and what we might now understand as an economic 'venture'. This extract also exemplifies one of the century's abiding images of imperial trade – the 'ocean' is a metaphor for commerce and a providential agent for British imperial dominance.[1]

The Commerce of the World, especially as it is now carried on, is an unbounded Ocean of Business; Trackless and unknown, like the Seas it is managed upon; the Merchant is no more to be follow'd in his Adventures, than a maze or Labyrinth is to be trac'd out without a Clue.

The Author of this Work is not quite so arrogant, after a Complaint of this Nature, as to tell you he shall present to you this universal Plan, for the whole Trade of the World: It is enough, if he is able to offer a Plan for the Trade of our own Country, in which it is but too true, there are many that talk of the general Commerce to one that understands it.

Nor even in this Plan of our Commerce, does he direct what the Trade of Europe, in general is with us; but what and how great our particular Commerce is; how it is arriv'd to its present Magnitude; how to be maintained and supported in its full

---

[1]   Text from 'The Preface', vii–viii, ix–xiv.

Extent; (and which is, or ought to be, the true End of all such Attempts:) How it may yet be improv'd and enlarg'd.

We have loud Complaints among us of the Decay of our Trade, the declining of our Manufactures, and especially of our woollen Manufacture; the contrary of which is, I think, evidently prov'd in this Tract, and the Reasons given for it, will not be easily refuted. It is not any little Negative put upon our Manufactures, as to their Consumption in this or that petty Province or Country in Germany, *or else where: Our Manufacture, like a flowing Tide, if 'tis bank't out in one Place, it spreads by other Channels at the same Time into so many different Parts of the World, and finds every Day so many new Outlets, that the Obstruction is not felt; but like the Land to the Sea, what it loses in one Place, it gains in another.*

[...]

This is the Substance of this Tract; 'tis the original Thought which gave Birth to the whole Work; if our Trade is the Envy of the World, and they are conspiring to break in upon it, either to anticipate it, or block it out, we are the more engaged to look out for its Support; and we have Room enough: The World is wide: There are new Countries, and new Nations, who may be so planted, so improv'd, and the People so manag'd, as to create new Commerce; and Millions of People shall call for our Manufacture, who never call'd for it before.

Nothing is to me more evident, than that the civilizing the Nations where we and other Europeans *are already settled; bringing the naked Savages to Clothe, and instructing barbarous Nations how to live, has had a visible Effect already, in this very Article. Those Nations call upon us every Year for more Goods, than they did the Year before, as well wollen Manufactures, as others. The* Portuguese *Colonies in the Brazils, and on the East Coasts of Africa, are an unanswerable Proof of this. The* European *Manufactures now sent to those Colonies, are above five Times as many as were sent to the same Places, about 30 to 40 Years ago; and yet the* European *Inhabitants in those Colonies are not encreased in Proportion. We might give Instances of the like in other Places abroad, and that not a few.*

New planting Colonies then, and farther improving those already settled, will effectually encrease this Improvement; for like Causes, will have like Effects; Clothing new Nations cannot fail of encreasing the Demand for Goods, because it encreases the Consumption, and that encreased Demand is the Prosperity of our Trade.

Here then is an undiscover'd Ocean of Commerce laid open to us, and some Specimens are offer'd, which if entered upon, with the Authority, Power, and Vigor of the Publick, would open such new Channels of Trade among us, as it would be very hard for our Manufacturers to overstock the Market, and as no petty Prohibitions in Europe could stop the Current of.

It is surprizing that in a Nation where such Encouragments are given for planting and improving, where Colonies have been settled, and Plantations made with such Success; where we may truly be said to have filled the World with the Wonders of our growing Possessions, and where we have added not Provinces only, but Kingdoms to the British *Dominium, and have launched out even to an Ocean of*

Commerce. That now, I say, We should, as it were, put a full Stop at once to all our great Designs; check the Humour of Encreasing,[2] *and from a kind of a mysterious unaccountable Stupidity turn indolent on a suddain. Not as if we found no more Room to launch out, for the Contrary to that is apparent; but as if we had enough, and sought no more Worlds in Trade to conquer.*

In all other Cases, and among all other Nations Success encourages Men to go on; encreasing, they endeavour to encrease, Crescit amor nummi,[3] *&c. – So in Trade, the growing and enlarging the Bounds of a Plantation, the swelling and thriving of Commerce, and the Advantages to the Merchant and Planter in all those Things, certainly encreases the Desire of planting, enlarges the Commerce and fires the Merchant with the Desires of enlarging his Adventures, searching out new Colonies, forming new Adventures, and pushing at new Discoveries for the Encrease of his Trading Advantages.*

It is so in other Nations, and it seems wonderful it should not be so here; the Spaniards *tho' an indolent Nation, whose Colonies were really so rich, so great, and so far extended, as were enough even to glut their utmost Avarice; yet gave not over, till, as it were, they sat still, because they had no more Worlds to look for; or till at least, there were no more Gold or Silver Mines to discover.*

The Portuguese, *tho' an effeminate, haughty, and as it were, a decay'd Nation in Trade; yet how do they go on Daily encreasing their Colonies in the* Brazils, *in* Africa, *as well on the East Side, as the West? And how do they encrease their Commerce in all those Countries, by reducing the numerous Nations in* Melinda, *in* Zanguebar, *in* Congo, *in* Angola, *in the* Brazils, *as well North as South, and every where else, to the Christian Oeconomy,*[4] *and to the Government of Commerce! by which they subdue whole Nations of Savages to a regular Life, and by that Means bring them to be subservient to Trade as well as to Government.*

But how little have we done of this kind? How little have we gain'd upon the Natives of America *in all our Colonies? How few of them are brought to live among us, how few to be subject to us? How little Progress of that kind can we boast of? All our Colonies seem to be carried on upon the meer Strength*[5] *of our own People. Nor can we say we have any one considerable Nation reduced to entire Obedience and brought to live under the Regularity and Direction of a Civil Government, in all our Plantations; a few (very few) in* New England *only excepted.*

As for new Colonies and Conquests, how do we seem entirely to give over, even the Thoughts of them, tho' the Scene is so large, tho' the Variety is so great, and the Advantage so many? On the Contrary, we seem to forget the glorious Improvements of our Ancestors, such as the great Drake, Cavendish, Smith, Greenfield, Somers, *and above all, the yet greater*

---

2   *Humour*: as in mood or attitude.
3   *Crescit amor nummi*: 'the love of money grows stronger'.
4   *Oeconomy*: in its most general meaning, economy was the 'disposition of things; regulation'.
      Samuel Johnson, *Dictionary* (1755).
5   *upon the meer Strength*: 'solely upon the strength'.

Sir Walter Raleigh,[6] *upon the Foot of whose Genius almost all the* English *Discoveries were made, and all the Colonies and Plantations, which now form what they call the* English Empire *in* America *were settled and established. These I say we seem to sit down with, as if we had done our utmost, were fully satisfied with what we have, that the enterprising Genius was buried with the old Discoverers, and there was neither Room in the World or Inclination in our People to look any farther.*

Whereas on the Contrary, the World presents us with large Scenes of Trade, new Platforms for Business, enough to prompt our Ambition, and even to glut our Avarice; yet we seem to have no Heart for the Adventure.

Nor is there any want of People among us; on the contrary, here are Thousands of Families who want Business, want Employment, want Encouragement, and many that want no Stocks to carry with them, and are ready to go abroad, were the adventuring Spirit reviv'd, and some Men fired with Warmth for the Undertaking, and but vigorous enough to make the Beginning.

This is the Way to raise new Worlds of Commerce, to enlarge and extend new Funds of Trade, to open Doors for an Encrease of Shipping and Manufacture; the Places are so many and the Advantages so great for the making such Attempts; that I say nothing is more wonderful of its kind, than to see how backward we are to push on our own Advantages, and to plant in the most agreeable Climates in the World, in a manner so advantageous as never to be supplanted, and such as should make the English *Possessions abroad five Times as Great, as Opulent and as Profitable to* Old England, *as they have been yet.*

James Thomson, *Britannia.*
A Poem (1729)

James Thomson (1700–48), the highly influential Scottish-born poet and playwright, rose to literary fame through his four-book poem *The Seasons* (1730), a sublime

---

[6]   *Drake ... Raleigh*: Sir Francis Drake (*c.* 1540–96), privateer (a pirate with a Government license) who who harried Spanish colonies, circumnavigated the world, and commanded the English fleet which defeated the Spanish Armada in 1588. Thomas Cavendish (1560–92) was a circumnavigator. John Smith (1580–1631) founded the colony of Virginia and was later famously mythologised as the lover of Pocahontas. Sir Richard Greenfield or Grenville (1542–91) was one of Raleigh's naval officers. Sir George Somers (1554–1610), a founder of the South Virginia Company, discovered the Bermudas in 1610 and claimed them for the English crown. Sir Walter Raleigh (1552–1618) introduced potatoes and tobacco into England from America, explored Trinidad and the river Orinoco in what is now Venezuela in 1595, and in 1616 led an expedition to explore South America in search of the mythical land of riches, El Dorado.

visual meditation that is kaleidoscopic in its juxtaposition of nature, history, politics and science. Through the politics of *Britannia* (1729), he came to the notice of George Lyttelton, leading figure of the Patriot Whig Opposition, who became his patron and friend and introduced him to Frederick, Prince of Wales. Thomson's other notable poems were the five-book *Liberty* (1735–36), a fervent account of the decline of liberty from ancient Greece to present-day Italy and its future in Britain, and *The Castle of Indolence* (1748), a Spenserian allegory of a land corrupted by luxury and saved by arts and industry. His politics continued in his plays and found a succinct expression in 'Rule Britannia' in the masque *Alfred* (1740), co-written with David Mallet.

The occasion of *Britannia* was the outcry against the Spanish attacks on British trading ships operating in the Spanish American colonies. From the Spanish coastguards' point of view, their attacks and seizures were entirely justified after the Treaty of Utrecht (see *Windsor-Forest*) limited trading concessions in the Americas. British merchants, however, felt it their right to trade freely and to benefit from this very prosperous traffic. Such episodes became a focus for a deeply felt hostility by the Patriot Opposition, for whom Robert Walpole's (Prime Minister 1721–42) non-aggressive foreign policy throughout the late 1720s and 1730s exemplified all that was corrupt in British politics. Thomson's depiction of the nation's 'manly soul' corrupted by 'waste Luxury' was a constant in apocalyptic warnings to the nation and owes its rhetorical force to the notion of 'civic virtue'. An antidote to corruption was a nostalgia for the Elizabethan golden age of sea-power. The poem's ideological complexity can be seen when Thomson includes the obligatory paean to an empire based upon peace and 'liberty' (in contrast to other empires secured by 'conquest'), yet the context of the poem forces him problematically to align British liberty with visions of imperial dominance and military might.

The poem opens with a description of a tattered Britannia, who then begins her long lament of the present state of the British nation and its empire.

> —*Et tantas audetis tollere Moles?*
> *Quos Ego – sed motos præstat componere Fluctus.*
> *Post mihi non simili Pæna commissa luetis.*
> *Maturate Fugam, Regique hæc dicite vestro:*
> *Non illi Imperium Pelagi, Sævumque Tridentem,*
> *Sed mihi forte datum.*— Virg.[1]

As on the Sea-beat Shore BRITANNIA sat,
Of her degenerate Sons the faded Fame,
Deep in her anxious Heart revolving sad:

---

[1] *Et tantus … datum*: Virgil, *Aeneid*, 1: 134–39, Neptune speaks: 'And do you dare to raise so great a storm? Whom I – but it is better first to calm the troubled waves; hereafter with another penalty you will pay me for your wrongdoing. Speed your flight, and bear this word to your king: not to him, but to me were given by lot the lordship of the sea and the dread trident.'

Bare was her throbbing Bosom to the Gale,
That hoarse, and hollow, from bleak Surge blew;   5
Loose flow'd her Tresses; Rent her Azure Robe.
Hung o'er the Deep, from her Majestick Brow
She tore the Laurel, and she tore the Bay.[2]
Nor ceas'd the copious Grief to bathe her Cheek;
Nor ceas'd her Sobs to murmur to the Main.   10
Peace discontented nigh, departing, stretch'd
Her Dove-like Wings. And *War*, tho' greatly rous'd,
Yet mourn'd his fetter'd Hands. While thus the *Queen*
Of Nations spoke; and what she said the *Muse*
Recorded, faithful, in unbidden Verse.   15

      Even not yon Sail, that, from the Sky-mixt Wave,
Dawns on the Sight, and wafts the ROYAL YOUTH,[3]
A Freight of future Glory to my Shore;
Even not the flattering View of golden Days,
And rising Periods yet of bright Renown,   20
Beneath the PARENTS, and their endless Line
Thro' late revolving Time, can sooth my Rage;
While, unchastis'd, the insulting *Spaniard* dares
Infest the trading Flood, full of vain War
Despise my *Navies*, and my *Merchants* seize;   25
As, trusting to false Peace, they fearless roam
The World of Waters wild, made, by the Toil,
And liberal Blood of glorious Ages, mine:
Nor bursts my sleeping Thunder on their Head.
Whence this unwonted Patience? This weak Doubt?   30
This tame Beseeching of rejected Peace?
This meek Forebearance? This unnative Fear,
To generous *Britons* never known before?
And sail'd my *Fleets* for this; on *Indian* Tides
To float, unactive, with the veering Winds?   35
The Mockery of War! While foul Disease,
And Sloth distemper'd, swept off burning Crowds,
For Action ardent; and amid the Deep,
Inglorious, sunk Them in a watry Grave.
There now they lie beneath the rowling Flood,   40
Far from their Friends, and Country unaveng'd;
And back the weeping *War-Ship* comes again,

---

[2] *laurel*: the 'crown of Laurel', the foliage from the bay tree, was a symbol of victory and distinction.

[3] *Royal Youth*: King George II's son, Frederic, Prince of Wales. Father and son were hostile towards each other, and Frederic aligned himself with the Patriot Opposition.

Dispirited, and thin; her Sons asham'd
Thus idly to review their native Shore;
With not one Glory sparkling in their Eye,   45
One Triumph on their Tongue. A Passenger,
The violated *Merchant* comes along;
That far-sought Wealth, for which the noxious Gale
He drew, and sweat beneath Equator Suns,
By lawless Force detain'd; a Force that soon   50
Would melt away, and every Spoil resign,
Were once the *British Lyon* heard to roar.
Whence is it that the proud *Iberian* thus,
In their own well-asserted Element,
Dares rouze to Wrath the *Masters of the Main*?   55
Who told him, that the big, incumbent *War*
Would not, ere this, have rowl'd his trembling Ports
In smoaky Ruin? And his guilty Stores,
Won by the Ravage of a butcher'd World,
Yet unatton'd, sunk in the swallowing Deep,   60
Or led the glittering Prize into the *Thames*?

    There was a Time (Oh let my languid Sons
Resume their Spirit at the rouzing Thought!)
When all the Pride of *Spain*, in one dread Fleet,
Swell'd o'er the labring Surge; like a whole Heaven   65
Of Clouds, wide-roll'd before the boundless Breeze.[4]
Gaily the splendid *Armament* along
Exultant plow'd, reflecting a red Gleam,
As sunk the Sun, o'er all the flaming Vast;
Tall, gorgeous, and elate; drunk with the Dream   70
Of easy Conquest; while their bloated War,
Stretch'd out from Sky to Sky, the gather'd Force
Of Ages held in its capacious Womb.
But soon, regardless of the cumbrous Pomp,
My dauntless *Britons* came, a gloomy Few,   75
With Tempest black, the goodly Scene deform'd,
And laid their Glory waste. The Bolts of Fate
Resistless thunder'd thro' their yielding Sides;
Fierce o'er their Beauty blaz'd the lurid Flame;
And seiz'd in horrid Grasp, or shatter'd wide,   80
Amid the mighty Waters, deep they sunk.
Then too from every Promontory chill,
Rank Fen, and Cavern where the wild Wave works,

---

[4]   Lines 62–89: Britannia begins to relate the battle of the Spanish Armada in 1588.

I swept confederate Winds, and swell'd a Storm.
Round the glad Isle, snatch'd by the vengeful Blast,   85
The scatter'd Remnants drove; on the blind Shelve,
And pointed Rock, that marks the indented Shore,
Relentless dash'd, where loud the *Northern Main*
Howls thro' the fractur'd *Caledonian* Isles.

    Such were the Dawnings of my liquid Reign;   90
But since how vast it grew, how absolute,
Even in those troubled Times, when dreadful *Blake*[5]
Aw'd angry Nations with the *British Name*,
Let every humbled State, let *Europe* say,
Sustain'd, and ballanc'd, by my *Naval Arm*.   95
Ah what must these immortal Spirits think
Of your poor Shifts? These, for their Country's Good,
Who fac'd the blackest Danger, knew no Fear,
No mean Submission, but commanded Peace.
Ah how with Indignation must they burn?   100
(If ought, but Joy, can touch æthereal Breasts)
With Shame? With Grief? To see their feeble Sons
Shrink from that Empire o'er the conquer'd Seas,
For which their Wisdom plann'd, their Councils glow'd,
And their Veins bled thro' many a toiling Age.   105

    Oh first of human Blessings! and Supreme!
Fair PEACE! how lovely, how delightful thou!
By whose wide Tie, the kindred Sons of Men,
Like Brothers live, in Amity combin'd,
And unsuspicious Faith; while honest *Toil*   110
Gives every Joy, and to those Joys a Right,
Which idle, barbarous *Rapine* but usurps.
Pure is thy Reign; when, unaccurs'd by Blood,
Nought, save the Sweetness of indulgent Showers,
Trickling distils into the vernant Glebe;   115
Instead of mangled Carcasses, sad-seen,
When the blithe Sheaves lie scatter'd o'er the Field;
When only shining Shares, the crooked Knife,
And Hooks imprint the vegetable Wound;
When the Land blushes with the Rose alone,   120
The falling Fruitage, and the bleeding Vine.
Oh, PEACE! thou Source, and Soul of social Life;

---

5   *Blake*: Robert Blake (1599–1657), famous English naval commander and son of a merchant. His inclusion here is probably a reference to his victory against a Spanish treasure-fleet off Tenerife in 1657.

Beneath whose calm, inspiring Influence,
Science his Views inlarges, *Art* refines,
And swelling *Commerce* opens all her Ports;   125
Blest be the *Man divine*, who gives us Thee!
Who bids the Trumpet hush his horrid Clang,
Nor blow the giddy Nations into Rage;
Who sheaths the murdrous Blade; the deadly Gun
Into the well-pil'd Armoury returns;   130
And, every Vigour, from the Work of Death,
To grateful Industry converting, makes
The City flourish, and the Country smile.
Unviolated, Him[6] the Virgin sings;
And Him the smiling Mother to her Train.   135
Of Him the Shepherd, in the peaceful Dale,
Chaunts; and, the Treasures of his Labour sure,
The Husbandman of Him, as at the Plow,
Or Team, He toils. With Him the Sailor sooths,
Beneath the trembling Moon, the Midnight Wave;   140
And the full City, warm, from Street to Street,
And Shop to Shop, responsive, rings of Him.
Nor joys one Land alone; his Praise extends
Far as the Sun rolls the diffusive Day;
Far as the Breeze can bear the Gifts of Peace,   145
Till all the happy Nations catch the Song.

     What would not, PEACE! the *Patriot* bear for Thee?
What painful Patience? What incessant Care?
What mixt Anxiety? What sleepless Toil?
Even from the rash Protected what Reproach?   150
For He thy Value knows; thy Friendship He
To human Nature: but the better thou,
The richer of Delight, sometimes the more
Inevitable WAR; when ruffian force
Awakes the Fury of an injur'd State.   155
Then the good easy Man, whom Reason rules;
Who, while unhurt, knew nor Offence, nor Harm,
Rouz'd by bold Insult, and injurious Rage,
With sharp, and sudden Check, th' astonish'd Sons
Of Violence confounds; firm as his Cause,   160
His bolder Heart; in awful Justice clad;
His Eyes effulging a peculiar Fire:
And, as he charges thro' the prostrate War,

---

[6]   *Him*: in other words, 'the *Man divine*' of line 126.

His keen Arm teaches faithless Men, no more
To dare the sacred Vengeance of the Just.   165

      And what, my thoughtless *Sons*, should fire you more,
Than when your well-earn'd Empire of the Deep
The least beginning Injury receives?
What better Cause can call your Lightning forth?
Your Thunder wake? Your dearest Life demand?   170
What better Cause, than when your Country sees
The sly Destruction at her Vitals aim'd?
For Oh it much imports you, 'tis your All,
To keep your *Trade* intire, intire the Force,
And Honour of your *Fleets*; o'er that to watch,   175
Even with a Hand severe, and jealous Eye.
In Intercourse[7] be gentle, generous, just,
By Wisdom polish'd, and of Manners fair;
But on the Sea be terrible, untam'd,
Inconquerable still: let none escape,   180
Who shall but aim to touch your Glory there.
Is there a Man, into the Lyon's Den
Who dares intrude, to snatch his Young away?
And is a *Briton* seiz'd? and seiz'd beneath
The slumbring Terrors of a *British Fleet*?   185
Then ardent rise! Oh great in Vengeance rise!
O'erturn the Proud, teach Rapine to restore:
And as you ride sublimely round the World,
Make every Vessel stoop, make every State
At once their Welfare and their Duty know.   190
This is your Glory; this your Wisdom; this
The native Power for which you were design'd
By *Fate*, when *Fate* design'd the firmest State,
That e'er was seated on the subject Sea;
A State, alone, where LIBERTY should live,   195
In these late Times, this Evening of Mankind,
When *Carthage, Rome,* and *Athens* are no more,[8]
The World almost in slavish Sloth dissolv'd.
For this, these Rocks around your Coast were thrown;
For this, your Oaks, peculiar harden'd, shoot   200
Strong into sturdy Growth; for this, your Hearts
Swell with a sullen Courage, growing still

---

[7] *intercourse*: here, meaning social communication, and perhaps commercial dealings.
[8] *Carthage, Rome, and Athens*: the capital cities of the ancient Phoenician, Roman and Greek empires. These were often evoked as examples of once great empires ruined by tyranny and luxury.

As Danger grows; and Strength, and Toil for this
Are liberal pour'd o'er all the fervent Land.
Then cherish this, this unexpensive Power,   205
Undangerous to the *Publick*, ever prompt,
By lavish *Nature* thrust into your Hand:
And, unencumber'd with the Bulk immense
Of Conquest, whence huge Empires rose, and fell,
Self-crush'd, extend your Reign from Shore to Shore,   210
Where-e'er the Wind your high Behests can blow,
And fix it deep on this eternal Base.
For should the sliding Fabrick once give Way,
And on the Brink of Fate begin to nod,
Soon slacken'd quite, and past Recovery broke,   215
It gathers *Ruin* as it rowls along,
Steep-rushing down to that devouring Gulph,
Where many a mighty Empire buried lies.
And should the big redundant Flood of *Trade*,
In which ten thousand thousand *Labours* join   220
Their several Currents, 'till the boundless Tide
Rolls in a radiant Torrent o'er the Land,
Fruitful of Wealth, Magnificence, and Joy,
Of every glittering Harvest, richer far
Than what *Hesperian* Gardens bore of old;[9]   225
Should this bright Stream, the least inflected, point
Its Course another Way, o'er other Lands
The *various Treasure* would resistless pour,
Ne'er to be won again; its antient Tract
Left a vile Channel, desolate, and dead,   230
With all around a miserable Waste.
Not *Egypt*,[10] were, her better Heaven, the *Nile*
Turn'd in the Pride of Flow; when o'er his Rocks,
And roaring Cataracts, beyond the Reach
Of dizzy Vision pil'd, in one wide Flash   235
An *Ethiopian* Deluge foams amain;
(Whence wond'ring *Fable* trac'd him from the Sky)
Even not that Prime of Earth, where Harvests croud
On untill'd Harvests, all the teeming Year,
If of the fat, o'erflowing Culture robb'd,   240
Were then a more uncomfortable Wild,
Steril, and void; than of her Trade depriv'd,
Britons, your boasted Isle: Her Princes sunk;

---

[9]   Lines 223–5 omitted in later editions.
[10]   *Not Egypt*: the Egyptian civilisation is used as another example of a state that overreached
        itself.

Her high-built Honour moulder'd to the Dust;
Unnerv'd her Force; her Spirit vanish'd quite;   245
With rapid Wing her Riches fled away;
Her unfrequented Ports alone the Sign
Of what she was; her Merchants scatter'd wide;
Her hollow Shops shut up; and in her Streets,
Her Fields, Woods, Markets, Villages, and Roads,   250
The chearful Voice of Labour heard no more.

    Oh let not then waste *Luxury* impair
That manly Soul of Toil, which strings your Nerves,
And your own proper Happiness creates!
Oh let not the soft, penetrating Plague   255
Creep on the free-born Mind! And working there,
With the sharp Tooth of many a new-form'd Want,
Endless, and idle all, eat out the Heart
Of LIBERTY; the high Conception blast;
The noble Sentiment, th' impatient Scorn   260
Of base Subjection, and the swelling Wish
For general Good, erazing from the Mind:
While nought save narrow *Selfishness* succeeds,
And low Design, the gloomy Passions all
Let loose, and reigning in the rankled Breast.   265
Induc'd at last, by scarce-perceiv'd Degrees,
Sapping the very Frame of Government,
And Life, a total *Dissolution* comes:
Sloth, Ignorance, Dejection, Flattery, Fear,
Oppression raging o'er the Waste He makes;   270
The human Being almost quite extinct;
And the whole State in broad *Corruption* sinks.
Oh shun that Gulph! That gaping Ruin shun!
And countless Ages roll it far away
From you, ye Heaven-belov'd! May LIBERTY,   275
The Light of Life! the Sun of human kind!
Whence *Heroes*, *Bards*, and *Patriots* borrow Flame,
Even where the keen depressive *North* descends,
Still spread, exalt, and actuate your Powers!
While slavish *Southern* Climates beam in vain.[11]   280
And may a *publick* Spirit from the THRONE,
Where every *Virtue* sits, go copious forth

---

[11]   *depressive North ... Southern climates*: Thomson draws upon the climate theory of the day, in which the character and government of nations was linked to their climate and their latitude. Thomson draws a distinction between the countries of Southern Europe (and the 'torrid zones' of more distant countries) and those of Northern Europe (including England and Scotland).

Wide o'er the Land! the *finer Arts* inspire;
Make thoughtful *Science* raise his pensive Head,
Blow the fresh *Bay*, bid *Industry* rejoice,   285
And the rough *Sons* of lowest *Labour* smile.
As when, profuse of Spring, the loosen'd *West*
Lifts up the pining Year, and luscious breathes
Youth, Life, Love, and Beauty o'er the World.

But haste We from these melancholly Shores,   290
Nor to deaf Winds, and Waves, our fruitless Plaint
Pour out; the Country claims our active Aid;
That let Us roam; and where we find a Spark
Of *publick Virtue*, blow it into a Flame.
The THRONE be chief our Care; th' ætherial Streams   295
Of Wisdom, Justice, and Benevolence,
That issue thence, refreshing all the Land,
Joyous to swell: and o'er the lovely Round
Of ROYAL BEAUTY, which about it glows,
To hover fond, prophetick of those Days   300
That, FREDERICK! dawn delightful in thy Eye.[12]
And now my *Sons*, the *Sons of Freedom*! meet
In awful Senate; thither let us fly;
Burn in the *Patriot*'s Thought, flow from his Tongue
In fearless Truth; myself, transform'd, *preside*,   305
And shed the Spirit of BRITANNIA round.

This said; her fleeting Form, and airy Train,
Sunk in the Gale; and nought but ragged Rocks
Rush'd on the broken Eye; and nought was heard
But the rough Cadence of the dashing Wave.   310

George Lillo, from *The London Merchant: Or, The History of George Barnwell* (1731)

George Lillo (1693–1739) was a dramatist whose play *The London Merchant*, with its depiction of the merchant-as-hero, instigated a strand of domestic middle-class

---

[12]   Lines 295–301 omitted in later editions.

tragedy (other plays include *The Christian Hero*, 1735, and *The Fatal Curiosity*, 1736). The play's origin was in the popular ballad 'George Barnwell', and concerns the story of Barnwell, an apprentice to the merchant Thorowgood, and his corruption by the seductress Millwood, who persuades him first to rob his employer and then to rob and murder his uncle. Millwood and Barnwell's capture and hanging provides the play's moral coda. The play attempts to mythologise the merchant as the vanguard and mainstay of British virtue. In the following extract Thorowgood talks to Trueman, one of his apprentices. The listing of the 'Blessings' of imperial produce that are disposed by 'Heaven' and the hymn to commerce as promoting 'mutual Love', exemplify a typically British ideology of empire.[1]

Thor. Methinks I wou'd not have you only learn the Method of Merchandize, and practise it hereafter, merely as a Means of getting Wealth.—'Twill be well worth your Pains to study it as a Science.—See how it is founded in Reason, and the Nature of Things.—How it has promoted Humanity, as it has opened and yet keeps up an Intercourse between Nations, far remote from one another in Situation, Customs and Religion; promoting Arts, Industry, Peace and Plenty; by mutual Benefits diffusing mutual Love from Pole to Pole.

Tr. Something of this I have consider'd, and hope, by your Assistance, to extend my Thoughts much farther.—I have observ'd those Countries, where Trade is promoted and encouraged, do not make Discoveries to destroy, but to improve Mankind,—by Love and Friendship, to tame the fierce, and polish the most savage,—to teach them the Advantages of honest Traffick,—by taking from them, with their own Consent, their useless Superfluities, and giving them, in Return, what, from their Ignorance in manual Arts, their Situation, or some other Accident they stand in need of.

Thor. 'Tis justly observ'd:—The populous East, luxuriant, abounds with glittering Gems, bright Pearls, aromatick Spices, and Health-restoring Drugs: The late found Western World glows with unnumber'd Veins of Gold and Silver Ore.—On every Climate, and on every Country, Heaven has bestowed some good peculiar to it self.—It is the industrious Merchant's Business to collect the various Blessings of each Soil and Climate, and, with the Product of the Whole, to enrich his native Country.

---

[1]   Text from Act III, Sc. I, pp. 28–9.

James Thomson and David Mallet, *Rule Britannia* (1740)

Rule Britannia was originally from the masque *Alfred,* which was first performed for Prince Frederick in 1740 and opened on Drury Lane the following year. The masque was a collaboration between Thomson and fellow Scot, David Mallet (?1705–65). The play celebrates the heroic resistance of Alfred the Great – king of the West Saxons from 871 until his death in 899 – to the Danes (alluding to the contemporary tensions between the English and the Spanish). Alfred was often represented in Patriot Opposition writings in the 1730s as a law-giver hero who exemplified Saxon liberty and Christian benevolence (in contrast to the prime minister Robert Walpole). The masque's climax occurs when the figure of the Hermit prophesies the future glory of England, and the Bard sings 'An ODE' which we now know as *Rule Britannia.*[1]

1.

When Britain *first, at heaven's command,*
 Arose from out the azure main;
This *was the charter of the land,*
 And guardian Angels sung this strain:
  'Rule, Britannia, *rule the waves;*   5
  Britons *never will be slaves.'*

2.

The nations, not so blest as thee,
 Must, in their turns, to tyrants fall:
While thou shalt flourish great and free,
 The dread and envy of them all.   10
  'Rule, Britannia, *rule the waves;*
  Britons *never will be slaves.'*

3.

Still more majestic shalt thou rise,
 More dreadful, from each foreign stroke:
As the loud blast that tears the skies,   15
 Serves but to root thy native oak.
  'Rule, Britannia, *rule the waves;*
  Britons *never will be slaves.'*

---

[1]   Text from *Alfred: A Masque* (1741), pp. 142–4.

4.

Thee haughty tyrants ne'er shall tame:
    All their attempts to bend thee down,   20
Will but arouse thy generous flame;
    But work their woe, and thy renown.
        'Rule, Britannia, rule the waves;
        Britons never will be slaves.'

5.

To thee belongs the rural reign;   25
    Thy cities shall with commerce shine:
All thine shall be the subject main,
    And every shore it circles thine.
        'Rule, Britannia, rule the waves;
        Britons never will be slaves.'   30

6.

The Muses, still with freedom found,
    Shall to thy happy coast repair:
Blest isle! with matchless beauty crown'd,
    And manly hearts to guard the fair.
        'Rule, Britannia, rule the waves,   35
        Britons never will be slaves.'

John Dyer, from *The Ruins of Rome* (1740)

John Dyer (1699–1757) was a native of Wales, whose landscape he celebrated in his popular poem *Grongar Hill* (1726). His other significant work was *The Fleece* (1757), a four-book poem written in the style of Virgil's *Georgics* in which the celebration of Britain's wool industry is intertwined with a detailed and comprehensive prospect of Britain's commercial networks and prosperity across the globe. Dyer travelled to Italy in 1724 and it is this trip which shaped the melancholic yet awe-inspiring vision of ancient Rome in *The Ruins of Rome*. The Roman Empire, for eighteenth-century writers, provided an emblem of imperial decay. Mobilised as both a contrast and a warning to the British Empire, the fate of Rome offered lessons in national and imperial conduct. Dyer's poem begins with a scene of the ruins of Roman civilisation, then proceeds to narrate the history of its rise and downfall. The excerpts below are from the opening and end of the poem. In the fate of the Roman Empire, writers – and Dyer's poem is no exception – saw a number of inter-related causes

and symptoms: a fatal slide into apathy, the downfall of virtuous political rule,
luxurious pleasure and even effeminacy.

> Enough of *Grongar*,[1] and the shady Dales
> Of winding *Towy, Merlin's* fabled haunt,
> I sung inglorious. Now the Love of Arts,
> And what in Metal or in Stone remains
> Of proud Antiquity, through various Realms   5
> And various Languages and Ages fam'd,
> Bears me remote, o'er *Gallia's*[2] woody Bounds,
> O'er the Cloud-piercing Alps, remote; beyond
> The Vale of *Arno* purpled with the Vine,
> Beyond the *Umbrian*, and *Etruscan* Hills,   10
> To *Latium's* wide Champain,[3] forlorn and waste,
> Where yellow *Tiber* his neglected wave
> Mournfully rolls. Yet once again, my Muse,
> Yet once again, and soar a Loftier flight;
> Lo the resistless Theme, Imperial *Rome*.   15
>   Fall'n, fall'n, a silent Heap; her Heroes all
> Sunk in their Urns; behold the Pride of Pomp,
> The Throne of Nations fall'n; obscur'd in dust;
> Ev'n yet Majestical: The solemn Scene
> Elates the soul, while now the rising Sun   20
> Flames on the Ruins, in the purer air
> Tow'ring aloft, upon the glitt'ring plain,
> Like broken Rocks, a vast circumference;
> Rent Palaces, crush'd Columns, rifted Moles,
> Fanes roll'd on Fanes,[4] and Tombs on buried Tombs.   25

> [...]

> The City gleam'd
> With pretious Spoils: Alas Prosperity!
> Ah baneful State! yet ebb'd not all their Strength
> In soft luxurious Pleasures; proud Desire
> Of boundless Sway, and fev'rish Thirst of Gold   455
> Rous'd them again to Battle; beauteous *Greece*,
> Torn from her joys, in vain with languid arm

---

1   *Grongar*: Dyer's poem *Grongar Hill* (1726).
2   *Gallia*: France. In lines 7–11 Dyer's imagination travels over France, the Alps and to Italy.
3   *champain*: open country.
4   *Fanes*: temples.

Half rais'd her rusty Shield; nor could avail
The Sword of *Dacia*, nor the *Parthian* Dart;[5]
Nor yet the Car of that fam'd *British* Chief,[6]   460
Which seven brave years beneath the doubtful Wing
Of Vict'ry dreadful roll its griding Wheels
Over the bloody War: The *Roman* Arms
Triumph'd, 'till Fame was silent of their Foes.
  And now the World unrival'd they enjoy'd   465
In proud Security: The crested Helm,
The plated Greave[7] and Corselet hung unbrac'd;
Nor clank'd their Arms, the Spear and sounding Shield,
But on the glitt'ring Trophy to the Wind.
  Dissolv'd in Ease and soft Delights they lie   470
'Till ev'ry Sun annoys, and ev'ry Wind
Has chilling force, and ev'ry Rain offends;
For now the Frame no more is girt with strength
Masculine, nor in Lustiness of heart,
Laughs at the winter storm, and summer beam,   475
Superior to their rage: enfeebling Vice
Withers each Nerve, and opens ev'ry Pore
To painful feeling: flow'ry Bow'rs they seek,
(As Æther prompts, as the sick Sense approves)
Or cool Nymphean Grots; or tepid Baths   480
(Taught by the soft *Ionians*) they, along
The lawny Vale, of ev'ry beauteous stone,
Pile in the roseat air with fond Expence:
Through silver channels glide the fragrant Waves,
And fall on silver Beds chrystalline down,   485
Melodious murmuring; while Luxury
Over their naked limbs, with wanton hand,
Sheds Roses, Odors, sheds unheeded Bane.
  Swift is the Flight of Wealth; unnumber'd Wants,
Brood of voluptousness, cry out aloud   490
Necessity, and seek the splendid Bribe;
The citron Board; the Bowl emboss'd with Gems,

---

5 *Dacia … Parthian dart*: Dacia, occupying the region later known as Translyvania, posed a
 serious threat to Rome, until they were defeated in two wars by emporer Marcus Trajanus
 (*c*.53–117). Parthia, around the region of modern Iran, was the centre of an empire that
 occupied most of Western Asia, until finally ground down by Roman generals in the
 second century.

6 *British chief*: Caratacus, or Caradoc (d.54), British chieftain who fought against the Romans
 between 43–50, but was eventually taken and exhibited in Rome in 51.

7 *Greave*: armour for the shin.

And tender Foliage, wildly wreath'd around,
Of seeming Ivy, by that artful Hand,
Corinthian Thericles;[8] whate'er is known   495
Of rarest acquisition; *Tyrian* Garbs,[9]
Neptunian Albion's high testaceous Food,[10]
And flavour'd *Chian* Wines, with Incense fum'd
To slake Patrician Thirst: For These their Rights
In the vile streets they prostitute to sale;   500
Their antient Rights, their Dignities, their Laws,
Their native glorious Freedom. Is there none,
Is there no Villain, that will bind the Neck
Stretch'd to the Yoke? they come; the Market throngs.
But who has most by Fraud or Force amass'd?   505
Who most can charm Corruption with his Doles?
He be the Monarch of the State; and lo
Didius, vile Us'rer; through the Croud he mounts;[11]
Beneath his Feet the *Roman* Eagle cow'rs,
And the red Arrows fill his grasp uncouth.   510
O *Britons*, O my Countrymen, beware,
Gird, gird your Hearts; the *Romans* once were Free,
Were Brave, were Virtuous.—Tyranny howe'er
Deign'd to walk forth a while in pageant state,
And with licentious pleasures fed the Rout,   515
The thoughtless Many: To the wanton Sound
Of Fifes and Drums they danc'd, or in the shade
Sung *Cæsar*, great and terrible in War,
Immortal *Cæsar*! lo, a God, a God,
He cleaves the yielding skies! *Cæsar* mean while   520
Gathers the Ocean Pebbles; or the Gnat
Enrag'd pursues; or at his lonely Meal
Starves a wide Province; tastes, dislikes, and flings
To Dogs and Sycophants: A God, a God!
The flow'ry Shades and Shrines obscene return.   525
    But see along the North the Tempest swell
O'er the rough Alps, and darken all their Snows!

---

8   *Corinthian Thericles*: Thericles was a potter of fine and much copied cups. An inhabitant of
Corinth in Greece was traditionally associated with licentiousness.
9   *Tyrian garbs*: this associates the colour, Tyrian purple, with the robes worn as a mark of
dignity and high rank in Ancient Greek and Roman culture.
10 *testaceous food*: shell-fish.
11 '*Didius Julianus* who bought the Empire' [Dyer's note]. Didius Julianus (*c*.135–193) was a
soldier who bought the Roman empire, after the Praetorian Guards put it up for sale on
the death of emperor Pertinax in 193. He reigned as emperor for only two months.

Sudden the *Goth* and *Vandal*, dreaded Names,
Rush as the Breach of waters, whelming all
Their Domes, their Villas; down the festive Piles,   530
Down fall their Parian Porches, Gilded Baths,
And roll before the Storm in clouds of dust.
    Vain end of human Strength, of human Skill,
Conquest, and Triumph, and Domain, and Pomp,
And Ease, and Luxury. O Luxury,   535
Bane of elated Life, of affluent States,
What dreary Change, what Ruin is not thine?
How doth thy Bowl intoxicate the Mind?
To the soft Entrance of thy Rosy Cave
How do'st thou lure the Fortunate and Great,   540
Dreadful Attraction! while behind thee gapes
Th' unfathomable Gulph where *Ashur*[12] lies
O'erwhelm'd, forgotten; and high-boasting *Cham*;[13]
And *Elam*'s haughty Pomp,[14] and beauteous *Greece*;
And the great Queen of Earth, Imperial *Rome*.   545

Joseph Warton, *The Dying Indian* (1755)

Joseph Warton (1722–1800) was a poet and critic in a family of poets and critics: his father, Thomas Warton the elder, was Professor of Poetry at Oxford and a friend of the poets Alexander Pope and Matthew Prior; his brother Thomas wrote the influential poem *The Pleasures of Melancholy* (1747). Joseph's writings included his poetic manifesto *Odes on Various Subjects* (1746) and his famous *An Essay on the Writings and Genius of Pope* (1756). His poetics stressed the power of imagination, pathos, and the sublime, breaking away from the emphasis on wit and moral didacticism in poetry. *The Dying Indian* (published with a companion poem *The Revenge of America*) is in

---

12   *Ashur*: ancient God of Assyria, associated with the Phoenician civilisation.
13   *Cham*: the title of the Prince of Tartary, who was also known as Khan.
14   *Elam*: one of the oldest civilisations, which was then successively conquered, it was in the region of what is now south-western Iran.

the tradition of the noble savage: the pathos of the speaker underlines the dominant perception of the Spanish empire in the eighteenth century.[1]

> The dart of Izdabel prevails! 'twas dipped
> In double poison—I shall soon arrive
> At the blest island, where no tigers spring
> On heedless hunters; where anana's bloom[2]
> Thrice in each moon; where rivers smoothly glide,   5
> Nor thundering torrents whirl the light canoe
> Down to the sea; where my forefathers feast
> Daily on the hearts of Spaniards!—O my son,
> I feel the venom busy in my breast,
> Approach, and bring my crown, decked with the teeth   10
> Of that bold christian who first dar'd deflour
> The virgins of the sun; and, dire to tell!
> Robb'd Vitzipultzi's statue[3] of its gems!
> I mark'd the spot where they interr'd this traitor,
> And once at midnight I stole to his tomb,   15
> And tore his carcass from the earth, and left it
> A prey to poisonous flies. Preserve this crown
> With sacred secrecy: if e'er returns
> Thy much-lov'd mother from the desart woods
> Where, as I hunted late, I hapless lost her,   20
> Cherish her age. Tell her I n'er have worship'd
> With those that eat their God. And when disease
> Preys on her languid limbs, then kindly stab her
> With thine own hands, nor suffer her to linger,
> Like christian cowards, in a life of pain.   25
> I go! great Copac beckons me! farewell![4]

---

[1] Text from Robert Dodsley, ed., *A Collection of Poems*, vol. IV (1755), pp. 209–10.

[2] *anana's bloom*: the pineapple.

[3] *Vitzipultzi*: Aztec war god. Warton seems to have confused Aztec (Mexican) and Inca (Peruvian) civilisations. From the 1763 edition, this was 'Pachacamac's altar'. Pachacamac was the Peruvian's supreme god of fire.

[4] *Copac*: Manco Capac was the first ruler or Inca of the Peruvians, and was held to be the source of all their beliefs.

John Brown, from
An Estimate of the Manners and Principles of the Times (1757)

John Brown (1715–66) was born in Newcastle and was a clergyman there for most of his life. He is principally famous for his *Estimate*, though he produced a wide variety of other writings, including, *An Essay on Satire* (1745); the tragedy *Barbarossa* (1754); *Sermons on Various Subjects* (1764); and *Thoughts on Civil Liberty* (1765). Before he died he conceived an ambitious plan to civilise Russia.

Written in the wake of the fall of Minorca to the French in the first year of the Seven Years' War (1756–63), Brown's apocalyptic survey of Britain's manners echoed public fears that the nation did not have the requisite martial vigour to win. Brown pointed the finger at the nation's lack of religiosity, lack of public virtue and its dissolute manners. His central concern was that an increasing tide of luxurious pleasures – clothes, gaming, dancing, food, Italian opera – were sapping the spirit of the nation's men. In his gloomy assessment luxury was inextricable from the national *malaise* of effeminacy (best conceived as a corruption of an ideal masculinity or manliness). For Brown, it was the very success of the British empire that sustained this luxurious corruption. At the end of his analysis, only a 'GREAT MINISTER' can save the nation.[1]

As it appears therefore, from this Delineation, that SHOW and PLEASURE are the main Objects of Pursuit: As the general Habit of *refined Indulgence* is *strong*, and the habit of *induring* is *lost*: As the general Sprit of *Religion*, *Honour*, and *public Love*, are weakened or vanished; as these Manners are therefore left to their own Workings, uncontrouled by *Principle*; we may with Truth and Candour conclude, that the ruling Character of the present Times is that of 'a vain, *luxurious, and selfish* EFFEMINACY'.

[...]

The Effects of Commerce on Manners have by most Writers, I think, been considered as *uniform*. Even the sage and amiable MONTESQUIEU says only, in general Terms, 'That Commerce polishes Manners, but corrupts Manners'.[2]

---

[1]   Text from pp. 66–7, 152–3, 159, 181–2. The 'GREAT MINISTER' is from p. 221.

[2]   'L'Esprit des Loix, I, XX.C.I.' [Brown's footnote]. Charles Montesquieu's (1689–1755) *De l'esprit des lois* ('The Spirit of Laws'; 1748) was a highly influential work that traced the origin and development of the laws of nations. It held that the influence of climate was key and also proposed England's constitution as an exemplar of liberty.

Whereas, from a candid View of its Nature and Effects, we shall probably find, that in its first and middle Stages it is beneficent; in its last, dangerous and fatal.

If we view Commerce in its first Stages, we shall see, that it supplies mutual Necessities, prevents mutual Wants, extends mutual Knowledge, eradicates mutual Prejudice, and spreads mutual Humanity.

If we view it in its middle and more advanced Period, we shall see, it provides Conveniences, increaseth Numbers, coins Money, gives Birth to Arts and Science, creates equal Laws, diffuses general Plenty and general Happiness.

If we view it in its third and highest Stage, we shall see it change its Nature and Effects. It brings in Superfluity and vast Wealth; begets Avarice, gross Luxury, or effeminate Refinement among the higher Ranks, together with general Loss of Principle.

[...]

Thus as the Character of a State altogether commercial in the highest Degree, is that of Industry and Avarice; so, in a Nation of Extended territory, where Commerce is in its highest Period, while its trading Members retain their Habits of Industry and Avarice, the natural Character of its landed Ranks, its Nobility and Gentry, is that of 'a vain, luxurious, and selfish Effeminacy'.

[...]

Thus our present exorbitant Degree of Trade and Wealth, in a mixed state like that of *England*, naturally tends to produce luxurious and effeminate Manners in the higher Ranks, together with a general Defect of *Principle*. And as the internal Strength of a Nation will always depend chiefly on the Manners and Principles of its leading Members, so these effeminate Manners and this Defect of Principle operate powerfully, and fatally, on the national Conduct and Affairs. They have produced a general Incapacity, have weakened the national Spirit of Defence, have heightened the national Disunion: And this national Disunion, besides its proper and immediate Effects, being founded in Avarice for the Ends of Dissipation, hath again weakened the small Remainder of publick Capacity and Defence; and thus seems to have fitted us for a Prey to the Insults and Invasions of our most powerful Enemy.[3]

---

[3] *Enemy*: undoubtedly France.

Lady Mary Wortley Montagu,
from *Letters of the Right Honourable*
Lady M—y W—y M—e: Written,
during her Travels in Europe,
Asia and Africa (1763)

Self-educated, witty and brilliant, Lady Mary Wortley Montagu (1689–1762) was well known in the literary circles of such as Joseph Addison and Alexander Pope. Aside from the *Letters*, her most famous writings are the satirical poems on contemporary manners *Six Town Eclogues* written in 1714–16 (published 1747). In 1712, she married Edward Wortley Montagu MP (against her father's wishes), and in 1716 he was appointed Ambassador Extraordinary to the Court of Turkey – he was also to represent the Levant Company trade interests in the Near East. This was a posting to the heart of the Ottoman empire, an important region for British political and economic strategy.

Lady Mary accompanied him on this trip (which also took in Holland, Austria, Hungary and Tunisia) and they finally settled in Adrianople. They set out in August 1716 and returned to England in 1718. Lady Mary initially prepared the letters from this period as the 'Turkish Embassy Letters', but she decided against publication (an unauthorised edition appeared in 1763, the year after her death). As an aristocratic woman with diplomatic connections, her privileged access to Turkish court life offered an unprecedented glimpse of the life of women in the upper echelons of an Islamic state. She was well aware that she was entering what was traditionally represented as an exotic, heathen land of sexual licence: Pope wrote to her on her journey asking, 'How do your Christian Virtues hold out in so long a Voyage? You have already ... out-travelled the Sin of Fornication, and are happily arrived at the free Region of Adultery'.[1] While Lady Mary undoubtedly eroticised Turkish women, she also criticised previous writers' misrepresentations, seeing in the women's ostensible oppression a utopian sexual freedom not available to their European counterparts. Her description (in the last extract) of Tunisians on the fringes of the Ottoman empire offers an interesting contrast to the aristocratic and metropolitan milieux of Turkey.

Vol. I. Letter XXIV.
To the Lady [Rich].[2]

Adrianople, April 1, 1717.

I am now got into a new world, where everything I see, appears to me a change of scene; and I write to your ladyship with some content of mind,

---

1   Pope to Lady Mary Wortley Montagu, 10 November 1716; *The Correspondence of Alexander Pope*, ed. George Sherburn, 3 vols (Clarendon Press, 1956), vol. 1, p. 368.
2   *To the Lady [Rich]*: Lady Rich, Elisabeth Griffin (1692–1773), wife of Sir Robert Rich, Lady-in-Waiting to Queen Charlotte.

hoping, at least, that you will find the charm of novelty in my letters, and no longer reproach me, that I tell you nothing extraordinary. I won't trouble you with a relation of our tedious journey; but I must not omit what I saw remarkable at *Sophia*,[3] one of the most beautiful towns in the Turkish Empire, and famous for its hot baths, that are resorted to both for diversion and health. I stop'd here one day, on purpose to see them; and designing to go *incognito*, I hired a Turkish coach. These voitures are not at all like ours, but much more convenient for the country, the heat being so great that glasses would be very troublesome. They are made a good deal in the manner of the Dutch stage coaches, having wooden lattices painted and gilded; the inside being also painted with baskets and nosegays of flowers, intermixed commonly with little poetical mottos. They are covered all over with scarlet cloth, lined with silk, and very often richly embroidered and fringed. This covering entirely hides the persons in them, but may be thrown back at pleasure, and thus permit the ladies to peep through the lattices. They hold four people very conveniently, seated on cushions, but not raised.

In one of these covered wagons; I went to the *Bagnio* about ten o clock. It was already full of women. It is built of stone, in the shape of a dome, with no windows but in the roof, which gives light enough. There were five of these domes joined together, the outmost being less than the rest, and serving only as a hall, where the *Portress* stood at the door. Ladies of quality generally give this woman a crown or ten shillings, and I did not forget that ceremony. The next room is a very large one, paved with marble, and all round it are two raised Sofas of marble, one above another. There were four fountains of cold water in this room, falling first into marble basons, and then running on the floor in little channels made for that purpose, which carried the streams into the next room, something less than this, with the same sort of marble Sofas, but so hot with steams of sulphur proceeding from the baths joining to it, 'twas impossible to stay there with one's cloaths on. The two other domes were the hot baths, one of which had cocks of cold water turning into it, to temper it to what degree of warmth the bathers pleased to have.

I was in my travelling habit, which is a riding dress, and certainly appeared very extraordinary to them. Yet there was not one of them that shewed the least surprize or impertinent curiosity, but received me with all the obliging civility possible. I know no European court, where the ladies would have behaved themselves in so polite a manner to such a stranger. I believe, upon the whole, there were two hundred women, and yet none of those disdainful smiles, and satirical whispers, that never fail in our assemblies, when any body appears that is not dressed exactly in the fashion. They repeated over and over to me: 'UZELLE, PEK, UZELLE,' which is nothing but, '*Charming, very charming.*'—The first Sofas were covered with cushions

---

3   *Sophia*: Sofia, capital of Bulgaria. It had been in the Ottoman empire since 1392.

and rich carpets, on which sat the ladies; and on the second, their slaves behind them, but without any distinction of rank by their dress, all being in the state of nature, that is, in plain English, stark naked, without any beauty or defect concealed. Yet there was not the least wanton smile or immodest gesture amongst them. They walked and moved with the same majestic grace, which Milton describes our General Mother with.[4] There were many amongst them, as exactly proportioned as ever any goddess was drawn, by the pencil of a Guido or Titian,[5]—And most of their skins shiningly white, only adorned by their beautiful hair, divided into many tresses, hanging on their shoulders, braided either with pearl or ribbon, perfectly representing the figures of the graces.

I was here convinced of the truth of a reflection I have often made, *that if it were the fashion to go naked, the face would be hardly observed.* I perceived that the ladies of the most delicate skins and finest shapes, had the greatest share of my admiration, though their faces were sometimes less beautiful than those of their companions. To tell you the truth, I had wickedness enough, to wish secretly, that Mr. *Gervais*[6] could have been there invisible. I fancy it would have very much improved his art to see so many fine women naked, in different postures, some in conversation, some working, others drinking coffee or sherbet, and many negligently lying on their cushions, while their slaves (generally pretty girls of seventeen, or eighteen) were employ'd in braiding their hair in several pretty fancies. In short, 'tis the women's coffee-house, where all the news of the town is told, scandal invented, &c.—They generally take this diversion once a week, and stay there at least four or five hours, without getting cold, by immediate coming out of the hot-bath into the cool room, which was very surprising to me. The lady, that seemed the most considerable amongst them, entreated me to sit by her, and would fain have undressed me for the bath. I excused myself with some difficulty. They being however all so earnest in persuading me, I was at last forced to open my shirt, and shew them my stays, which satisfied them very well; for, I saw, they believed I was locked up in that machine, and that it was not in my own power to open it, which contrivance they attributed to my husband.—I was charmed with their civility and beauty, and should have been very glad to pass more time with them; but Mr. W—resolving to pursue his journey next morning early, I was in haste to see the ruins of Justinian's church,[7] which

---

[4] *General Mother*: Eve. In their pre-lapsarian state, Adam and Eve are without shame: that only comes after the fall; see John Milton's *Paradise Lost* (1667), 4: 288–324.

[5] *Guido or Titian*: Guido Reni (1575–1642) painter from Bologna; Titian (c.1488–1576) Venetian painter.

[6] *Gervais*: Charles Jervas (?1675–1739), portrait painter at the centre of literary life and a friend of Lady Mary.

[7] *Justinian's church*: church erected in Constantinople by Justinian I (c.482–565) emperor of the East Roman empire from 527.

did not afford me so agreeable a prospect as I had left, being little more than a heap of stones.

Adieu, Madam, I am sure I have now entertained you, with an account of such a sight as you never saw in your life and what no book of travels could inform you of, as 'tis no less than death for a man to be found in one of these places.

[…]

Vol. II. Letter XXVII
To the Countess of B[ristol].[8]

Adrianople, April 1 [1717].

As I never can forget the smallest of your ladyship's commands, my first business here, has been to enquire after, the stuffs, you ordered me to look for, without being able to find what you would like. The difference of the dress here and at London is so great, the same sort of things are not proper for *Caftans* and *Manteaus*. However, I will not give over my search, but renew it again at Constantinople, though I have reason to believe there is nothing finer than what is to be found here, as this place is at present the residence of the court. The Grand Signior's[9] eldest daughter was married some few days before I came hither, and upon that occasion, the Turkish Ladies display all their magnificence. The bride was conducted to her husband's house in very great splendor. She is widow of the late Vizier, who was killed at Peterwaradin,[10] though that ought rather to be called a *contract*, than a *marriage*, since she never has lived with him; however, the greatest part of his wealth is hers. He had the permission of visiting her in the Seraglio; and being one of the handsomest men in the Empire, had very much engaged her affections.—When she saw this second husband, who is at least fifty, she could not forbear bursting into tears. He is indeed a man of merit, and the declared favorite of the Sultan (which they call *Mosayp*) but that is not enough to make him pleasing in the eyes of a girl of thirteen.

The government here is entirely in the hands of the army. The Grand Signior, with all his absolute power, is as much a slave as any of his subjects, and trembles at a Janizarie's frown.[11] Here is, indeed, a much greater

---

8   *To the Countess of B[ristol]*: Lady Bristol, Elizabeth Fenton (1676–1741), wife of John Hervey, First Earl of Bristol. She was a close friend of Montagu's and was Lady of the Bedchamber to Queen Charlotte. In the 1763 text this is incorrectly dated as 1718.

9   *Grand Signior*: the Sultan, Ahmed III (1673–1736).

10   *late Vizier … Peterwaradin*: Ali Pasha (*c.*1667–1716). In 1716 Austrian forces had defeated a huge Turkish army at Peterwardien in Hungary. His widow was Princess Fatima who was to be married to the new Grand Vizier, Ibrahim Pasha (*c.*1666–1730).

11   *Janizaries' frown*: a janizary (sometimes spelt janissary) is a Turkish soldier specifically to guard the Sultan.

appearance of subjection than amongst us; a minister of state is not spoke to, but upon the knee; should a reflection on his conduct be dropt in a coffee-house (for they have spies every where) the house would be raz'd to the ground, and perhaps the whole company put to the torture. No *huzzaing mobs, senseless pamphlets, and tavern disputes about politics;*

> A consequential ill that freedom draws;
> A bad effect, – but from a noble cause.[12]

None of our harmless calling names! but when a minister here displeases the people, in three hours time he is dragged even from his master's arms. They cut off his hands, head and feet, and throw them before the palace gate, with all the respect in the world; while the Sultan (to whom they all profess an unlimited adoration) sits trembling in his apartment, and dare neither defend nor revenge his favorite. This is the blessed condition of the most absolute monarch upon earth, who owns no *Law* but his *Will*.

I cannot help wishing, in the loyalty of my heart, that the Parliament would send hither a ship load of your passive obedient men,[13] that they might see arbitrary government in its clearest strongest light, where 'tis hard to judge, whether the Prince, People, or Ministers, are most miserable. I could make many reflections on this subject; but I know, Madam, your own good sense, has already furnished you with better than I am capable of.

[...]

Letter XXXIX.
To the Countess of [Mar].[14]

Adrianople, April 1, 1717.

... I never saw in my life, so many fine heads of hair. In one lady's, I have counted a hundred and ten of the tresses, all natural; but, it must be owned, that every kind of beauty is more common here than with us. 'Tis surprising to see a young woman that is not very handsome. They have naturally the most beautiful complexions in the world, and generally large black eyes. I can assure you with great truth, that the court of England (though

---

12   *A consequential ... cause*: Montagu's own verse, repeated in a later poem by her on Walpole.

13   *passive obedient men*: passive obedience was a political doctrine, most often espoused by Tory High Church Anglicans in late seventeenth- and early eighteenth-century England. It held that subjects should not resist the commands of the monarch however unlawful, but that they may refuse to act and submit passively to punishment in this world in the hope of just rewards in the next.

14   *To the Countess of [Mar]*: Lady Mar, Frances Pierrepont (1690–1761), Montagu's younger sister who married John Erskine, Earl of Mar.

I believe it the fairest in Christendom) does not contain so many beauties as are under our protection here. They generally shape their eye brows, and both Greeks and Turks have the custom of putting round their eyes a black tincture, that, at distance, or by candle-light, adds very much to the blackness of them. I fancy many of our ladies would be overjoyed to know this secret; but 'tis too visible by day. They dye their nails a rose-colour; but I own, I cannot enough accustom myself to this fashion, to find any beauty in it.

As to their morality or good conduct, I can say, like Harlequin, that 'tis just as 'tis with you;[15] and the Turkish ladies don't commit one sin the less for not being Christians. Now that I am little acquainted with their ways, I cannot forbear admiring, either the exemplary discretion, or extreme stupidity of all the writers that have given accounts of them. 'Tis very easy to see, they have in reality more liberty than we have. No woman, of what rank soever, is permitted to go into the streets without two *Murlins*, one that covers her face, all but her eyes; and another, that hides the whole dress of her head, and hangs half way down her back. Their shapes are also wholly concealed, by a thing they call a *Ferigee*, which no woman of any sort appears without; this has strait sleeves, that reach to their fingers ends, and it laps all round them, not unlike a riding-hood. In winter, 'tis of cloth; and in summer, of plain stuff or silk. You may guess then, how effectually this disguises them, so that there is no distinguishing the great lady from her slave. 'Tis impossible for the most jealous Husband to know his wife, when he meets her, and no man dare touch or follow a woman in the street.

This perpetual masquerade gives them entire liberty of following their inclination without danger of discovery. The most usual method of intrigue is, to send an appointment to the lover to meet the lady at a Jew's shop, which are as notoriously convenient as our Indian-houses; and yet, even those who don't make use of them, do not scruple to go to buy penny-worths, and tumble over rich goods, which are chiefly to be found amongst that sort of people. The great ladies seldom let their gallants know who they are; and 'tis so difficult to find it out, that they can very seldom guess at her name, whom they have corresponded with for above half a year together. You may easily imagine the number of faithful wives very small in a country where they have nothing to fear from a lover's indiscretion, since we see so many have the courage to expose themselves to that in this world, and all the threatned punishment of the next, which is never preached to the Turkish damsels. Neither have they much to apprehend from the resentment of their husbands; those ladies that are rich, having all their money in their own hands. Upon the whole, I look upon the Turkish women, as the only free people in the Empire; the very Divan pays a respect to them, and the Grand Signior himself, when a *Bassa* is executed, never violates the privileges of the *Haram*

---

[15]   *Harlequin*: a character in Aphra Behn's farce *The Emperor of the Moon* (1687); in the play it is said that morality is the same on the moon as it is on the earth.

(or women's apartment) which remains unsearched and entire to the widow. They are Queens of their slaves, whom the husband has no permission so much as to look upon, except it be an old woman or two that his lady chuses. 'Tis true, their law permits them four wives, but there is no instance of a man of quality that makes use of this liberty, or of a woman of rank that would suffer it. When a husband happens to be inconstant (as those things will happen) he keeps his mistress in a house apart, and visits her as privately as he can, just as 'tis with you. Amongst all the great men here, I only know the *Testerdar* (*i.e.* Treasurer) that keeps a number of the slaves, for his own use (that is, on his own side of the house, for a slave once given to serve a lady, is entirely at her disposal) and he is spoke of as a libertine, or what we should call a rake; and his wife won't see him, though she continues to live in his house. Thus you see, dear sister, the manners of mankind do not differ so widely, as our voyage writers would make us believe. Perhaps, it would be more entertaining to add a few surprising customs of my own invention; but nothing seems to me so agreeable as truth, and I believe nothing so acceptable to you. I conclude therefore, with repeating the great truth of my being.

Dear Sister, &c.

[...]

Vol. III. Letter XLII.
To the Countess of—.[16]

[*Pera, Constantinople*, May 1718].

I am now preparing to leave Constantinople, and perhaps you will accuse me of hypocrisy, when I tell you, 'tis with regret; but as I am used to the air, and have learnt the language, I am easy here; and as much as I love travelling, I tremble at the inconveniences attending so great a journey, with a numerous family, and a little infant hanging at the breast. However, I endeavour, upon this occasion, to do as I have hitherto done in all the odd turns of my life; turn them, if I can, to my diversion. In order to this, I ramble every day, wrapped up in my *Ferige* and *Asmak*,[17] about Constantinople, and amuse myself with seeing all that is curious in it. I know you will expect that this declaration should be followed with some account of what I have seen. But I am in no humour to copy what has been writ so often over. To what purpose should I tell you, that Constantinople is the antient Bizantium? that 'tis at present the conquest of a race of people, supposed Scythians? that there are five or six thousand mosques in it? that *Sancta Sophia* was founded by Justinian? &c. I'll assure you 'tis not for want of learning, that I forbear writing all these bright

---

16   *To the Countess of—*: there is no date and place in the 1763 text. The letter is possibly to Lady Bristol. See Malcolm Jack, ed., *Turkish Embassy Letters* (Pickering, 1993).

17   *Asmak*: a yasmak is a double veil worn over the face by Muslim ladies in public.

things. I could also, with very little trouble, turn over *Knolles* and Sir *Paul Rycaut*,[18] to give you a list of Turkish Emperors; but I will not tell you what you may find in every author that has writ of this country. I am more inclined, out of a true female spirit of contradiction, to tell you the falsehood of a great part of what you find in authors; as for example, in the admirable Mr. *Hill*,[19] who so gravely asserts, that he saw in *Sancta Sophia*, a sweating pillar, very balsamic for disordered heads. There is not the least tradition of any such matter; and I suppose it was revealed to him in vision, during his wonderful stay in the Egyptian Catacombs; for I am sure he never heard of any such miracle here. 'Tis also very pleasant to observe how tenderly he and all his brethren voyage-writers, lament the miserable confinement of the Turkish ladies, who are perhaps more free than any ladies in the universe, and are the only women in the world, that had a life of uninterrupted pleasure, exempt from cares, their whole time being spent in visiting, bathing, or the agreeable amusement of spending money and inventing new fashions. A husband would be thought mad that exacted any degree of œconomy from his wife, whose expenses are no way limited but by her own fancy. 'Tis his business to get money, and hers to spend it; and this noble prerogative extends itself to the very meanest of the sex. Here is a fellow that carries embroidered handkerchiefs upon his back to sell. And as a miserable a figure as you may suppose such a mean dealer; yet I'll assure you, his wife scorns to wear any thing less than cloth of gold; has her ermine furs, and a very handsome set of jewels for her head. 'Tis true, they have no places but the bagnios, and these can only be seen by their own sex; however, that is a diversion they take great pleasure in.

[...]

Letter XLIV.
To the Abbott of—.[20]

Tunis, July 31, 1718.

... While I sat here, from the town of *Tents* not far off many of the women flocked in to see me, and we were equally entertain'd with viewing one another. Their posture in sitting, the colour of their skin, their lank black hair falling on each side of their faces, their features and the shape of their limbs, differ so little from their country people the baboons, 'tis hard to fancy them a distinct race; I could not help thinking there had been some ancient alliances between them.

---

18 *Knolles ... Paul Rycaut*: Richard Knolles (1550–1610) wrote *A Generall Historie of the Turks* in 1603; Paul Rycaut's *The History of the Turks* (1700) was a continuation.
19 *Hill*: Aaron Hill (1685–1750) wrote *A Full and Just Account of the Present State of the Ottoman Empire* (1709).
20 *To the Abbott of*—: Abbé Conti, or Antonio Conti (1677–1749) met Montagu in England in 1715. He translated the poems of Alexander Pope and was a dramatist.

William Smith, from
An Historical Account of the Expedition Against the Ohio Indians (1766)

William Smith (1727–1803), born in Aberdeen, was a clergyman, amateur astronomer, tutor and provost of the College of Philadelphia. He journeyed to America in 1751 as a tutor to the two sons of the planter Josiah Martin.

In the wake of the British victories in North America during the Seven Years' War – also known, significantly, as the 'French and Indian War' – there were increasing encroachments on American Indian land. Some were sympathetic: in 1763 a proclamation sought to limit this westward expansion. It was not in time to stop the rising under the Ottawa chief Pontiac, which overran most of the frontier forts, and caused others to confirm their beliefs in American Indian savagery. Smith's popular *Account* (it ran to many editions) reproduces these ambivalent reactions. In part, the purpose of his narrative of the expedition undertaken by Brigadier General Henry Bouquet in 1764 is to vindicate the British army's actions and even its beneficence against the 'perfidy' of the Ohio tribes. In the extracts below, the hymn to British mercy, and the hints of the Native Americans' 'usual' temper, indicate Smith's belief in the improving effect of imperial contact. However, the extract depicting the return of captives also shows the extent to which the differences between Native American and colonist became blurred (206 captives were returned in 1764; some had lived with the tribes for up to ten years). Smith, mobilising the highly literary mode of sentiment, depicts white captives as unwilling to part with their adopted, weeping American Indian families. Such scenarios indicate the extent to which captivity transformed identity on the frontiers of the British empire in America.[1]

[Speech of Colonel Henry Bouquet to the Seneca, Delaware, and Shawnee; October 1764]

'Your former allies, the Ottawas, Chipwas, Wyandots, and others, have made their peace with us. The Six Nations have joined us against you. We now surround you, having possession of all the waters of the Ohio, the Missisippi, the Miamis, and the lakes. All the French living in those parts are now subjects to the king of Great-Britain, and dare no longer assist you. It is therefore in our power totally to extirpate you from being a people— But the English are a merciful and generous nation, averse to shed the blood, even of their most cruel enemies; and if it was possible that you

---

[1]   Text from pp. 16–17, 26–9.

could convince us, that you sincerely repent of your past perfidy, and that we could depend on your good behaviour for the future, you might yet hope for mercy and peace—If I find that you faithfully execute the following preliminary conditions, I will not treat you with the severity you deserve.

'I give you twelve days from this date to deliver into my hands at Wakatamake all the prisoners in your possession, without any exception; Englishmen, Frenchmen, women and children; whether adopted in your tribes, married, or living amongst you under any denomination and pretence whatsoever, together with all negroes. And you are to furnish the said prisoners with cloathing, provisions, and horses, to carry them to Fort Pitt.

'When you have fully complied with these conditions, you shall then know on what terms you may obtain the peace you sue for'.—

This speech made an impression on the minds of the savages, which, it is hoped, will not soon be eradicated. The firm and determined spirit with which the Colonel delivered himself, their consciousness of the aggravated injuries they had done us, and the view of the same commander and the army that had so severely chastised them at Bushy-Run the preceding year, now advanced into the very heart of their remote settlements, after penetrating through wildernesses which they had deemed impassable by regular troops—all these things contributed to bend the haughty temper of the savages to the lowest degree of abasement; so that even their speeches seem to exhibit but few specimens of that strong and ferocious eloquence, which their inflexible spirit of independency has on former occasions inspired. And though it is not to be doubted, if an opportunity had offered, but they would have fallen upon our army with their usual fierceness, yet when they saw the vigilance and spirit of our troops were such, that they could neither be attacked nor surprized with any prospect of success, their spirits seemed to revolt from the one extreme of insolent boldness, to the other of abject timidity. And happy will it be for them and for us, if the instances of our humanity and mercy, which they experienced in that critical situation, shall make as lasting impressions on their savage dispositions, as it is believed the instances of our bravery and power have done; so that they may come to unite, with their fear of the latter, a love of the former; and have their minds gradually opened, by such examples, to the mild dictates of peace and civility.

[...]

[The return of captives, November 1764]

And here I am to enter on a scene, reserved on purpose for this place, that the thread of the foregoing narrative might not be interrupted—a scene, which language indeed can but weakly describe; and to which the Poet or Painter might have repaired to enrich their highest colourings of the variety of human passions; the Philosopher to find ample subject for his most serious reflections; and the Man to exercise all the tender and sympathetic feelings of the soul.

The scene I mean, was the arrival of the prisoners in the camp; where were to be seen fathers and mothers recognizing and clasping their once-lost babes; husbands hanging round the necks of their newly recovered wives; sisters and brothers unexpectedly meeting together after long separation, scarce able to speak the same language, or, for some time, to be sure that they were children of the same parents! In all these interviews, joy and rapture inexpressible were seen, while feelings of a very different nature were painted in the looks of others;—flying from place to place in eager enquiries after relatives not found! trembling to receive an answer to their questions! distracted with doubts, hopes and fears, on obtaining no account of those they fought for! or stiffened into living monuments of horror and woe, on learning their unhappy fate!

The Indians too, as if wholly forgetting their usual savageness, bore a capital part in heightening this most affecting scene. They delivered up their beloved captives with the utmost reluctance; shed torrents of tears over them, recommending them to the care and protection of the commanding officer. Their regard to them continued all the time they remained in camp. They visited them from day to day; and brought them what corn, skins, horses and other matters, they had bestowed on them, while in their families; accompanied with other presents, and all the marks of the most sincere and tender affection. Nay, they did not stop here, but, when the army marched, some of the Indians solicited and obtained leave to accompany their former captives all the way to Fort-Pitt, and employed themselves in hunting and bringing provisions for them on the road. A young Mingo[2] carried this still further, and gave an instance of love which would make a figure even in romance. A young woman of Virginia was among the captives, to whom he had formed so strong an attachment, as to call her his wife. Against all remonstrances of the imminent danger to which he exposed himself by approaching to the frontiers, he persisted in following her, at the risk of being killed by the surviving relations of many unfortunate persons, who had been captivated or scalped by those of his nation.

Those qualities in savages challenge our just esteem. They should make us charitably consider their barbarities as the effects of wrong education, and false notions of bravery and heroism; while we should look on their virtues as sure marks that nature has made them fit subjects of cultivation as well as us; and that we are called by our superior advantages to yield them all the helps we can in this way. Cruel and unmerciful as they are, by habit and long example, in war, yet whenever they come to give way to the native dictates of humanity, they exercise virtues which Christians need not

---

[2]   *Mingo*: a tribe of the Six Nations or Iroquois in Ohio.

blush to imitate. When they once determine to give life, they give every thing with it, which, in their apprehension, belongs to it. From every enquiry that has been made, it appears—that no woman thus saved is preserved from base motives, or need fear the violation of her honour. No child is otherwise treated by the persons adopting it than the children of their own body. The perpetual slavery of those captivated in war, is a notion which even their barbarity has not yet suggested to them. Every captive whom their affection, their caprice, or whatever else, leads them to save, is soon incorporated with them, and fares alike with themselves.

These instances of Indian tenderness and humanity were thought worthy of particular notice. The like instances among our own people will not seem strange; and therefore I shall only mention one, out of a multitude that might be given on this occasion.

Among the captives, a woman was brought into the camp at Muskingham, with a babe about three months old at her breast. One of the Virginia-volunteers soon knew her to be his wife, who had been taken by the Indians about six months before. She was immediately delivered to her overjoyed husband. He flew with her to his tent, and cloathed her and his child in proper apparel. But their joy, after the first transports, was soon damped by the reflection that another dear child of about two years old, captivated with the mother, and separated from her, was still missing, altho' many children had been brought in.

A few days afterwards, a number of other prisoners were brought to the camp, among whom were several more children. The woman was sent for, and one, supposed to be hers, was produced to her. At first sight she was uncertain, but viewing the child with great earnestness, she soon recollected its features; and was so overcome with joy, that literally forgetting her sucking child she dropt it from her arms, and catching up the new found child in an extasy, pressed it to her breast, and bursting into tears carried it off, unable to speak for joy. The father seizing up the babe she had let fall, followed her in no less transport and affection.

Among the children who had been carried off young, and had long lived with the Indians, it is not to be expected that any marks of joy would appear on being restored to their parents or relatives. Having been accustomed to look upon the Indians as the only connexions they had, having been tenderly treated by them, and speaking their language, it is no wonder that they considered their new state in the light of a captivity, and parted from the savages with tears.

But it must not be denied that there were even some grown persons who shewed an unwillingness to return. The Shawanese were obliged to bind several of their prisoners and force them along to the camp; and some women, who had been delivered up, afterwards found means to escape and run back to the Indian towns. Some, who could not make their escape, clung to their savage acquaintance at parting, and continued many days in bitter lamentations, even refusing sustenance.

For the honour of humanity, we would suppose those persons to have been of the lowest rank, either bred up in ignorance and distressing penury, or who had lived so long with the Indians as to forget all their former connections. For, easy and unconstrained as the savage life is, certainly it could never be put in competition with the blessings of improved life and the light of religion, by any persons who have had the happiness of enjoying, and the capacity of discerning, them.

James Albert Ukawsaw Gronniosaw, from *A Narrative of the Most Remarkable Particulars in the Life of James Albert Ukawsaw Gronniosaw, An African Prince, as related by Himself* [1770]

Ukawsaw Gronniosaw was born in the city of Borno, in the north of what is now Nigeria. Taken from his homeland when he was fifteen, he was bought by a Dutchman in Barbadoes, and taken to New England. There he was bought by a pastor, Mr Freedlandhouse, in New York, who was a friend to the famous Methodist evangelist George Whitefield. It is at this point that Gronniosaw experienced his religious awakening. Although he was freed by Freedlandhouse, he continued to serve several masters, until he was commandeered by an officer to serve in the British armed forces against the French during the Seven Years War. After service he was discharged and made his way to England where he took the name James Albert and married a weaver called Betty. The *Narrative* ends with a moving account of his family's painful destitution under the trials of irregular employment (he was a navvy and carpenter at times) and the vagaries of human charity. Gronniosaw's *Narrative* was dictated to a lady of Leominster when he was 60 and is only the second published slave narrative. As Louis Gates has pointed out, it is the first with the 'trope of the Talking Book', and this encounter with Western knowledge is recounted in the first extract.[1] In the second extract, the England of his imagination is tested when he encounters the reality.[2]

---

[1]   For the trope of the talking book, see Henry Louis Gates, Jnr., *The Signifying Monkey: A Theory of African-American Literary Criticism* (Oxford University Press, 1988), pp. 127–69.

[2]   Text from the second edition (1785), pp. 15, 30–32.

I was now washed, and clothed in the Dutch or English manner.—My master grew very fond of me, and I loved him exceedingly. I watched every look, was always ready when he wanted me, and endeavoured to convince him, by every action, that my only pleasure was to serve him well.—I have since thought that he must have been a serious man. His actions corresponded very well with such a character.—He used to read prayers in public to the ship's crew every Sabbath day; and when first I saw him read, I was never so surprised in my whole life as when I saw the book talk to my master; for I thought it did, as I observed him to look upon it, and move his lips.—I wished it would do so to me.—As soon as my master had done reading I followed him to the place where he put the book, being mightily delighted with it, and when nobody saw me, I opened it and put my ear down close upon it, in great hope that it would say something to me; but was very sorry and greatly disappointed when I found it would not speak, this thought immediately presented itself to me, that every body and every thing despised me because I was black.

[...]

I continued some time with Mr. Dunscum as his servant; he was very kind to me.—But I had a vast inclination to visit ENGLAND, and wished continually that it would please providence to make a clear way for me to see this island.[3] I entertained a notion that if I could get to ENGLAND, I should never more experience either cruelty or ingratitude, so that I was very desirous to get among Christians. I knew Mr. Whitfield[4] very well—I had heard him preach often at NEW YORK.—In this disposition I listed in the twenty eighth regiment of foot, who were designed for Martinico in the late war.—We went in Admiral Pocock's[5] fleet from New York to Barbados; from thence to Martinico.—When that was taken we proceeded to the Havannah, and took that place likewise.—There I got discharged.

I was then worth about thirty pounds, but I never regarded money in the least; not would I tarry to receive my prize-money, lest I should lose my chance of going to England—I went with the Spanish prisoners to Spain; and came to Old England with the English prisoners[6]—I cannot describe

---

3   *this land*: he had noted earlier, 'I imagined that all the inhabitants of this island were *holy*', p. 27.
4   *Mr Whitfield*: George Whitefield (1714–70), the famous Calvinist evangelist and one of the founders of Methodism. He was initially minister of Savannah, Georgia, and after his return to England, he still made several preaching tours of America. One of his most ardent English supporters was Selina Hastings, Countess of Huntingdon (1707–91) who made Whitefield her chaplain in 1748, and who Gronniosaw dedicated his *Narrative* to. (Huntingdon was also patron to the black writers Phillis Wheatley, John Marrant, and Olaudah Equiano).
5   *Admiral Pocock*: Sir George Pocock (1706–92), commander-in-chief of the expedition in 1762 to capture Spanish-held Havana, Cuba.
6   *I went ... English prisoners*: presumably, an exchange of prisoners between Spain and England.

my joy when we were within sight of Portsmouth. But I was astonished when we landed, to hear the inhabitants of that place curse and swear, and otherwise profane. I expected to find nothing but goodness, gentleness, and meekness, in this Christian Land. I then suffered great perplexities of mind.

I enquired if any serious Christian people resided there. The woman I made this enquiry of answered me in the affirmative; and added, that she was one of them. I was heartily glad to hear her say so. I thought I could give her my whole heart. She kept a public house.—I deposited with her all the money I had not an immediate occasion for; as I thought it would be safer with her.—It was twenty-five guineas; but six of them I desired her to lay out to the best advantage to buy me some shirts, a hat, and some other necessaries. I made her a present of a very handsome large looking-glass, that I had brought with me from Martinico, in order to recompence her for the trouble I had given her. I must do this woman the justice to acknowl-edge, that she did lay out some little for my use; but the nineteen guineas, and part of the six, with my watch, she would not return, but denied that I ever gave it her.

I soon perceived that I was got among bad people, who defrauded me of my money and watch; and that all my promised happiness was blasted. I had no friend but GOD, and I prayed to Him earnestly. I could scarcely believe it possible that the place where so many eminent Christians had lived and preached, could abound with so much wickedness and deceit. I thought it worse than *Sodom* (considering the great advantages they have).

Samuel Foote, *The Nabob;*
a comedy, in Three Acts (1772)

In his plays, such as *The Minor* (1760) and *Piety in Pattens* (1773), Samuel Foote (1727–77) often combined controversial personal attack with general social satire. He had a gift for comic mimicry, and he often used the form of an 'afterpiece': a short three-act play added on to a bill which would include a larger, main attraction. *The Nabob*, first performed in 1772, focuses on the 'nabob' – the returning East India Company man who was perceived as an avaricious and barbaric *parvenu*, corrupted by unfettered access to power, riches and vice in India. In an important sense Indian culture, as much as the nabob himself, was perceived as the source of corruption. The play's reversals of social order – and the sentimental ending which restores order – echo the kind of concerns found in many debates on the relationship between Britain and India. The nabob of the title is the character Sir Matthew Mite, who has been variously thought to refer to Robert Clive,

General Richard Smith, or Sir Matthew White, all of whom worked for the East India Company. Clive, in particular, was the *bête noire* of the times – an archetypal nabob who, while substantially consolidating British influence in India, netted himself fabulous riches. Foote's play is topical: the year before its performance the East India Company and Clive in particular were under investigation by the Government for corrupt commercial practices. *The Nabob* begins with the Oldham family lamenting their situation: Sir John has spent a fortune on bringing charges of corruption against Sir Matthew Mite's election to Parliament. However, he has obviously borrowed heavily and, to make matters worse, that lender's credit has been taken over by Mite – so now Sir John is in debt to Sir Matthew, and at the start of the play, Sir Matthew has asked for his daughter's hand in marriage.[1]

ACT I.

A Chamber.

Enter Lady Oldham and Sir John Oldham.

Lady Oldham. Not a syllable more will I hear!

Sir John. Nay, but, my dear—

L. Old. I am amazed, Sir John, at your meanness! or that you could submit to give his paltry proposals so much as a reading!

Sir John. Nay, my dear, what would you have had me done?

L. Old. Done? returned them with the contempt they deserved. But, come, unfold! I am calm: Reveal the pretty project your precious head has produced.

Sir John. Nay, my dear, as to that, my head produced—

L. Old. Nay, I don't wonder that shame has tied up your tongue! But, come; I will spare the confusion, and tell you what you would say. Here, Lady Oldham, Sir Matthew Mite has just sent me a letter, modestly desiring that, in return for the ruin he has brought on me and my house, I would be so kind as to bestow upon him my darling daughter, the hopes of my— And is it possible you can be mean enough to think of such an alliance? Will you, Sir John, oblige me with an answer to a few short questions?

Sir John. Without doubt.

L. Old. I suppose you consider yourself as sprung from a family at least as ancient as any in the country you live in?

Sir John. That I fancy will not be denied.

L. Old. Nor was it, I fancy, dishonoured by an alliance with mine?

Sir John. My Lady, the very reverse.

---

[1]   Text from the first edition (1778).

L. Old. You succeeded, Sir, to a patrimony, which though the liberal and hospitable spirit of your predecessors would not suffer to encrease, yet their prudence took care should never be diminished?

Sir John. True.

L. Old. From the public and private virtues of your ancestors, the inhabitants of the neighbouring borough thought their best and dearest interests in no hands so secure as in theirs?

Sir John. Right.

L. Old. Nor till lately were they so tainted by the fashion of the times, as to adopt the egregious absurdity, That to be faithfully served and protected above, it was necessary to be largely bribed and corrupted below?

Sir John. Why, I can't say, except now and then a bit of venison, or an annual dinner, they have ever put me to any great—

L. Old. Indulge me yet a moment, Sir John! In this happy situation, did the last year chearfully close; our condition, though not opulent, affluent, and you happy in the quiet possession of your family honours.

Sir John. There is no gainsaying of that.

L. Old. Now, look at the dismal, shocking reverse!

Sir John. There is but too much reason in what your ladyship says.

L. Old. And consider, at the same time, to whom you are obliged.

Sir John. Why, what could we do? your ladyship knows there was nobody more against my giving up than yourself.

L. Old. Let me proceed. At this crisis, preceded by all the pomp of Asia, Sir Matthew Mite, from the Indies, came thundering amongst us; and, profusely scattering the spoils of ruined provinces, corrupted the virtue and alienated the affections of all the old friends to the family.

Sir John. That is nothing but truth.

L. Old. Compelled by the same means to defend those that were employed in attacking your interest, you have been obliged deeply to encumber your fortune; his superior address has procured a return, and probably your petition will complete the ruin his opposition began.[2]

Sir John. Let us hope all for the best.

L. Old. And who can tell, but you may be soon forced to part with your patrimony, to the very insolent worthless individual, who has been the author of your distress?

---

2   *Compelled … began*: Sir John is trying to nullify Sir Matthew Mite's election, on the grounds of corruption, by appealing to Parliament. But Sir John seems to have spent all his own fortune in pursuing this campaign, and if he fails, the costs will ruin him.

Sir John. I would sooner perish, my Lady!

L. Old. Parallel instances may be produced; nor is it at all unlikely, but Sir Matthew, taking a liking to your family mansion, has pursued this very method to compel you to sell it.

Sir John. It is, my dear, to avoid this necessity that I wish you to give his letter a reading.

L. Old. Is it possible, not to mention the meanness, that you can be weak enough to expect any real service from that infamous quarter?

Sir John. Who can tell, my love, but a consciousness of the mischief he has done us, may have roused some feelings that—

L. Old. His feelings! will he listen to a private complaint, who has been deaf to the cries of a people? or drop a tear for particular distress, who owes his rise to the ruin of thousands?

Sir John. Well, Lady Oldham, I find all that I say signifies nothing.—But here comes brother Thomas; two heads are better than one; let us take his opinion, my love.

L. Old. What need of any opinion? the case is too clear; nor indeed, if there had been a necessity for consulting another, should I have thought your brother the properest man to advise with on the occasion.

Sir John. And why not? there is not a merchant whose judgment would be sooner taken.

L. Old. Perhaps not, on the value of merchandize, or the goodness of a Bill of Exchange: But there is a nicety, a delicacy, an elevation of sentiment, in this case, which people who have narrowed their notions with commerce, and considered during the course of their lives their interest alone, will scarce comprehend.

Enter Mr. Thomas Oldham.

Thomas. So, sister! what! upon your old topic, I find?

L. Old. Sir!

Thomas. Some pretty comparisons, I suppose, not much to the honour of trade.

L. Old. Nay, brother, you know I have always allowed merchants to be a useful body of men; and considered commerce, in this country, as a pretty resource enough for the younger shoots of a family.

Thomas. Exceedingly condescending, indeed! And yet, sister, I could produce you some instances where the younger shoots have flourished and throve, when the reverend trunk has decayed.

L. Old. Perhaps, brother Thomas—

Thomas. Nay, nay, don't let us revive our antient disputes!—You seem warm; no misunderstanding, I hope?

Sir John. No, no; none, in the least: You know, my lady's temper's apt to be lively now and then.

Thomas. Nay, sister—But, come! what has occasioned this mighty debate?

Sir John. You know, brother, how affairs stand between Sir Matthew and us.

Thomas. Well!

Sir John. He has sent us here a kind of a compromise; I don't know well what to call it; a sort of a treaty.[3]

Thomas. That in your hand?

Sir John. Yes; and I can't prevail on my lady to give it a reading.

Thomas. And why not?

L. Old. To what end?

Thomas. A very natural one; in order to know the contents.

L. Old. Of what importance can they be to us?

Thomas. That the letter will tell you. But surely, Lady Oldham, you are rather too nice. Give it me!

Sir John. Is it your ladyship's pleasure?

Thomas. Psha! here's a rout, indeed!—One would be apt to suspect that the packet was pestilential, and came from the Archipelago, instead of the Indies. Now let us see what this formidable memorial contains! [*opens the letter*]. 'To Sir John Oldham. Sir Matthew Mite having lately seen, at Lady Levant's rout, the eldest Miss Oldham, and being struck with her personal charms, proposes to her father the following treaty.'

L. Old. A very monarchical address!

Thomas. '*Imprimis*; Upon a matrimonial union between the young lady and him, all hostilities and contention shall cease, and Sir John be suffered to take his seat in security.'

L. Old. That he will do, without an obligation to him.

Thomas. Are you, sister, certain of that?

L. Old. You don't harbour the least doubt of our merits?

Thomas. But do they always prevail?

L. Old. There is now, brother Thomas, no danger to dread; the restraint the popular part of government[4] has in this instance laid on itself, at the same time that it does honour to them, distributes equal justice to all.

---

3   *Treaty*: the 'looting' of India by the East India Company had been accomplished by so-called Trade Treaties.

4   *Government*: a reference to Lord North's government (prime minister 1770–82).

Thomas. And are you aware what the expence will be to obtain it?—But, pray, let me proceed!—'Secondly, as Sir Matthew is bent upon a large territorial acquisition in England, and Sir John Oldham's finances are at present a little out of repair, Sir Matthew Mite will make up the money already advanced in another name, by way of future mortgage upon his estate, for the entire purchase, five lacks of roupees.'

L. Old. Now, Sir John! was I right in my guess?

Sir John. Your ladyship is never out.—But, brother Thomas, these same lacks—to what may they amount?

Thomas. Sixty thousand, at least.

Sir John. No inconsiderable offer, my lady.

L. Old. Contemptible! But pray, Sir, proceed.

Thomas. 'Or if it should be more agreeable to the parties, Sir Matthew will settle upon Sir John and his Lady, for their joint lives, a jagghire.'

Sir John. A jagghire?

Thomas. The term is Indian, and means an annual income.

L. Old. What strange jargon he deals in!

Thomas. His stile is a little Oriental, I must own; but most exceedingly clear.

L. Old. Yes, to Cossim Ali-Khan, or Mier Jaffeir. I hope you are near the conclusion.

Thomas. But two articles more. [reads] 'And that the principals may have no cares for the younger parts of their family, Sir Matthew will, at his own expence, transport the two young ladies, Miss Oldham's two sisters, to Madrass or Calcutta, and there procure them suitable husbands.'

L. Old. Madrass, or Calcutta!

Thomas. Your patience, dear sister!—'And as for the three boys, they shall be either made supercargoes, ships' husbands, or go out cadets and writers in the Company's service.'

L. Old. Why, he treats my children like a parcel of convicts: Is this their method of supplying their settlements?

Thomas. This, with now and then a little kidnapping, dear sister.—Well, madam, you have now the means of getting rid of all your offspring at once: Did not I tell you the paper was worth your perusal? You will reply to his wish; you can have no doubts, I suppose.

L. Old. Not the least, as I will shew you. [*Tears the letter.*] And, if Sir John has the least spirit or pride, he will treat the insolent principal as I do his proposals.

Thomas. But that method, as things stand, may not be altogether so safe. I am sorry you were so hasty in destroying the letter: If I remember rightly, there is mention made of advancing money in another man's name.

L. Old. We have been compelled to borrow, I own; but I had no conception that he was the lender.

Thomas. That's done by a common contrivance; not a country lawyer but knows the doctrine of transfer.—How much was the sum?

Sir John. Ten thousand pounds.

Thomas. And what, Sir John, were the terms?

Sir John. As I could give no real security, my estate being settled till my son John comes of age, I found myself obliged to comply with all that was asked.

Thomas. A judgment, no doubt.[5]

Sir John. They divided the sum, and I gave them a couple.

Thomas. Which will affect not only your person, but personal property; so they are both in his power.

Sir John. Too true, I am afraid!

Thomas. And you may be sent to a gaol, and your family turned into the streets, whenever he pleases.

L. Old. How! Heaven forbid!

Thomas. Not the least doubt can be made.— This is an artful project: No wonder that so much contrivance and cunning has been an overmatch for a plain English gentleman, or an innocent Indian. And what is now to be done? Does your daughter Sophy know of this letter?

L. Old. Sir John?

Sir John. It reached my hands not ten minutes ago.

Thomas. I had some reason to think, that, had you complied, you would not have found her very eager to second your wishes.

L. Old. I don't know that, brother: Young girls are easily caught with titles and splendor; magnificence has a kind of magick for them.

Thomas. I have a better opinion of Sophy. You know, Lady Oldham, I have often hinted, that my boy was fond of his cousin; and possibly my niece not totally averse to his wish; but you have always stopp'd me short, under a notion that the children were too nearly allied.

L. Old. Why, brother, don't you think—

Thomas. But that, sister, was not the right reason; you could have easily digested the *cousins*, but the *compting-house* stuck in his way: Your favourite maxim has been, that citizens are a distinct race, a sort of creatures that should mix with each other.

L. Old. Bless me, brother, you can't conceive that I—

---

[5]   *judgment*: a 'judgment' meant that the debtor waived all legal rights against foreclosure. In other words, Sir John's goods and property could be seized and himself imprisoned.

Thomas. Nay, no apology, good Lady Oldham! perhaps you have a higher alliance in view; and let us now consider what is to be done. You are totally averse to this treaty?

L. Old. Can that be a question?

Thomas. Some little management is necessary, as to the mode of rejection: As matters now stand, it would not be prudent to exasperate Sir Matthew.

L. Old. Let Sir John discharge the debt due to him at once.

Thomas. But where shall we get materials?

L. Old. Can that be a difficult task?

Thomas. Exceedingly so, as I apprehend: But few can be found to advance so large a sum on such slender security; nor is it to be expected, indeed, unless from a friend to relieve, or a foe to ruin.

L. Old. Is it possible Sir Matthew can have acted from so infernal a motive, to have advanced the money with a view of distressing us deeper?

Thomas. Sir Matthew is a profound politician, and will not stick at trifles to carry his point.

L. Old. With the wealth of the East, we have too imported the worst of its vices. What a horrid crew!

Thomas. Hold, sister! don't gratify your resentment at the expence of your justice; a general conclusion from a single instance is but indifferent logick.

L. Old. Why, is not this Sir Matthew—

Thomas. Perhaps as bad a subject as your passion can paint him: But there are men from the Indies, and many too, with whom I have the honour to live, who dispense nobly and with hospitality here, what they have acquired with honour and credit elsewhere; and, at the same time they have increased the dominions and wealth, have added virtues too to their country.

L. Old. Perhaps so: But what is to be done? Suppose I was to wait on Sir Matthew myself.

Thomas. If your ladyship is secure of commanding your temper.

Sir John. Mercy on us, brother Thomas, there's no such thing as trusting to that!

L. Old. You are always very obliging, Sir John! if the embassy was to be executed by you—

Thomas. Come, come, to end the dispute, I will undertake the commission myself.

L. Old. You will take care, brother, to make no concessions that will derogate from—

Thomas. Your dignity, in my hands, will have nothing to fear.—But should not I see my niece first? she ought to be consulted, I think.

Sir John. By all means.

Thomas. For, if she approves of the knight, I don't see any thing in the alliance so much to be dreaded.

L. Old. I will send Sophy to her uncle directly; but I desire the girl may be left to herself; no undue influence!

[*Exit.*

Thomas. The caution was needless.

Sir John. Why, really, now, brother, but that my lady's too warm, I don't see any thing so very unreasonable in this same paper here that lies scattered about. But, I forget, did he mention any thing of any fortune he was to have with the girl?

Thomas. Pho! a paltry consideration, below his concern.

Sir John. My lady herself must own there is something generous in that.

Thomas. Will you stay and represent the case to Sophy yourself?

Sir John. She is here!

Enter Sophy.

Your uncle, child, has something to say to you: You know he loves you, my dear, and will advise you for the best.

[*Exit.*

Thomas. Come hither, Sophy, my love! don't be alarmed. I suppose my lady has opened to you, that Sir Matthew has sent a strange kind of a romantic letter.

Sophy. But she did not seem, Sir, to suppose that it deserved much attention.

Thomas. As matters now stand, perhaps more than she thinks. But come, my good girl, be explicit: Suppose the affairs of your family should demand a compliance with this whimsical letter, should you have any reluctance to the union proposed?

Sophy. Me, Sir? I never saw the gentleman but once in my life.

Thomas. And I don't think that would interest you much in his favour.

Sophy. Sir!

Thomas. No prepossession? no prior object that has attracted your notice?

Sophy. I hope, Sir, my behaviour has not occasioned this question.

Thomas. Oh, no, my dear; it naturally took its rise from the subject. Has your cousin lately been here?

Sophy. Sir!

Thomas. Tom Oldham, my son?

Sophy. We generally see him, Sir, every day.

Thomas. I am glad to hear that: I was afraid some improper attachment had drawn him from the city so often of late.

Sophy. Improper! I dare say, Sir, you will have nothing of that kind to fear from my cousin.

Thomas. I hope not: And yet I have had my suspicions, I own; but not unlikely you can remove 'em: Children rarely make confidants of their fathers.

Sophy. Sir!

Thomas. Similarity of sentiments, nearness of blood, and the same season of life, perhaps may have induced him to unbosom to you.

Sophy. Do you suppose, Sir, that he would discover to me, what he chose to conceal from so affectionate a father?

Thomas. Nay, prithee, Sophy, don't be grave! What, do you imagine I should think his preferring your ear to mine, for a melting passionate tale, any violent breach of his duty?

Sophy. You are merry, Sir.

Thomas. And who knows but you might repay the communication with a similar story? You blush, Sophy.

Sophy. You are really pleased to be so very particular, that I scarce know what answer to make.

Thomas. Come, my good niece, I will perplex you no longer: My son has concealed nothing from me; and did the completion of your wishes depend on my approbation alone, you would have but little to fear: But my lady's notions are so very peculiar, you know, and all her principles so determined and fixed—

Sophy. The merits of my cousin, which she herself is not slow to acknowledge, and time, might, I should hope, soften my mother.

Thomas. Why then, my dear niece, leave it to time, in most cases the ablest physician. But let your partiality for Tom be a secret!—I must now endeavour to learn when I can obtain an audience from Sir Matthew.

Sophy. An audience from him?

Thomas. Yes, child; these new gentlemen, who from the caprice of Fortune, and a strange chain of events, have acquired immoderate wealth, and rose to uncontroled power abroad, find it difficult to descend from their dignity, and admit of any equal at home. Adieu, my dear niece! But keep up your spirits! I think I foresee an event that will produce some change in our favour.

[*Exeunt.*

Sir Matthew Mite's Hall.
Janus and Conserve discovered.[6]

Cons. I own the place of a porter, if one can bear the confinement—And then, Sir Matthew has the character of—[*low tap.*] Use no ceremony, Mr. Janus; mind your door, I beseech you.

---

6   *Janus:* alluding to the Roman god of portals who had two faces. To be Janus-faced, then, was to be hypocritical. It also sounds very much like a Janissery, the personal guard of Muslim princes.

Janus. No hurry! keep your seat, Mr. Conserve; it's only the tap of a tradesman: I make those people stay till they collect in a body, and so let in eight or ten at a time; it saves trouble.

Cons. And how do they brook it?

Janus. Oh, wonderfully well, here with us. In my last place, indeed, I thought myself bound to be civil; for as all the poor devils could get was good words, it would have been hard to have been sparing of them.

Cons. Very considerate!

Janus. But here we are rich; and as the fellows don't wait for their money, it is but fair they should wait for admittance.

Cons. Or they would be apt to forget their condition.

Janus. True.

Cons. Upon the whole, then, you do not regret leaving my lord?

Janus. No; Lord Levee's place had its sweets, I confess; perquisites pretty enough: But what could I do? they wanted to give me a rider.

Cons. A rider?

Janus. Yes; to quarter Monsieur Frissart, my Lady's valet de chambre, upon me; so you know I could not but in honour resign.

Cons. No; there was no bearing to be rid by a Frenchman; there was no staying in after that.

Janus. It would have been quoted as a precedent against the whole corps.

Cons. Yes. Pox on 'em! our masters are damned fond of encroachments. Is your present duty severe?

Janus. I drudge pretty much at the door; but that, you know, is mere bodily labour: But then, my mind is at ease; not obliged to rack my brain for invention.

Cons. No?

Janus. No; not near the lying here, as in my last place.

Cons. I suppose not, as your master is but newly in town; but you must expect that branch to encrease.

Janus. When it does, I shall insist the door be done by a deputy.

[*Two raps.*

Cons. Hark! to your post!

Janus. No; sit still! that is some aukward body out of the city; one of our people from Leadenhall-Street; perhaps a director; I sha'n't stir for him.[7]

---

7   *director*: reflecting the perception that East India Company officers and factors in India ignored the orders of the directors in London (the offices of the East India Company were in Leadenhall street).

Cons. Not for a director? I thought he was the commanding officer, the Great Captain's captain.

Janus. No, no; quite the reverse; the tables are turned, Mr. Conserve: In acknowledgment for appointing us their servants abroad, we are so obliging as to make them directors at home.

[*A loud rapping.*

Cons. That rap will rouse you, I think.

Janus. Let me take a peep at the wicket. Oh, oh! is it you, with a pox to you? How the deuce came your long legs to find the way hither? —I shall be in no haste to open for you.

Cons. Who is it?

Janus. That eternal teizer, Sir Timothy Tallboy. When once he gets footing, there is no such thing as keeping him out.

Cons. What, you know him then?

Janus. Yes, rot him, I know him too well! he had like to have lost me the best place I ever had in my life.

Cons. How so?

Janus. Lord Lofty had given orders on no account to admit him. The first time, he got by me under a pretence of stroking Keeper the house-dog; the next, he nick'd me by desiring only just leave to scratch the poll of the parrot, Poll, Poll, Poll! I thought the devil was in him if he deceived me a third; but he did, notwithstanding.

Cons. Prithee, Janus, how?

Janus. By begging to set his watch by Tompion's clock in the Hall; I smoaked his design, and laid hold of him here: [*taking hold of his coat*]. As sure as you are alive, he made but one leap from the stairs to the study, and left the skirt of his coat in my hand?

Cons. You got rid of him then?

Janus. He made one attempt more; and, for fear he should slip by me (for you know he is as thin as a slice of beef at Marybone-Gardens), I slapped the door in his face, and told him, the dog was mad, the parrot dead, and the clock stood; and, thank Heaven, I have never sat eyes on him since.

[*Knock louder.*

Cons. But the door!

Janus. Time enough.—You had no particular commands, master Conserve?

Cons. Only to let you know that Betsy Robins has a rout and supper on Sunday next.

Janus. Constant still, Mr. Conserve, I see. I am afraid I can't come to cards; but shall be sure to attend the repast. A nick-nack, I suppose?

Cons. Yes, yes; we all contribute, as usual: The substantials from Alderman Sirloin's; Lord Frippery's cook finds fricasees and ragouts; Sir Robert Bumper's butler is to send in the wine; and I shall supply the desert.

Janus. There are a brace of birds and a hare, that I cribbed this morning out of a basket of game.[8]

Cons. They will be welcome.—[*Knock louder.*] But the folks grow impatient!

Janus. They must stay till I come.—At the old place, I suppose?

Cons. No; I had like to have forgot! Betsy grew sick of St. Paul's, so I have taken her a house amongst the new buildings; both the air and the company is better.[9]

Janus. Right.

Cons. To say truth, the situation was disagreeable on many accounts. Do you know, though I took care few people should behave better at Christmas, that because he thought her a citizen, the housekeeper of Drury-Lane Theatre, when his master mounted, refused her a side-box?

Janus. No wonder Miss Betsy was bent upon moving.—What is the name of her street?

Cons. Rebel-Row: It was built by a messenger who made his market in the year forty-five.[10] But shall Miss Robins send you a card?

Janus. No, no; I shall easily find out the place. [*Knock.*] Now let us see; who have we here? Gads my life, Mrs. Match'em! my master's amorous agent: It is as much as my place is worth to let her wait for a minute.

[*Opens the door. Exit Cons.*

Enter Mrs. Match'em, some Tradespeople, who bow low to Janus, and Thomas Oldham.

Match. So, Sir! this is pretty treatment, for a woman like me to dangle at your gate, surrounded by a parcel of tradespeople!

Janus. I beg pardon; but, madam—

Match. Suppose any of my ladies had chanced to drive by: In a pretty situation they'd have seen me! I promise you I shall make my complaints to Sir Matthew.

Janus. I was receiving some particular commands from my master.

Match. I shall know that from him. Where is he? let him know I must see him directly; my hands are so full I have not a moment to spare.

---

8   *Substantials … game*: the servants are eating the very best.
9   *Betsy*: archetypal name for a serving maid. Betsy has moved out of the disreputable area around St Paul's church, Covent Garden.
10   *made his market*: someone who has come up in the world by buying cheap land during the Jacobite rebellion of 1745.

Janus. At that door the groom of the chamber will take you in charge; I am sure you'll be admitted as soon as announced.

Match. There is as much difficulty to get a sight of this signior, as of a member when the parliament's dissolved!

[*Exit.*

Janus. Soh! what, you have brought in your bills? damned punctual, no doubt! The steward's room is below.—And, do you hear? when you are paid, be sure to sneak away without seeing me.

All Trades. We hope you have a better opinion—

Janus. Well, well, march! [*Exe. Tradesmen.*] So, friend; what is your business, pray?

Thomas. I have a message to deliver to Sir Matthew.

Janus. You have? and pray what is the purport?

Thomas. That's for his ear alone.

Janus. You will find yourself mistaken in that.

Thomas. How?

Janus. It must make its way to his, by passing thro' mine.

Thomas. Is that the rule of the house?

Janus. Ay; and the best way to avoid idle and impertinent pratlers.

Thomas. And of that you are to judge?

Janus. Or I should not be fit for my post. But, you are very importunate; who are you? I suppose a Jew broker, come to bring my master the price of the stocks?

Thomas. No.

Janus. Or some country cousin, perhaps?

Thomas. Nor that neither.

Janus. Or a voter from our borough below? we never admit them but against an election.

Thomas. Still wide of the mark.— [*Aside.*] There is but one way of managing here; I must give the Cerberus a sop, I perceive.[11]—Sir, I have really business with Sir Matthew, of the utmost importance; and if you can obtain me an interview, I shall think myself extremely obliged.

[*Gives money.*

Janus. As I see, Sir, by your manner, that it is a matter of moment, we will try what can be done; but you must wait for his levee; there is no seeing him yet.

---

11   *Cerberus*: in classical mythology the three-headed dog that guards the entrance to the infernal regions.

Thomas. No?

Janus. He is too busy at present; the waiter at Almack's has just brought him home his macaroni dress for the hazard-table, and is instructing him to throw the dice with a grace.[12]

Thomas. Then where can I wait?

Janus. If you will step into that room, I will take care to call you in time. [*Exit Mr. Old.*]—[*Looking at the money.*] A good sensible fellow! At first sight, how easily one may be mistaken in men!

[*Exit.*

ACT II.

A Chamber. Sir Matthew Mite in his gaming dress, a Waiter attending.

Mite. Main and chance?

Waiter. Five to nine, please your honour.

Mite. I am at all that is set. How must I proceed?

Waiter. With a tap, as the chances are equal; then raise the box genteelly and gently, with the finger and thumb.

Mite. Thus?

Waiter. Exactly, your honour. Cinque and quarter: You're out.

Mite. What is next to be done?

Waiter. Flirt the bones with an air of indifference, and pay the money that's set.

Mite. Will that do?

Waiter. With a little more experience, your honour.

Mite. Then pass the box to my neighbour?

Waiter. Yes; or you make a back hand, if you please.

Mite. Cou'dn't you give me some general rules? for then, you know, I might practise in private.

Waiter. By all means. Seven, Sir, is better nicked by a stamp.

Mite. So?

Waiter. Yes. When you want to throw six and four, or two cinques, you must take the long gallery, and whirl the dice to the end of the table.

---

12   *Almacks, … macaroni*: Almacks was a gaming club. A macaroni was a fop; a man who was perceived to be overly concerned with dress and imputed to be effeminate. This is an allusion to the financial crisis of 1772 precipitated by the collapse of the private bank involving Alexander Fordyce: he was perceived to be gambling with investor's money. Popular prints of Fordyce equate him with East India company nabobs and their 'macaroni' style, and also allude to the nabobs' dubious riches (my thanks to Daniel O'Quinn for this point).

Mite. Thus?

Waiter. Pretty well, please your honour. When your chance is low, as tray, ace, or two deuces, the best method is to dribble out the bones from the box.

Mite. Will that do?

Waiter. Your honour comes rapidly on.

Mite. So that, perhaps, in a couple of months, I shall be able to tap, flirt, stamp, dribble, and whirl, with any man in the club?

Waiter. As your honour has a genius, you will make a wonderful progress, no doubt: But these nice matters are not got in a moment; there must be parts, as well as practice, your honour.

Mite. What! parts for the performance of this?

Waiter. This? Why, there's Sir Christopher Clumsey, in the whole losing his fortune, (and I believe he was near a twelvemonth about it) never once threw, paid, or received, with one atom of grace.

Mite. He must have been a dull devil, indeed.

Waiter. A mere dunce! got no credit by losing his money; was ruined without the least reputation.

Mite. Perhaps so. Well, but, Dick, as to the oaths and phrases that are most in use at the club?

Waiter. I have brought them here in this paper: As soon as your honour has got them by heart, I will teach you when and in what manner to use them.

Mite. [*after looking at the paper.*] How long do you apprehend before I may be fit to appear at the table?

Waiter. In a month or six weeks. I would advise your honour to begin in the Newmarket week, when the few people left do little better than piddle.

Mite. Right: So I shall gain confidence against the club's coming to town.

Enter Servant.

Serv. Mrs. Crocus, from Brompton, your honour.

Mite. Has she brought me a bouquet?

Serv. Your honour?

Mite. Any nosegays, you blockhead?

Serv. She has a boy with a basket.

Mite. Shew her in! [*Exit Servant.*]—Well, Dick, you will go down to my steward, and teach him the best method of making a rouleau. And, do you hear? let him give you one for your pains.[13]

Waiter. Your honour's obedient! You'd have me attend every morning?

---

[13]   *roleau*: a stack of coins in a roll of paper.

Mite. Without doubt: It would be madness to lose a minute, you know.

[*Exit Waiter*.

Enter Mrs. Crocus.

Well, Mrs. Crocus; let us see what you have brought me. Your last bouquet was as big as a broom, with a tulip strutting up like a magistrate's mace; and, besides, made me look like a devil.

Crocus. I hope your honour could find no fault with the flowers? It is true, the polyanthuses were a little pinched by the easterly winds; but for pip, colour, and eye, I defy the whole parish of Fulham to match'em.

Mite. Perhaps not; but it is not the flowers, but the mixture, I blame. Why, here now, Mrs. Crocus, one should think you were out of your senses, to cram in this clump of jonquils!

Crocus. I thought your honour was fond of their smell.

Mite. Damn their smell! it is their colour I talk of. You know my complexion has been tinged by the East, and you bring me here a blaze of yellow, that gives me the jaundice. Look! do you see here, what a fine figure I cut? You might as well have tied me to a bundle of sun-flowers!

Crocus. I beg pardon, your honour!

Mite. Pardon! there is no forgiving faults of this kind. Just so you served Harry Hectic; you stuck into his bosom a parcel of hyacinths, though the poor fellow's face is as pale as a primrose.

Crocus. I did not know—

Mite. And there, at the opera, the poor creature sat in his side-box, looking like one of the figures in the glass-cases in Westminster-Abbey; dead and drest!

Crocus. If gentlemen would but give directions, I would make it my study to suit 'em.

Mite. But that your cursed climate won't let you. Have you any pinks or carnations in bloom?

Crocus. They are not in season, your honour. Lillies of the valley—

Mite. I hate the whole tribe! What, you want to dress me up like a corpse! When shall you have any rose-buds?

Crocus. The latter end of the month, please your honour.

Mite. At that time you may call.

Crocus. Your honour has no further commands?

Mite. None, You may send nosegays for my chairmen, as usual. [*Exit Mrs. Crocus*.] Piccard! Here, take that garland away: I believe the woman thought she was dressing a may-pole. Make me a bouquet with the artificial flowers I brought from Milan.

Enter Servant.

Serv. Would your honour please to see Madam Match'em?

Mite. Introduce her this instant.

Enter Mrs. Match'em.

My dear Match'em! Well, what news from Cheapside?[14]

Match. Bad enough; very near a total defeat.

Mite. How so? you were furnished with ample materials.

Match. But not of the right kind, please your honour. I have had but little intercourse with that part of the world: My business has chiefly lain on this side of the Bar; and I was weak enough to think both cities alike.[15]

Mite. And arn't they?

Match. No two nations can differ so widely! Though money is supposed the idol of merchants, their wives don't agree in the worship.

Mite. In that article I thought the whole world was united.

Match. No; they don't know what to do with their money; a Pantheon subscription,[16] or a masquerade ticket, is more negotiable there than a note from the Bank.

Mite. What think you of a bracelet, or a well-fancied aigret?

Match. I should think they must make their way.

Mite. I have sent some rough diamonds to be polished in Holland; when they are returned, I will equip you, Match'em, with some of these toys.

Match. Toys? how light he makes of these things!—Bless your noble and generous soul! I believe for a trifle more I could have obtained Lady Lurcher last night.

Mite. Indeed?

Match. She has been pressed a good deal to discharge an old score, long due to a knight from the North; and play-debts, your honour knows, there is no paying in part: She seemed deeply distressed; and I really believe another hundred would have made up the sum.

Mite. And how came you not to advance it?

Match. I did not chuse to exceed my commission; your honour knows the bill was only for five.

---

14   *Cheapside*: a district of the old City of London.

15   *the Bar*: the boundary between the old City of London and Westminster was Temple Bar, so that Match'em is referring to Mite's residence as being in the newer and more affluent part of the metropolis west of the City.

16   *Pantheon*: concert rooms.

Mite. Oh, you should have immediately made it up; you know I never stint myself in these matters.

Match. Why, had I been in cash, I believe I should have ventured, your honour. If your honour approves, I have thought of a project that will save us both a good deal of trouble.

Mite. Communicate, good Mrs. Match'em!

Match. That I may not pester you with applications for every trifle I want, suppose you were to deposit a round sum in my hands.

Mite. What, Match'em, make you my banker for beauty? Ha, ha, ha!

Match. Exactly, your honour. Ha, ha, ha!

Mite. Faith, Match'em, a very good conceit.

Match. You may depend on my punctuality in paying your drafts.

Mite. I don't harbour the least doubt of your honour.

Match. Would you have me proceed in Patty Parrington's business? She is expected from Bath in a week.

Mite. And what becomes of her aunt?

Match. That Argus[17] is to be left in the country.

Mite. You had better suspend your operations for a while. Do you know, Mrs. Match'em, that I am a-going to be married?

Match. Married? your honour's pleased to be pleasant: That day I hope never to see.

Mite. The treaty wants nothing but her friends' ratification; and I think there is no danger of their with-holding that.

Match. Nay, then, the matter is as good as concluded: I was always in dread of this fatal stroke!

Mite. But, Match'em, why should you be so averse to the measure?

Match. Can it be thought, that with dry eyes I could bear the loss of such a friend as your honour? I don't know how it is, but I am sure I never took such a fancy to any man in my life.

Mite. Nay, Match'em!

Match. Something so magnificent and princely in all you say or do, that a body has, as I may say, a pleasure in taking pains in your service.

Mite. Well, but prithee, child—

Match. And then, when one has brought matters to bear, no after-reproaches, no grumblings from parties, such general satisfaction on all sides!

---

[17]   *Argus*: someone who is jealously watchful. In Grecian legend, Argus had 100 eyes.

I am sure, since the death of my husband, as honest a man, except the thing he died for—

Mite. How came that about, Mrs. Match'em?

Match. Why, Kit was rather apt to be careless, and put a neighbour's name to a note without stopping to ask his consent.

Mite. Was that all?

Match. Nothing else. Since that day, I saw no mortal has caught my eye but your honour.

Mite. Really, Match'em?

Match. I can't say, neither, it was the charms of your person—though they are such as any lady might like—but it was the beauties of your mind, that made an impression upon me.

Mite. Nay, prithee, Match'em, dry up your tears! you distress me! Be persuaded you have nothing to fear.

Match. How!

Mite. Why, you don't suppose that I am prompted to this project by passion?

Match. No?

Mite. Pho! no; only wanted a wife to complete my establishment; just to adorn the head of my table.

Match. To stick up in your room, like any other fine piece of furniture?

Mite. Nothing else; as an antique bust or a picture.

Match. That alters the case.

Mite. Perhaps, I shall be confined a little at first; for when you take or bury a wife, decency requires that you should keep your house for a week: After that time, you will find me, dear Match'em, all that you can wish.

Match. Ah! that is more than your honour can tell. I have known some of my gentlemen, before marriage, make as firm and good resolutions not to have the least love or regard for their wives; but they have been seduced after all, and turned out the poorest tame family fools!

Mite. Indeed?

Match. Good for nothing at all.

Mite. That shall not be my case.

Enter Servant.

Serv. Your honour's levee is crouded.[18]

---

[18] *levee*: this was a reception for guests and visitors, traditionally in the mornings after rising from bed.

Mite. I come. Piccard, give me my coat!—I have had some thoughts of founding in this town a seraglio;[19] they are of singular use in the Indies: Do you think I could bring it to bear?

Match. Why, a customer of mine did formerly make an attempt; but he pursued too violent measures at first; wanted to confine the ladies against their consent; and that too in a country of freedom.

Mite. Oh, fy! How the best institutions may fail, for want of a man proper to manage!

Match. But your honour has had great experience. If you would bestow the direction on me—

Mite. Impossible, Match'em! in the East we never confide that office to your sex or complexion. I had some thoughts of importing three blacks from Bengal, who have been properly prepared for the service; but I sha'n't venture till the point is determined whether those creatures are to be considered as mere chattels, or men.[20]

[*Exeunt.*

A Saloon.
Enter Mayor, Touchit, Nathan, Moses, &c.

Serv. Walk in, gentlemen! his honour will be presently here.

Touchit. Do you see, Mr. Mayor? look about you! here are noble apartments!

Mayor. Very fine, very curious, indeed! But, after all, Master Touchit, I am not so over-fond of these Nabobs; for my part, I had rather sell myself to somebody else.

Touchit. And why so, Mr. Mayor?

Mayor. I don't know—they do a mortal deal of harm in the country: Why, wherever any of them settles, it raises the price of provisions for thirty miles round. People rail at seasons and crops; in my opinion, it is all along with them there folks, that things are so scarce.

Touchit. Why, you talk like a fool! Suppose they have mounted the beef and mutton a trifle; a'n't we obliged to them too for raising the value of boroughs? You should always set one against t'other.

Mayor. That, indeed, is nothing but fair. But how comes it about? and where do these here people get all their wealth?

---

[19]   *seraglio*: a word borrowed from the Italian for enclosure, it traditionally meant the Sultan's buildings in Constantinople, including his harem. The term became short-hand for a brothel.

[20]   *I had ... or men*: in 1772, the year *The Nabob* was first performed, the Somerset case was debating whether a slave who had run away could be legally re-enslaved on British soil. The eventual ruling was perceived to outlaw slavery in Britain.

Touchit. The way is plain enough; from our settlements and possessions abroad.

Mayor. Oh, may be so. I've been often minded to ask you what sort of things them there settlements are; because why, as you know, I have been never beyond sea.

Touchit. Oh, Mr. Mayor, I will explain that in a moment: Why, here are a body of merchants that beg to be admitted as friends, and take possession of a small spot in a country, and carry on a beneficial commerce with the inoffensive and innocent people, to which they kindly give their consent.

Mayor. Don't you think now that is very civil of them?

Touchit. Doubtless. Upon which, Mr. Mayor, we cunningly encroach, and fortify by little and by little, till at length, we growing too strong for the natives, we turn them out of their lands, and take possession of their money and jewels.

Mayor. And don't you think, Master Touchit, that is a little uncivil in us?

Touchit. Oh, nothing at all: These people are but a little better than Tartars or Turks.

Mayor. No, no, Master Touchit; just the reverse; it is they have caught the Tartars in us.

Touchit. Ha, ha, ha! well said, Mr. Mayor. But, hush! here comes his honour. Fall back!

Enter Sir Matthew Mite.

Mite. Oh, Nathan! are you there? You have split the stock, as I bid you?[21]

Nathan. I vas punctually obey your directions.

Mite. And I shall be in no danger of losing my list?

Nathan. Dat is safe, your honour; we have noting to fear.

Mite. Moses Mendoza! You will take care to qualify Peter Pratewell and Counsellor Quibble? I shall want some speakers at the next General Court.

Moses. Please your honour, I shall be careful of dat.

Mite. How is the stock?

Moses. It vas got up the end of the veek.

Mite. Then sell out till you sink it two and a half. Has my advice been followed for burning the tea?

---

21   *Split the stock … General Court*: to 'split the stock' is to split up a large block of stock in the East India Company into separate 'qualifications' which create extra votes in a company election. 'List': a list of candidates up for election in the company. 'General Court': a meeting of shareholders. Mite is manipulating the elections to the next shareholders' meeting of the company. See also Burke.

Moses. As to dat matter, I vas not enquire dat; I believe not.

Mite. So that commodity will soon be a drug. The English are too proud to profit by the practice of others: What would become of the spice trade, if the Dutch brought their whole growth to market?

Moses. Dat is very true. Your honour has no farder commands?

Mite. None at present, master Mendoza.

[*Exit Mendoza.*

Nathan. For de next settlement, would your honour be de bull or de bear?[22]

Mite. I shall send you my orders to Jonathan's. Oh, Nathan! did you tell that man in Berkshire, I would buy his estate?

Nathan. Yes; but he say he has no mind, no occasion to sell it; dat de estate belong to great many faders before him.

Mite. Why, the man must be mad; did you tell him I had taken a fancy to the spot, when I was but a boy?

Nathan. I vas tell him as much.

Mite. And that all the time I was in India, my mind was bent upon the purchase?

Nathan. I vas say so.

Mite. And now I'm come home, am determined to buy it?

Nathan. I make use of de very vords.

Mite. Well then! what would the booby be at?

Nathan. I don't know.

Mite. Give the fellow four times the value, and bid him turn out in a month.—[*To Touchit.*] May I presume, Sir, to ask who you are, and what your business may be?

Touchit. My name, Sir, is Touchit, and these gentlemen some friends and neighbours of mine. We are ordered by the Christian Club, of the borough of Bribe'em, to wait upon your honour, with a tender of the nomination of our two members at the ensuing election.[23]

Mite. Sir, I accept their offer with pleasure; and am happy to find, notwithstanding all that has been said, that the union still subsists between Bengal and the ancient corporation of Bribe'em.

---

[22]   *bull … bear*: a bull is 'a person who buys shares hoping to sell them at a higher price later'; a bear is 'a person who sells shares hoping to buy them back later at a lower price'. OED.

[23]   *Christian Club*: alluding to an actual Christian club at Shoreham. The ensuing dialogue satirises the corrupt practices of some eighteenth-century parliamentary elections: the Mayor of Brib'em has come to offer his borough's parliamentary seats for sale.

Touchit. And if they ever are severed, I can assure your honour the Christian Club will not be to blame. Your honour understands me, I hope?

Mite. Perfectly. Nor shall it, I promise you, be my fault, good Mr. Touchit. But, (you will forgive my curiosity, Sir!) the name your club has adopted, has at first a whimsical sound; but you had your reasons, no doubt.

Touchit. The very best in the world, please your honour: From our strict union and brotherly kindness, we hang together; like the primitive Christians too, we have all things in common.

Mite. In common? I don't apprehend you.

Touchit. Why, please your honour, when the bargain is struck, and the deposit is made, as a proof that we love our neighbours as well as ourselves, we submit to an equal partition; no man has a larger share than another.

Mite. A most Christian-like dispensation!

Touchit. Yes; in our borough all is unanimity now: Formerly, we had nothing but discontents and heart-burnings amongst us; each man jealous and afraid that his neighbour got more and did better than him.

Mite. Indeed?

Touchit. Ay, and with reason sometimes. Why, I remember, at the election some time ago, when I took up my freedom, I could get but thirty guineas for a new pair of jack-boots; whilst Tom Ramskin over the way had a fifty-pound note for a pair of wash-leather breeches.[24]

Mite. Very partial indeed!

Touchit. So, upon the whole, we thought it best to unite.

Mite. Oh, much the best. Well, Sir, you may assure your principals that I shall take care properly to acknowledge the service they do me.

Touchit. No doubt, no doubt. But—will your honour step a little this way?— Though no question can be made of your honour's keeping your word, yet it has always been the rule with our club to receive the proper acknowledgment before the service is done.

Mite. Ay, but, Mr. Touchit, suppose the service should never be done?

Touchit. What then must become of our consciences? We are Christians, your honour.

Mite. True; but, Mr. Touchit, you remember the proverb?

Touchit. What proverb, your honour?

Mite. There are two bad pay-masters; those who pay before, and those who never pay.

---

[24] *jack-boots … breeches*: indirect bribery often took the form of paying inflated prices for voters' goods.

Touchit. True, your honour; but our club has always found, that those who don't pay before are sure never to pay.

Mite. How! impossible! the man who breaks his word with such faithful and honest adherents, deserves richly a halter. Gentlemen, in my opinion, he deserves to be hanged.

Touchit. Hush! have a care what you say.

Mite. What is the matter?

Touchit. You see the fat man that is behind; he will be the returning officer at the election.

Mite. What then?

Touchit. On a gibbet at the end of our town there hangs a smuggler, for robbing the custom-house.

Mite. Well?

Touchit. The mayor's own brother, your honour: Now, perhaps, he may be jealous that you meant to throw some reflection on him or his family.

Mite. Not unlikely.—I say, gentlemen, whoever violates his promise to such faithful friends as you are, in my poor opinion, deserves to be damned!

Touchit. That's right! stick to that! for tho' the Christian Club may have some fears of the gallows, they don't value damnation of a farthing.

Mite. Why should they, as it may be so long before any thing of that kind may happen, you know?

Touchit. Good! good again! Your honour takes us rightly, I see: I make no doubt, it won't be long before we come to a good understanding.

Mite. The sooner the better, good master Touchit; and, therefore, in one word, pray what are your terms?

Touchit. Do you mean for one, or would your honour bargain for both?

Mite. Both, both.

Touchit. Why, we could not have afforded you one under three thousand at least; but as your honour, as I may say, has a mind to deal in the gross, we shall charge you but five for both.

Mite. Oh fy! above the market, good Mr. Touchit!

Touchit. Dog-cheap; neck-beef; a penny-loaf for a halfpenny! Why, we had partly agreed to bring in Sir Christopher Quinze and major Match'em for the very same money; but the major has been a little unlucky at Almack's, and at present can't deposit the needful; but he says, however, if he should be successful at the next Newmarket meeting, he will faithfully abide by the bargain: But the turf, your honour knows, is but an uncertain estate, and so we can't depend upon him.

Mite. True. Well, Sir, as I may soon have occasion for all the friends I can make, I shall haggle no longer; I accept your proposals: In the next room we will settle the terms.

Touchit. Your honour will always find the Christians steady and firm.—But, won't your honour introduce us to his Worship whilst we are here?

Mite. To his Worship? to whom?

Touchit. To the gentleman in black.

Mite. Worship? you are mad, Mr. Touchit! That is a slave I brought from the Indies.

Touchit. Good lack! may be so! I did not know but the gentleman might belong to the tribe, who, we are told by the papers, conferred those splendid titles upon your honour in India.

Mite. Well, Master Touchit, what then?

Touchit. I thought it not unlikely, but, in return to that compliment, your honour might chuse to make one of the family member for the corporation of Bribe'em.

Mite. Why, you would not submit to accept of a Negro?

Touchit. Our present members, for aught we know, may be of the same complexion, your honour; for we have never set eyes on them yet.

Mite. That's strange! But, after all, you could not think of electing a black?

Touchit. That makes no difference to us: The Christian Club has ever been persuaded, that a good candidate, like a good horse, can't be of a bad colour.

[*Exit with friends.*

Enter Thomas Oldham and others.

Mite [*to Oldham*]. What is your business, and name?

Thomas. Oldham.

Mite. The brother of Sir John? I have heard of you: You are, if I mistake not, a merchant?

Thomas. I have that honour; Sir Matthew.

Mite. Um! honour!—Well, Sir; and what are your commands?

Thomas. I wait on you in the name of my brother, with—

Mite. An answer to the message I sent him. When do we meet to finish the matter? It must be tomorrow, or Sunday; for I shall be busy next week.

Thomas. Tomorrow?

Mite. Ay; it is not for a man like me to dangle and court, Mr. Oldham.

Thomas. Why, to be plain, Sir Matthew, it would, I am afraid, be but losing your time.

Mite. Sir?

Thomas. As there is not one in the family, that seems the least inclined to favour your wish.

Mite. No? ha, ha, ha! that's pleasant enough! ha, ha, ha! And why not?

Thomas. They are, Sir Matthew, no strangers to your great power and wealth; but corrupt as you may conceive this country to be, there are superior spirits living, who would disdain an alliance with grandeur obtained at the expence of honour and virtue.

Mite. And what relation has this sentimental declaration to me?

Thomas. My intention, Sir Matthew, was not to offend; I was desired to wait on you with a civil denial.

Mite. And you have faithfully discharged your commission.

Thomas. Why, I'm a man of plain manners, Sir Matthew; a supercilious air, or a sneer, won't prevent me from speaking my thoughts.

Mite. Perfectly right, and prodigiously prudent!—Well, Sir; I hope it won't be thought too presuming, if I desire to hear my sentence proceed from the mouth of the father and daughter.

Thomas. By all means; I will wait on you thither.

Mite. That is not so convenient, at present. I have brought from Italy, antiques, some curious remains, which are to be deposited in the archives of this country: The Antiquarian Society have, in consequence, chosen me one of their body, and this is the hour of reception.

Thomas. We shall see you in the course of the day?

Mite. At the close of the ceremony. Perhaps, I shall have something to urge, that may procure me some favour from your very respectable family.— Piccard, attend Mr. A—a—a to the door.

Thomas. I guess your design.

                                                                    [*Exit.*

Mite. Who waits there?

                              Enter Servant.

Step to my attorney directly; bid him attend me within an hour at Oldham's, armed with all the powers I gave him.

                                                            [*Exit Servant.*

I will see if I can't bend to my will this sturdy race of insolent beggars!— After all, riches to a man who knows how to employ them, are as useful in England as in any part of the East: There they gain us those ends in spite and defiance of law, which, with a proper agent, may here be obtained under the pretence and colour of law.

                                                                    [*Exit.*

ACT III.

The Antiquarian Society.[25]

Secretary. Sir Matthew Mite, preceded by his presents, will attend this honourable Society this morning.

1 Ant. Is he apprised that an inauguration-speech is required, in which he is to express his love of vertù, and produce proofs of his antique erudition?

Sec. He has been apprised, and is rightly prepared.

2 Ant. Are the minutes of our last meeting fairly recorded and entered?

Sec. They are.

1 Ant. And the valuable antiques which have happily escaped the depredations of time ranged and registered rightly?

Sec. All in order.

2 Ant. As there are new acquisitions to the Society's stock, I think it is right that the members should be instructed in their several natures and names.

1 Ant. By all means. Read the list!

Sec. 'Imprimis, In a large glass-case, and in fine preservation, the toe of the slipper of Cardinal Pandulpho, with which he kick'd the breech of King John at Swinstead-Abbey, when he gave him absolution and penance.'

2 Ant. A most noble remains!

1 Ant. An excellent antidote against the progress of Popery, as it proves the Pontiff's insolent abuse of his power!—Proceed.

Sec. 'A pair of nut-crackers presented by Harry the Eighth to Anna Bullen the eve of their nuptials; the wood supposed to be walnut.'

1 Ant. Which proves that before the Reformation walnut-trees were planted in England.

Sec. 'The cape of Queen Elizabeth's riding-hood, which she wore on a solemn festival, when carried behind Burleigh to Paul's; the cloth undoubtedly Kidderminster.'

2 Ant. A most instructive lesson to us, as it proves that patriotic princess wore nothing but the manufactures of England!

Sec. 'A cork-screw presented by Sir John Falstaff to Harry the Fifth, with a tobacco-stopper of Sir Walter Raleigh's, made of the stern of the ship in which he first compassed the globe; given to the Society by a clergyman from the North-Riding of Yorkshire.'

---

[25]   *Antiquarian Society*: this section is a satire on the obscure pedantry of the Society of Antiquarians and of Mite's parvenu pretensions.

1 Ant. A rare instance of generosity, as they must have both been of singular use to the reverend donor himself!

Sec. A curious collection, in regular and undoubted succession, of all the tickets of Islington-Turnpike, from its first institution to the twentieth of May.

2 Ant. Preserve them with care, as they may hereafter serve to illustrate that part of the English History.

Sec. 'A wooden medal of Shakespeare, made from the mulberry-tree he planted himself; with a Queen Anne's farthing; from the Manager of Drury-Lane Playhouse.'

1 Ant. Has he received the Society's thanks?

Sec. They are sent.

Enter Beadle.

Beadle. Sir Matthew Mite attends at the door.

1 Ant. Let him be admitted directly.

> *Enter Sir Matthew Mite, preceded by four Blacks; first Black*
> *bearing a large book; second, a green chamber-pot; third, some lava*
> *from the mountain Vesuvius; fourth, a box. Sir Matthew takes his seat;*
> *Secretary receives the first present, and reads the label.*

Sec. 'Purchased of the Abbé Montini at Naples for five hundred pounds, an illegible manuscript in Latin, containing the twelve books of Livy, supposed to be lost.'

Mite. This invaluable treasure was very near falling into the hands of the Pope, who designed to deposit it in the Vatican Library, and I rescued it from idolatrous hands.

1 Ant. A pious, learned, and laudable purchase!

Sec. [*receives the second present, and reads the label.*] 'A sarcophagus, or Roman urn, dug from the temple of Concord.'

Mite. Supposed to have held the dust of Marc-Antony's coachman.

Sec. [*receives the third present, and reads.*] 'A large piece of the lava, thrown from the Vesuvian volcano at the last great eruption.'

Mite. By a chymical analysis, it will be easy to discover the constituent parts of this mass; which, by properly preparing it, will make it no difficult task to propagate burning mountains in England, if encouraged by premiums.

2 Ant. Which it will, no doubt!

Mite. Gentlemen! Not contented with collecting, for the use of my country, these inestimable relics, with a large catalogue of petrifactions, bones, beetles, and butterflies, contained in that box, [*pointing to the present borne by the fourth Black.*] I have likewise laboured for the advancement of national knowledge: For which end, permit me to clear up some doubts relative to a material and interesting point in the English history. Let others toil to illumine the dark annals of Greece, or of Rome; my searches are sacred only to the service of Britain! The point I mean to clear up, is an error crept into the life of that illustrious magistrate, the great Whittington, and his no-less-eminent Cat: And in this disquisition four material points are in question.

1st. Did Whittington ever exist?

2d. Was Whittington Lord-Mayor of London?

3d. Was he really possessed of a Cat?

4th. Was that Cat the source of his wealth?

That Whittington lived, no doubt can be made; that he was Lord-Mayor of London, is equally true; but as to his Cat, that, gentlemen, is the gordian knot to untie. And here, gentlemen, be it permitted me to define what a Cat is. A Cat is a domestic, whiskered, four-footed animal, whose employment is catching of mice; but let Puss have been ever so subtle, let Puss have been ever so successful, to what could Puss's captures amount? no tanner can curry the skin of a mouse, no family make a meal of the meat; consequently, no Cat could give Whittington his wealth. From whence then does this error proceed? be that my care to point out! The commerce this worthy merchant carried on, was chiefly confined to our coasts; for this purpose, he constructed a vessel, which, from its agility and lightness, he aptly christened a Cat. Nay, to this our day, gentlemen, all our coals from Newcastle are imported in nothing but Cats. From thence it appears, that it was not the whiskered, four-footed, mouse-killing Cat, that was the source of the magistrate's wealth, but the coasting, sailing, coal-carrying Cat; that, gentlemen, was Whittington's Cat.

1 Ant. What a fund of learning!

2 Ant. Amazing acuteness of erudition!

1 Ant. Let this discovery be made public directly.

2 Ant. And the author mentioned with honour.

1 Ant. I make no doubt but the city of London will desire him to sit for his picture, or send him his freedom in a fifty-pound box.

2 Ant. The honour done their first magistrate richly deserves it.

1 Ant. Break we up this assembly, with a loud declaration, that Sir Matthew Mite is equally skilled in arts as well as in arms.

2 Ant. Tam Mercurio quam Marti.

[*Exe. Ant.*

Mite. Having thus discharged my debt to the public, I must attend to my private affairs. Will Rapine, my attorney, attend as I bid him?

Serv. He will be punctual, your honour.

Mite. Then drive to Hanover-Square.

Putty [*without*]. I will come in!

Enter Servant.

Serv. There's a little shabby fellow without, that insists on seeing your honour.

Mite. Why, who and what can he be?

Serv. He calls himself Putty, and says he went to school with your honour.

Serv. [*within*.] His honour don't know you!

Putty. I will come in! Not know me, you oaf? what should ail him? Why, I tell you we were bred up together from boys. Stand by, or I'll—

Enter Putty.

Hey! yes, it is—no, it a'n't—yes, it is Matthew Mite.—Lord love your queer face! what a figure you cut! how you are altered! well, had I met with you by chance, I don't think I should ever have known you. I have had a deuced deal of work to get at you.

Mite. This is a lucky encounter!

Putty. There is a little fat fellow, that opens the door at your house, was as pert as a prentice just out of his time: He would not give me the least inkling about you; and I should have returned to Shoreditch as wise as I came, if some folks who are gazing at the fine gilt coach in the street, hadn't told me 'twas yours. Well, Master Mite, things are mainly changed since we were boys at the Blue-Coat:[26] Who could have thought that you would have got so up in the world? for you know you were reckoned a dull one at school.

Serv. Friend, do you know who you talk to?

Putty. Yes, friend, much better than you do. I am told he is become a Knight, and a Nabob; and what of all that? For your Nabobs, they are but a kind of outlandish creatures, that won't pass current with us; and as to knights, we have a few of them in the city, whom I dare speak to without doffing my hat. So, Mr. Scrapetrencher, let's have no more of your jaw!—I say, Mat, doesn't remember one Easter-Tuesday, how you tipt the barrow-woman into Fleet-Ditch, as we were going about with the hymns?

Mite. An anecdote that does me infinite honour!

Putty. How all the folks laughed to see how bolt upright she stood on her head in the mud! ha! ha! ha! And one fifth of November, I shall never forget! how you frightened a preaching methodist taylor, by throwing a cracker into the pulpit.

Mite. Another pretty exploit!

---

[26]   *Blue-Coat*: Christ's Hospital School (founded in 1572) for orphans and the children of the poor; so-called because of the pupil's blue cassocks.

Putty. At every bounce, how poor Stitch capered and jumped! Ah! many's the merry freak we have had! for this I must say, though Mat was but bad at his book, for mischiefful matters there wasn't a more ingenious, cuterer lad in the school.

Mite. Yes; I have got a fine reputation, I see!

Putty. Well, but Mat! what, be'st dumb? why doesn't speak to a school-fellow?

Mite. That at present is more than I'll own.— I fancy, Mr. A—a—a, you have made some mistake.

Putty. Some mistake?

Mite. I don't recollect that I ever had the honour to know you.

Putty. What, don't you remember Phil Putty?

Mite. No.

Putty. That was prentice to Master Gibson, the glazier in Shoreditch?

Mite. No.

Putty. That at the Blue-Coat-Hospital has often saved your bacon by owning your pranks?

Mite. No.

Putty. No! What, then, mayhap you ben't Mat Mite, son of old John and Margery Mite, at the Sow and Sausage in St. Mary Axe, that took the tarts from the man in Pye-corner, and was sent beyond sea, for fear worse should come on it?

Mite. You see, Mr. Putty, the glazier, if that is your name and profession, you are entirely out in this matter, so you need not repeat your visits to me.

[*Exit.*

Putty. Now here's a pretty purse-proud son of a—who, forsooth, because he is grown great by robbing the heathens, won't own an old friend and acquaintance, and one too of the livery beside! Dammee, the great Turk himself need not be ashamed to shake hands with a citizen! 'Mr. Putty the glazier!' well, what a pox am I the better for you? I'll be sworn our company has made more money by a single election at Brentford, than by all his exploits put together.[27]

[*Exit.*

Sir John Oldham's house.
Enter Mr. Thomas Oldham, followed by a Servant.

Thomas. Sir Matthew Mite is not come?

Serv. No, Sir.

---

[27]   *I'll be sworn … together:* since elections were often an occasion to break windows.

Thomas. Is Tom here?

Serv. Mr. Oldham is, I believe, with Miss in the parlour.

Thomas. Let him know I would see him. [*Exit Serv.*] Poor boy! Nay, I sincerely grieve for them both! this disappointment, like an untimely frost, will hang heavy on their tender years: To conquer the first and finest feelings of nature is an arduous task!

Enter Young Oldham.

So, Tom! still attached to this spot, I perceive?

Y. Old. Sir, I arrived but the instant before you.

Thomas. Nay, child, I don't blame you. You are no stranger to the almost-invincible bars that oppose your views on my niece; it would be therefore prudent, instead of indulging, to wean yourself by degrees.

Y. Old. Are there no hopes, then, Sir, of subduing my aunt?

Thomas. I see none: Nay, perhaps, as matters now stand, a compliance may be out of her power.

Y. Old. How is that possible, Sir? out of her power?

Thomas. I won't anticipate: Misfortunes come too soon of themselves; a short time will explain what I mean.

Y. Old. You alarm me! Would you condescend to instruct me, I hope, Sir, I shall have discretion enough—

Thomas. It would answer no end. I would have you both prepare for the worst: See your cousin again; and remember, this, perhaps, may be the last time of your meeting.

Y. Old. The last of our—

Thomas. But Sophy is here. I must go in to Sir John.

[*Oldham bows low to Sophy and retires.*

Enter Sophy.

Sophy. Sir! What can be the meaning of this? My uncle Oldham avoids me! you seem shocked! no additional misfortune, I hope?

Y. Old. My father has threatened me, in obscure terms, I confess, with the worst that can happen.

Sophy. How!

Y. Old. The total, nay, perhaps, immediate loss of my Sophy.

Sophy. From what cause?

Y. Old. That in tenderness he chose to conceal.

Sophy. But why make it a mystery? have you no guess?

Y. Old. Not the most distant conception. My lady's dislike would hardly prompt her to such violent measures. I can't comprehend how this can possibly be; but yet my father has too firm, too manly a mind, to encourage or harbour vain fears.

Sophy. Here they come. I suppose the riddle will soon be explained.

Enter Sir John, Lady, and Thomas Oldham.

L. Old. But what motive could he have for demanding this whimsical interview? he could not doubt your credentials, or think his presence could be grateful to us.

Thomas. I have delivered my message.

L. Old. Perhaps he depends on his rhetorical powers: I hear he has a good opinion of them. Stay, Sophy! Sir Matthew Mite, distrusting the message we begged your uncle to carry, desires to have it confirmed by ourselves: I fancy, child, you will do yourself no violence in rejecting this lover. He is an amiable swain, I confess!

Sophy. I shall be always happy in obeying your ladyship's orders.

L. Old. Are you sure of that, Sophy? a time may soon come for the trial.

Sir John. Well, in the main, I am glad of this meeting; it will not only put a final end to this business, but give us an opportunity of discussing other matters, my dear.

L. Old. Is that your opinion, Sir John? I fancy he will not be very fond of prolonging his visit.

Enter Servant.

Serv. Sir Matthew Mite!

L. Old. Shew him in!—Now, Sir John, be on your guard; support this scene with a dignity that becomes one of your birth and—

Sir John. Never fear my dignity, love. I warrant you I'll give him as good as he brings.

Enter Sir Matthew Mite.

Mite. I find the whole tribe is convened.—I hope I am not an intruder; but I confess the extraordinary answer I received from the mouth of this worthy citizen, to a message conveyed by my secretary, induced me to question its authenticity, unless confirmed by yourselves.

L. Old. And why should you think our reply so very extraordinary?

Mite. You must give me leave to smile at that question.

L. Old. A very decisive answer, I own!

Mite. You are, Lady Oldham, a woman of the world, and supposed not to be wanting in sense.

L. Old. Which this conduct of mine inclines you to doubt?

Mite. Why, to be plain, my condition and your own situation considered, prudence might have dictated a different reply.

L. Old. And yet, Sir Matthew, upon the maturest deliberation, all the parties, you see, persist in giving no other.

Mite. Is it so? You will permit me, Lady Oldham, to desire one of those reasons which influenced this august assembly upon the occasion?

L. Old. They will, I dare say, appear but trifling to you.

Mite. Let us have them, however.

L. Old. First, we think it right to have a little regard to her happiness, as she is indebted for her existence to us.

Mite. Which you think she risques in a union with me? [*Lady Oldham bows.*] And why so? I have the means to procure her, madam, those enjoyments with which your sex is chiefly delighted.

L. Old. You will, Sir Matthew, pardon my weakness; but I would much rather see my child with a competence, nay, even reduced to an indigent state, than voluptuously rioting in pleasures that derive their source from the ruin of others.

Mite. Ruin! what, you, I find, adopt the popular prejudice, and conclude that every man that is rich is a villain?

L. Old. I only echo the voice of the public. Besides, I would wish my daughter a more solid establishment: The possessions arising from plunder very rarely are permanent; we every day see what has been treacherously and rapaciously gained, as profusely and full as rapidly squandered.

Mite. I am sorry, madam, to see one of your fashion, concur in the common cry of the times; but such is the gratitude of this country to those who have given it dominion and wealth.

Thomas. I could wish even that fact was well founded, Sir Matthew. Your riches (which perhaps too are only ideal) by introducing a general spirit of dissipation, have extinguished labour and industry, the slow, but sure source of national wealth.

Mite. To these refinements I have no time to reply. By one of your ladyship's hints I shall profit at least: I shall be a little more careful of the plunder I have made. Sir John Oldham, you recollect a small sum borrowed by you?

Sir John. I do.

Mite. The obligations for which are in my possession at present.

Sir John. I understand as much by your letter.

Mite. As I find there is an end of our treaty, it would be right, I think, to discharge them directly.

Sir John. I can't say that is quite so convenient; besides, I understood the party was to wait till the time that Jack comes of age.

Mite. I am told the law does not understand what is not clearly expressed. Besides, the probable event of your death, or the young gentleman's shyness to fulfil the agreement, are enough to put a man on his guard.

Thomas. Now comes on the storm.

Mite. And, that my prudence might not suffer in that lady's opinion, I have taken some precautions which my attorney will more clearly unfold.— Mr. Rapine!

Enter Rapine.

You will explain this affair to Sir John: I am a military man, and quite a stranger to your legal manoeuvres.

Rap. By command of my client, Sir Matthew, I have issued here a couple of writs.

L. Old. Sir John!

Sir John. What?

Rap. By one of which, plaintiff possesses the person, by t'other goods and chattels, of Sir John the defendant.

Mite. A definition very clear and concise!

L. Old. Goods, Sir? what, must I be turned out of my house?

Rap. No, madam; you may stay here till we sell, which perhaps mayn't happen these two days. We must, indeed, leave a few of our people, just to take care that there is nothing embezzled.

L. Old. A short respite, indeed! For a little time, I dare say, my brother Oldham will afford us protection. Come, Sir John, nor let us indulge that monster's malice with a longer sight of our misery.

Rap. You, madam, are a wife, and may go where you please; but as to Sir John—

L. Old. Well!

Rap. He must not stir: We are answerable for the possession of him.

L. Old. Of him? a prisoner? then indeed is our ruin complete!

Sophy. Oh, uncle!—You have been pleased, Sir, to express an affection for me: Is it possible, Sir, you can be so cruel, so unkind to my parents—

Mite. They are unkind to themselves.

Sophy. Let me plead for mercy! suspend but a little!—My uncle, you, Sir, are wealthy too!—Indeed we are honest! you will not run the least risque.

Mite. There is a condition, Miss, in which you have a right to command.

Sophy. Sir!

Mite. It is in your power, and that of your parents, to establish one common interest amongst us.

L. Old. Never! after rejecting, with the contempt they deserved, the first arrogant offers you made, do you suppose this fresh insult will gain us?

Mite. I am answered.—I presume, Mr. Rapine, there is no longer occasion for me?

Sophy. Stop, Sir! Mr. Oldham teaches me what I should do. Can I see their distress? Heaven knows with what eagerness I would sacrifice my own peace, my own happiness, to procure them relief!

[*Kneels to Sir Matthew*.

Thomas. Rise, niece! nor hope to soften that breast, already made too callous by crimes! I have long seen, Sir, what your malice intended, and prepared myself to baffle its purpose. I am instructed, Sir, in the amount of this man's demands on my brother: You will there find a sum more than sufficient to pay it.—And now, my dear sister, I hope you will please to allow a citizen may be useful sometimes.

Mite. Mr. Rapine, is this manoeuvre according to law?

Rap. The law, Sir Matthew, always sleeps when satisfaction is made.

Mite. Does it? Our practice is different in the Mayor's Court at Calcutta.— I shall now make my bow; and leave this family, whom I wished to make happy in spite of themselves, soon to regret the fatal loss sustained by their obstinate folly.

Thomas. Nor can it be long, before the wisdom of their choice will appear; as by partaking of the spoil, they might have been involved in that vengeance, which soon or late can't fail to fall on the head of the author: And, Sir, notwithstanding your seeming security, perhaps the hour of retribution is near!

Mite. You must, Master Oldham, give me leave to laugh at your prophetic effusion. This is not Sparta, nor are these the chaste times of the Roman republic: Now-a-days, riches possess at least one magical power, that, being rightly dispensed, they closely conceal the source from whence they proceeded: That wisdom, I hope never to want.—I am the obsequious servant of this respectable family! Adieu!—Come along, Rapine!

[*Exit with Rapine*.

L. Old. Brother, what words can I use, or how can we thank you as we ought? Sir John! Sophy!

Thomas. I am doubly paid, Lady Oldham, in supplying the wants of my friends, and defeating the designs of a villain. As to the mere money, we citizens indeed are odd kind of folks, and always expect good security for what we advance.

L. Old. Sir John's person, his fortune, every—

Thomas. Nay, nay, nay, upon this occasion we will not be troubled with land: If you, sister, will place as a pledge my fair cousin in the hands of my son—

L. Old. I freely resign her disposal to you.

Sir John. And I.

Thomas. Then be happy, my children! And as to my young cousins within, I hope we shall be able to settle them without Sir Matthew's assistance: For, however praiseworthy the spirit of adventure may be, whoever keeps his post, and does his duty at home, will be found to render his country best service at last!

[*Exeunt.*

FINIS.

John Hawkesworth, from *An Account of the Voyages undertaken by the Order of His Present Majesty for Making Discoveries in the Southern Hemisphere* (1773)

John Hawkesworth (?1715–73) made his living from writing: he was a contributor to the *Gentleman's Magazine*, editor and contributor to *The Adventurer*, and published various works, including an adaptation of Thomas Southerne's play *Oroonoko* in 1759 (itself a version of Behn's nouvelle), and *Almoran and Hamet, an Oriental Tale* (1761). In 1771 James Cook had returned from his first expedition to the South Seas (primarily to observe the transit of Venus from the vantage point of Tahiti, but he also had secret instructions to forge alliances with natives and annexe new lands on behalf of Britain). Hawkesworth was appointed by the Admiralty to revise and publish an account of the voyages to the South Seas (including earlier ones by Byron, Wallis and Carteret).

His *Account* is a synthesis of the journals of Cook and the mission's botanist Joseph Banks, and Hawkesworth worked at marrying the style of the novel with experimental philosophy. However, such a mix was perceived to lack a clear moral grounding, and while it was a huge publishing success, it was severely condemned for its inaccuracies, its indecencies, its refusal to admit the hand of providence, and its philosophical relativism. In it, there are precarious negotiations between European desire and curiosity, the acknowledgement of cultural difference in the name of enlightened scientific knowledge, and patriotic utility. The first four extracts from the Dedication, Introduction, and Cook's rules of engagement reveal much about the tensions between the ideals of discovery and the realities of intercultural contact. The later extracts display what became dominant constructions of Pacific peoples as inhabiting an edenic land, possessing a child-like simplicity. To many readers, however, the scenes of unrestrained sexuality and infanticide merely confirmed the unredeemable barbarity of non-Europeans.[1]

[From the 'Dedication']

It is the distinguishing characteristic of Your Majesty to act from more liberal motives; and having the best fleet, and the bravest as well as the most able navigators in Europe, Your Majesty has, not with a view to the acquisition of treasure, or the extent of dominion, but the improvement of commerce and the increase and diffusion of knowledge, undertaken what has so long been neglected.

[...]

[From the 'General Introduction']

I cannot however dismiss my Readers to the following narratives, without expressing the regret with which I have recorded the destruction of poor naked savages, by our firearms, in the course of these expeditions, when they endeavoured to repress the invaders of their country; a regret which I am confident my Readers will participate with me: this however appears to be an evil which, if discoveries of new countries are attempted, cannot be avoided: resistance will always be made, and if those who resist are not overpowered, the attempt must be relinquished. It may perhaps be said, that the expense of life upon these occasions is more than is necessary to convince the natives that further contest is hopeless, and perhaps this may sometimes have been true: but it must be considered, that if such expeditions are undertaken, the execution of them must be intrusted to persons not exempt from human frailty; to men who are liable to provocation by sudden injury, to unpremeditated violence by sudden danger, to error by the defect of judgment or the strength of passion, and always disposed to transfer laws by which they are bound themselves, to others who are not

---

[1]   Text from vol. 1, 'Dedication', pp. xvi–xix; vol. 2: pp. 81–2, 101–5, 127–8, 206–9.

subject to their obligation; so that every excess thus produced is also an inevitable evil.

[...]

If the gratification of artificial wants, or the increase of knowledge, are justifiable causes for the risk of life, the landing by force on a newly discovered country, in order to examine its produce, may be justified; if not, every trade and profession that exposes life for advantages of the same kind is unlawful; and by what trade or profession is not life exposed? Let us examine all the multitudes that art has employed, from the refiner who sweats at the furnace to the sedentary artificer who grows pale at the loom, and perhaps none can be found in which life is not in some degree sacrificed to the artificial necessities of civil society. But will it therefore be said, that civil society, to which this sacrifice is made, is for that reason a combination contrary to the great original principles of morality, which are the basis of all duty? Will it be said, that to exercise the faculties which are the distinguishing characteristics of our nature is unnatural? And that being endowed with the various powers which in civil societies only can be brought into action, it was incongruous to the will of our Creator that any such society should be formed, and that it would be pleasing to him if, still continuing in a savage state, these powers should lie torpid in our nature, like life in an embrio, during the whole of our existence? This surely must appear extravagant and absurd in the highest degree, especially as it must be allowed, that although commerce and arts in some instances expose life, in others they preserve it; they supply the wants of Nature, without rapine and violence, and by producing a common interest, they prevent the inhabitants of the same country from being divided into different clans, which among savages are almost perpetually committing hostilities against each other, with a ferocious cruelty which is not to be found where civil government and literary knowledge have meliorated the manners of mankind. Upon the whole, therefore, it seems reasonable to conclude, that the increase of knowledge and commerce are ultimately common benefits; and that the loss of life which happens in the attempt, is among the partial evils which terminate in general good.

[...]

[13 April 1769]

Rules to be observed by every person in or belonging to his Majesty's Bark the Endeavour, for the better establishing a regular and uniform trade for provision, &c. with the inhabitants of George's Island.

'I. To endeavour, by every fair means, to cultivate a friendship with the natives; and to treat them with all imaginable humanity.

'II. A proper person, or persons, will be appointed to trade with the natives for all manner of provisions, fruit, and other productions of the earth; and no officer or seaman, or other person belonging to the ship, excepting such as are so appointed, shall trade or offer to trade for any sort of provision, fruit, or other productions of the earth, unless they have leave to do so.

'III. Every person employed on shore, on any duty whatsoever, is strictly to attend to the same; and if by any neglect he loseth any of his arms, or working tools, or suffers them to be stolen, the full value thereof will be charged against his pay, according to the custom of the navy in such cases, and he shall receive such farther punishment as the nature of the offence may deserve.

'IV. The same penalty will be inflicted on every person who is found to embezzle, trade, or offer to trade, with any part of the ship's stores of what nature soever.

'V. No sort of iron, or any thing that is made of iron, or any sort of cloth, or other useful or necessary articles, are to be given in exchange for any thing but provision.

'J. COOK.'

[...]

[25–28 April 1769]

Tubourai Tamaide, upon this demonstration of his innocence, expressed the strongest emotions of mind, both in his looks and gestures; the tears started from his eyes, and he made signs, with the knife, that, if he was ever guilty of such an action as had been imputed to him, he would submit to have his throat cut. He then rushed out of the lines, and returned hastily to Mr. Banks,[2] with a countenance that severely reproached him with his suspicions. Mr. Banks soon understood that the knife had been received from his servant, and was scarcely less affected at what had happened than the Chief; he felt himself to be the guilty person, and was very desirous to atone for his fault. The poor Indian, however violent his passions, was a stranger to sullen resentment; and upon Mr. Bank's spending a little time familiarly with him, and making him a few trifling presents, he forgot the wrong that had been done him, and was perfectly reconciled.

Upon this occasion it may be observed, that these people have a knowledge of right and wrong from the mere dictates of natural conscience; and involuntarily condemn themselves when they do that to others, which they would condemn others for doing to them. That Tubourai Tamaide felt the force of moral obligation, is certain; for the imputation of an action which he considered as indifferent, would not, when it appeared to be groundless, have moved him with such excess of passion. We must indeed estimate the

---

[2]   *Mr. Banks*: Sir Joseph Banks (1744–1820), president of the Royal Society from 1778 and botanist on this first expedition.

virtue of these people, by the only standard of morality, the conformity of their conduct to what in their opinion is right; but we must not hastily conclude that theft is a testimony of the same depravity in them that it is in us, in the instances in which our people were sufferers by their dishonesty; for their temptation was such, as to surmount would be considered as a proof of uncommon integrity amongst those who have more knowledge, better principles, and stronger motives to resist the temptations of illicit advantage: an Indian among penny knives, and beads, or even nails and broken glass, is in the same state of trial with the meanest servant in Europe among unlocked coffers of jewels and gold.

On the 26th, I mounted six swivel guns upon the fort, which I was sorry to see struck the natives with dread: some fishermen who lived upon the point removed farther off, and Owhaw told us, by signs, that in four days we should fire great guns.

On the 27th, Tubourai Tamaide, with a friend, who eat with a voracity that I never saw before, and the three women that usually attended him, whose names were TERAPO, TIRAO, and OMIE, dined at the fort: in the evening they took their leave, and set out for the house which Tubourai Tamaide had set up in the skirts of the wood; but in less than a quarter of an hour he returned in great emotion, and hastily seizing Mr. Bank's arm, made signs that he should follow him. Mr. Banks immediately complied, and they soon came up to a place where they found the ship's butcher, with a reaping-hook in his hand: here the Chief stopped, and, in a transport of rage which rendered his signs scarcely intelligible, intimated that the butcher had threatened, or attempted, to cut his wife's throat with the reaping-hook. Mr. Banks then signified to him, that if he could fully explain the offence, the man should be punished. Upon this he became more calm, and made Mr. Banks understand that the offender, having taken a fancy to a stone hatchet which lay in his house, had offered to purchase it of his wife for a nail: that she having refused to part with it upon any terms, he had catched it up, and throwing down the nail, threatened to cut her throat if she made any resistance: to prove this charge the hatchet and the nail were produced, and the butcher had so little to say in his defence that there was not the least reason to doubt of its truth.

Mr. Banks having reported this matter to me, I took an opportunity, when the Chief and his women, with other Indians, were on board the ship, to call up the butcher, and after a recapitulation of the charge and the proof, I gave orders that he should be punished, as well to prevent other offences of the same kind, as to acquit Mr. Banks of his promise; the Indians saw him stripped and tied up to the rigging with a fixed attention, waiting in silent suspence for the event; but as soon as the first stroke was given, they interfered with great agitation, earnestly entreating that the rest of the punishment might be remitted: to this, however, for many reasons, I could not consent, and when they found that they could not prevent by their intercession, they gave vent to their pity by tears.

Their tears indeed, like those of children, were always ready to express any passion that was strongly excited, and like those of children they also appeared to be forgotten as soon as shed; of which the following among many others, is a remarkable instance. Very early in the morning of the 28th, even before it was day, a great number of them came down to the fort, and Terapo being observed among the women on the outside of the gate, Mr. Banks went out and brought her in; he saw that the tears then stood in her eyes, and as soon as she entered they began to flow in great abundance: he enquired earnestly the cause, but instead of answering she took from under her garment a shark's tooth, and struck it six or seven times into her head with great force; a profusion of blood followed, and she talked loud, but in a most melancholy tone, for some minutes, without at all regarding his enquiries, which he repeated with still more impatience and concern, while the other Indians, to his great surprize, talked and laughed, without taking the least notice of her distress. But her own behaviour was still more extraordinary. As soon as the bleeding was over, she looked up with a smile, and began to collect some small pieces of cloth, which during her bleeding she had thrown down to catch the blood; as soon as she had picked them all up, she carried them out of the tent, and threw them into the sea, carefully dispersing them abroad, as if she wished to prevent the sight of them from reviving the remembrance of what she had done. She then plunged into the river, and after having washed her whole body, returned to the tents with the same gaiety and cheerfulness as if nothing had happened.

It is not indeed strange that the sorrows of these artless people should be transient, any more than that their passions should be suddenly and strongly expressed: what they feel they have never been taught either to disguise or suppress, and having no habits of thinking which perpetually recal the past, and anticipate the future, they are affected by all the changes of the passing hour, and reflect the colour of the time, however frequently it may vary: they have no project which is to be pursued from day to day, the subject of unremitted anxiety and solicitude, that first rushes into the mind when they awake in the morning, and is last dismissed when they sleep at night. Yet if we admit that they are upon the whole happier than we, we must admit that the child is happier than the man, and that we are losers by the perfection of our nature, the increase of our knowledge, and the enlargement of our views.

[…]

[14 May 1769]

On the 14th, which was Sunday, I directed that Divine Service should be performed at the fort: we were desirous that some of the principal Indians should be present, but when the hour came, most of them were returned home. Mr. Banks, however, crossed the river, and brought back Tubourai Tamaide and his wife Tomio, hoping that it would give occasion to some enquiries on their part, and some instruction on ours: having seated them, he placed himself between them, and during the whole service, they very attentively observed his behaviour, and very exactly imitated it; standing, sitting, or kneeling, as they saw him do: they were conscious that we were employed about somewhat serious and important, as appeared by their calling to the Indians without the fort to be silent; yet when the service was over, neither of them asked any questions, nor would they attend to any attempt that was made to explain what had been done.

Such were our Matins: our Indians thought fit to perform Vespers[3] of a very different kind. A young man, near six feet high, performed the rites of Venus[4] with a little girl about eleven or twelve years of age, before several of our people, and a great number of the natives, without the least sense of its being indecent or improper, but, as appeared, in perfect conformity to the custom of the place. Among the spectators were several women of superior rank, particularly Oberea,[5] who may properly be said to have assisted at the ceremony; for they gave instructions to the girl how to perform her part, which, young as she was, she did not seem much to stand in need of.

This incident is not mentioned as an object of idle curiosity, but as it deserves consideration in determining a question which has been long debated in philosophy; Whether the shame attending certain actions, which are allowed on all sides to be in themselves innocent, is implanted in Nature, or superinduced by custom? If it has its origin in custom, it will, perhaps, be found difficult to trace that custom, however general, to its source; if in instinct, it will be equally difficult to discover from what cause it is subdued or at least over-ruled among these people, in whose manners not the least trace of it is to be found.

[...]

[1769; summary of Tahiti]

In other countries, the girls and unmarried women are supposed to be wholly ignorant of what others upon some occasions may appear to know;

---

3   *Matins ... Vespers*: Matins is one of the canonical hours of prayer, here recited at daybreak. Vespers is the hour of prayer at evening.
4   *Venus*: Roman Goddess of love.
5   *Oberea*: or Purea, Queen of Tahiti. A series of scurrilous satires on Joseph Banks and Oberea followed the publication of *An Account*, particularly incited by Banks' presence at this 'rite' and his habit of sleeping in the Tahitians' houses (once, embrassingly, his clothes were stolen while sleeping at the house of Oberea).

and their conduct and conversation are consequently restrained within narrower bounds, and kept at a more remote distance from whatever relates to a connection with the other sex: but here, it is just contrary. Among other diversions, there is a dance, called *Timorodee*, which is performed by young girls, whenever eight or ten of them can be collected together, consisting of motions and gestures beyond imagination wanton, in the practice of which they are brought up from their earliest childhood, accompanied by words, which, if it were possible, would more explicitly convey the same ideas. In these dances they keep time with an exactness that is scarcely excelled by the best performers upon the stages of Europe. But the practice which is allowed to the virgin, is prohibited to the woman from the moment that she has put these hopeful lessons in practice, and realized the symbols of the dance.

It cannot be supposed that, amongst these people, chastity is held in much estimation. It might be expected that sisters and daughters would be offered to strangers, either as a courtesy, or for reward; and that breaches of conjugal fidelity, even in the wife, should not be otherwise punished than by a few hard words, or perhaps a slight beating, as indeed is the case: but there is a scale in dissolute sensuality, which these people have ascended, wholly unknown to every other nation whose manners have been recorded from the beginning of the world to the present hour, and which no imagination could possibly conceive.

A very considerable number of the principle people of Otaheite,[6] of both sexes, have formed themselves into a society, in which every woman is common to every man; thus securing a perpetual variety as often as their inclination prompts them to seek it, which is so frequent, that the same man and woman seldom cohabit together more than two or three days.

These societies are distinguished by the name of *Arreoy*;[7] and the members have meetings, at which no other is present, where the men amuse themselves by wrestling, and the women, notwithstanding their occasional connection with different men, dance the Timorodee in all its latitude, as an incitement to desires which it is said are frequently gratified upon the spot. This however is comparatively nothing. If any of the women happen to be with child, which in this manner of life happens less frequently than if they were to cohabit with only one man, the poor infant is smothered the moment it is born, that it may be no incumbrance to the father, nor interrupt the mother in the pleasures of her diabolical prostitution. It sometimes indeed happens, that the passion which prompts a woman to enter into this society, is surmounted when she becomes a mother, by that instinctive affection which Nature has given to all creatures for the preservation of

---

6   *Otaheite*: the usual eighteenth-century name for Tahiti.
7   *Arreoy*: or arioi, an elite society associated with the war-god Oro.

their offspring; but even in this case, she is not permitted to spare the life of her infant, except she can find a man who will patronise it as his child: if this can be done, the murder is prevented; but both the man and woman, being deemed by this act to have appropriated each other, are ejected from the community, and forfeit all claim to the privileges and pleasures of Arreoy for the future; the woman from that time being distinguished by the term *Whannownow,* 'bearer of children,' which is here a term of reproach; though none can be more honourable in the estimation of wisdom and humanity, of right reason, and every passion that distinguishes the man from the brute.

It is not fit that a practice so horrid and so strange should be imputed to human beings upon slight evidence, but I have such as abundantly justifies me in the account I have given. The people themselves are so far from con-cealing their connection with such a society as a disgrace, that they boast of it as a privilege; and both myself and Mr. Banks, when particular persons have been pointed out to us as members of the Arreoy, have questioned them about it, and received the account that has been here given from their own lips. They have acknowledged, that they had long been of this accursed society, that they belonged to it at that time, and that several of their children had been put to death.

But I must not conclude my account of the domestic life of these people without mentioning their personal cleanliness. If that which lessens the good of life and increases the evil is vice, surely cleanliness is a virtue: the want of it tends to destroy both beauty and health, and mingles disgust with our best pleasures. The natives of Otaheite, both men and women, constantly wash their whole bodies in running water three times every day; once as soon as they rise in the morning, once at noon, and again before they sleep at night, whether the sea or river is near them or at a distance. I have already observed, that they wash not only the mouth, but the hands at their meals, almost between every morsel; and their clothes, as well as their persons, are kept without spot or stain; so that in a large company of these people, nothing is suffered but heat, which, perhaps, is more than can be said of the politest assembly in Europe.

Phillis Wheatley

The poet Phillis Wheatley (1753–84) was born in west Africa and was carried as a slave to Boston in 1761. There she was bought by John and Susanna Wheatley who employed her as a domestic servant. Through their daughter Mary, she gained an unusual education that encompassed Classical and English literature, the Bible, geography and history; 'as to her Writing', John Wheatley noted, 'her own Curiosity led her to it'.[1] Phillis Wheatley's *Poems on Various Subjects, Religious and Moral* was published in London in 1773 with the patronage of Selina Hastings, the Countess of Huntingdon (patron to evangelist George Whitfield, and black writers such as Gronniosaw, John Marrant, and Olaudah Equiano). That year she had taken a trip there, intending to recover her health, see to the collection's publication, and visit her patron, but she was called back to tend her ailing mistress. She was granted her freedom shortly after her return to America in the same year.

The year of her trip to England was only a year after the momentous Somerset case which denied slave owners the right to remove a slave out of England: in effect the ruling rendered slavery illegal in England. The poems in this selection address the issue of liberty in a variety of ways. Wheatley's poem to King George III clearly looks to England as the font of liberty. *To the Right Honourable WILLIAM, Earl of DARTMOUTH* draws upon her own status as a black slave, re-appropriating the rhetoric of colonial domination over Americans: read in the light of the Somerset ruling, the poem hopes political liberty will lead to liberty for black slaves. In *A Farewel to AMERICA*, 'Britannia' is a source of hope, whereas the poem is ambivalent about America. (This optimism did not last, however: by the War of American Independence, she was on the side of the American Patriots). Phillis Wheatley's imagination moved around the Atlantic slave triangle, and her poems display complex meditations on her sense of identity, strung as it was between Africa, America and Britain.

To the KING's Most Excellent Majesty. 1768[2]

Your subjects hope, dread Sire —
The crown upon your brows may flourish long,
And that your arm may in your God be strong!
O may your sceptre num'rous nations sway,
And all with love and readiness obey!   5

But how shall we the *British* king reward!
Rule thou in peace, our father, and our lord!
Midst the remembrance of thy favours past,
The meanest peasants most admire the last.[3]
May *George*, belov'd by all the nations round,   10
Live with heav'ns choicest constant blessings crown'd!

---

[1] From *Poems on Various Subjects, Religious and Moral* (1773), 'Copy of a Letter sent by the Author's Master to the publisher'. This also included a list of people attesting to the writings as written by 'Phillis, a young Negro Girl'.

[2] From *Poems*, p. 17.

[3] 'The Repeal of the Stamp Act' [Wheatley's note]. The Stamp Act was introduced in 1765 as a tax on all legal documents throughout the British empire. It was universally detested and unenforceable, and was withdrawn in 1766. It provoked a series of crucial debates concerning the relationship between Britain and its American colonies in the years preceding the War of American Independence. See also Freeth and Peart.

Great God, direct, and guard him from on high,
And from his head let ev'ry evil fly!
And may each clime with equal gladness see
A monarch's smile can set his subjects free! 15

On being brought from AFRICA to AMERICA.[4]

'Twas mercy brought me from my *Pagan* land,
Taught my benighted soul to understand
That there's a God, that there's a *Saviour* too:
Once I redemption neither sought nor knew.
Some view our sable race with scornful eye, 5
'Their colour is a diabolic die.'
Remember, *Christians*, *Negros*, black as *Cain*,
May be refin'd, and join th' angelic train.

To the Right Honourable WILLIAM, Earl of DARTMOUTH, His Majesty's Principal Secretary of State for North-America, &c.[5]

Hail, happy day, when, smiling like the morn,
Fair *Freedom* rose *New-England* to adorn:
The northern clime beneath her genial ray,
Dartmouth, congratulates thy blissful sway:

Elate with hope her race no longer mourns, 5
Each soul expands, each grateful bosom burns,
While in thine hand with pleasure we behold
The silken reins, and *Freedom*'s charms unfold.
Long lost to realms beneath the northern skies
She shines supreme, while hated *faction* dies: 10
Soon as appear'd the *Goddess* long desir'd,
Sick at the view, she languish'd and expir'd;
Thus from the splendors of the morning light
The owl in sadness seeks the caves of night.

No more, *America*, in mournful strain 15
Of wrongs, and grievance unredress'd complain,
No longer shalt thou dread the iron chain,
Which wanton *Tyranny* with lawless hand
Had made, and with it meant t' enslave the land.

---

4 From *Poems*, p. 18.
5 From *Poems*, pp. 73–75. In 1772 William Legge (1731–1801) was appointed Secretary of State for the North American colonies, and president of the Board of Trade and Foreign Plantations. He was a friend of Countess Huntingdon.

Should you, my lord, while you peruse my song, 20
Wonder from whence my love of *Freedom* sprung,
Whence flow these wishes for the common good,
By feeling hearts alone best understood,
I, young in life, by seeming cruel fate
Was snatch'd from *Afric*'s fancy'd happy seat: 25
What pangs excruciating must molest,
What sorrows labour in my parent's breast?
Steel'd was that soul and by no misery mov'd
That from a father seiz'd his babe belov'd:
Such, such my case. And can I then but pray 30
Others may never feel tyrannic sway?

For favours past, great Sir, our thanks are due,
And thee we ask thy favours to renew,
Since in thy pow'r, as in thy will before,
To sooth the griefs, which thou did'st once deplore. 35
May heav'nly grace the sacred sanction give
To all thy works, and thou for ever live
Not only on the wings of fleeting *Fame*,
Though praise immortal crowns the patriot's name,
But to conduct to heav'ns refulgent fane, 40
May fiery coursers sweep th' ethereal plain,
And bear thee upwards to that blest abode,
Where, like the prophet, thou shalt find thy God.

A Farewel to AMERICA. To Mrs. S. W.[6]

I.

Adieu, *New-England's* smiling meads,
Adieu, the flow'ry plain:
I leave thine op'ning charms, O spring,
And tempt the roaring main.

II.

In vain for me the flow'rets rise, 5
And boast their gaudy pride,
While here beneath the northern skies
I mourn for *health* deny'd.

---

[6]   From *Poems*, pp. 119–22. *Mrs S.W.*: Susanna Wheatley.

III.

Celestial maid of rosy hue,
    O let me feel thy reign!   10
I languish till thy face I view,
    Thy vanish'd joys regain.

IV.

Susanna mourns, nor can I bear
    To see the crystal show'r,
Or mark the tender falling tear   15
    At sad departure's hour;

V.

Not unregarding can I see
    Her soul with grief opprest:
But let no sighs, no groans for me,
    Steal from her pensive breast.   20

VI.

In vain the feather'd warblers sing,
    In vain the garden blooms,
And on the bosom of the spring
    Breathes out her sweet perfumes,

VII.

While for *Britannia's* distant shore   25
    We sweep the liquid plain,
And with astonish'd eyes explore
    The wide-extended main.

VIII.

Lo! *Health* appears! celestial dame!
    Complacent and serene,   30
With *Hebe's* mantle o'er her Frame,[7]
    With soul-delighting mein.

---

[7]   *Hebe*: the Greek goddess of youth.

IX.

To mark the vale where *London* lies
   With misty vapours crown'd,
Which cloud *Aurora's* thousand dyes,   35
   And veil her charms around,

X.

Why, *Phoebus*, moves thy car so slow?
   So slow thy rising ray?
Give us the famous town to view,
   Thou glorious king of day!   40

XI.

For thee, *Britannia*, I resign
   New-England's smiling fields;
To view again her charms divine,
   What joy the prospect yields!

XII.

But thou! Temptation hence away,   45
   With all thy fatal train
Nor once seduce my soul away,
   By thine enchanting strain.

XIII.

Thrice happy they, whose heav'nly shield
   Secures their souls from harms,   50
And fell *Temptation* on the field
   Of all its pow'r disarms!

Boston, May 7, 1773

Edward Long, from
The History of Jamaica, or General Survey of the Antient and Modern State of that Island (1774)

Edward Long (1734–1813) was the son of a Jamaican planter and his family had connections with the island since the seventeenth century. At his father's death in Jamaica in 1757, Long travelled to the island and eventually became judge of the vice-admiralty in the West-Indies. Ill health forced him to leave in 1769 and he spent the rest of his life in England. Other writings included, *Candid Reflections upon the Judgments of the Court of King's Bench on what is commonly called the Negro-cause, by a Planter* (1772); *The Sentimental Exhibition, or Portraits and Sketches of the Times* (1774); and *Pamphlet on the Sugar Trade* (1782).

As a defender of the slave trade, Long's description of the Creoles (Jamaican-born whites) is generous, though it still reflects a number of common assumptions regarding their character. However, in the descriptions of the effect of climate, racial intermixture, and mere proximity of African slaves on the manners and behaviour of the Creoles, the first few extracts also reveal the anxieties of cultural degeneration in the contact zones of the empire. As a buffer against this, Long was particularly keen to emphasise the crucial role of women in the production of a virtuous planter-class. In the last few extracts, Long argues that Africans were created as a distinct species (polygenesis) and were hardly human at all – an early example of a form of categorisation we now call 'race'. The extremity of his racism is a product of both the peculiar conditions of Jamaica and his vehement defence of slavery. Long's *The History of Jamaica* is both more and less than a 'history': the contemporary description of one of Britain's foremost colonies was a complex mix of theories of human difference, bound up in a polemical package of racial anxieties and justifications.

[From 'Creoles'][1]

The inhabitants of this island may be distinguished under the following classes: Creoles, or natives; Whites, Blacks, Indians, and their varieties; European and other Whites; and imported or African Blacks.

The intermixture of Whites, Blacks, and Indians, has generated several different casts, which have all their proper denominations, invented by the

---

[1]   From vol. 2, pp. 260–3, 265, 267, 276–7, 278–80.

Spaniards, who make this a kind of science among them. Perhaps they will be better understood by the following table.

DIRECT linear Ascent from the Negro Venter.

White Man, = Negroe Woman.
|
White Man, = Mulatta.
|
White Man, = Terceron.
|
White Man, = Quateron.
|
White Man, = Quinteron.
|
WHITE

MEDIATE or STATIONARY, neither advancing nor receding.

Quateron, = Terceron.
|
Tente-enel-ayre

RETROGRADE

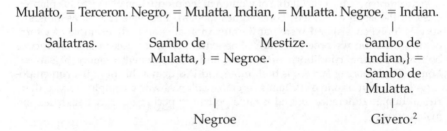

In the Spanish colonies, it is accounted most creditable to mend the breed by ascending or growing whiter; insomuch that a Quateron will hardly keep company with a Mulatto; and a Mestize values himself very highly in comparison with a Sambo. The Giveros lie under the imputation of having the worst inclinations and principles; and, if the cast is known, they are banished. These distinctions, however, do not prevail in Jamaica; for here the Terceron is confounded with the Quateron; and the laws permit all, that are above three degrees removed in lineal descent from the Negro ancestor,

---

2   'Perhaps from *Gisero*, a butcher' [Long's note].

to vote at elections, and enjoy all the privileges and immunities of his majesty's white subjects of the island.[3] The Dutch, I am informed, transcend the Spaniards very far in their refinement of these complexions. They add drops of pure water to a single drop of dusky liquor, until it becomes tolerably pellucid. But this needs the apposition of such a multitude of drops, that, to apply the experiment by analogy to the human race, twenty or thirty generations, perhaps, would hardly be sufficient to discharge the stain.

The native white men, or Creoles, of Jamaica are in general tall and well-shaped; and some of them rather inclined to corpulence. Their cheeks are remarkably high-boned, and the sockets of their eyes deeper than is commonly observed among the natives of England; by this conformation, they are guarded from those ill effects which an almost continual strong glare of sun-shine might otherwise produce. Their sight is keen and penetrating; which renders them excellent marksmen: a light-grey, and black, or deep hazel, are the more common colours of the pupil. The effect of climate is not only remarkable in the structure of their eyes, but likewise in the extraordinary freedom and suppleness of their joints, which enable them to move with ease, and give them a surprising agility, as well as gracefulness in dancing. Although descended from British ancestors, they are stamped with these characteristic deviations. Climate, perhaps, has had some share in producing the variety of feature which we behold among the different societies of mankind, scattered over the globe: so that, were an Englishman and woman to remove to China, and there abide, it may be questioned, whether their descendants, in the course of a few generations, constantly residing there, would not acquire somewhat of the Chinese cast of countenance and person? I do not indeed suppose, that, by living in Guiney, they would exchange hair for wool, or a white cuticle for a black: change of complexion must be referred to some other cause. I have spoken only of those Creoles who never have quitted the island; for they, who leave it in their infancy, and pass into Britain for education, where they remain until their growth is pretty well compleated, are not so remarkably distinguished either in their features or limbs. Confining myself to the permanent natives, or Creole men, I have this idea of their qualities; that they are in general sensible, of quick apprehension, brave, good-natured, affable, generous, temperate, and sober; unsuspicious, lovers of freedom, fond of social enjoyments, tender fathers, humane and indulgent masters; firm and sincere friends, where they once repose a confidence; their tables are covered with plenty of good cheer, and they pique themselves on regaling their guests with a profusion of viands; their hospitality is unlimited; they have lodging and entertainment always at the service of transient strangers and travelers; and receive in the most friendly manner those, with whose character and

---

[3]   *the laws … island*: the Jamaican legislature passed this law in 1733, which, uniquely for the British West Indies, effectively turned mulattos into white citizens.

circumstances they are often utterly unacquainted;[4] they affect gaiety and diversions, which in general are cards, billiards, backgammon, chefs, horse-racing, hog-hunting, shooting, fishing, dancing, and music; the latter in particular they are formed to enjoy with the nicest feelings; and their ear for melody is, for the most part, exceedingly correct. This, indeed, has also been remarked of the Creole Blacks, who, without being able to read a single note, are known to play twenty or thirty tunes, country-dances, minuets, airs, and even sonatas, on the violin; and catch, with an astonishing readiness, whatever they hear played or sung, especially if it is lively and striking.

[...]

With all these praise-worthy qualities, the Creoles have some foibles in their disposition. They are subject to frailties in common with the rest of mankind. They are possessed with a degree of supineness and indolence in their affairs, which renders them bad œconomists, and too frequently hurts their fortune and family. With a strong natural propensity to the other sex, they are not always the most chaste and faithful of husbands. They are liable to sudden transports of anger; but these fits, like hurricanes, though violent while they last, are soon over and subside into a calm: yet they are not apt to forget or forgive substantial injuries. A lively imagination brings every circumstance present to their remembrance, and agitates them almost as much as if it had occurred but immediately before. They are fickle and desultory in their pursuits; though unshaken in their friendships. From this cause perhaps it is, that various schemes, both in pleasure and business, have been eagerly started, and then suddenly dropped, and forgotten as if they had never existed. They have some tincture of vanity, and occasionally of haughtiness; though much less of the latter than formerly. That distant carriage, which was gained here insensibly by habit, when the planters employed six times the number of white servants, whom, together with their Negroes, they might think it prudent to keep under a due awe and subordination to authority, has worn away in course of time with the causes of it. They are too much addicted to expensive living, costly entertainments, dress, and equipage. Were they but more abstemious in these respects, and more attentive to good husbandry on their plantations, there are few who would not amass considerable fortunes, and render their posterity opulent.

[...]

The planters of this island have been very unjustly stigmatized with an accusation of treating their Negroes with barbarity. Some alledge, that these

---

4   'One obvious proof of this is, that there is scarcely one tolerable inn throughout the whole island, except at a great distance from any settlement' [Long's note].

slave-holders (as they are pleased to call them, in contempt) are lawless bashaws, West-India tyrants, inhuman oppressors, bloody inquisitors, and a long, &c. of such pretty names. The planter, in reply to these bitter invectives, will think it sufficient to urge, in the first place, that *he* did not make them slaves, but succeeded to the inheritance of their services in the same manner as an English 'squire succeeds to the estate of his ancestors; and that, as to his Africans, he buys their services from those who have all along pretended a very good right to sell; that it cannot be for his interest to treat his Negroes in the manner represented; but that it is so to use them well, and preserve their vigour and existence as long as he is able.[5]

[...]

Whilst I render all due praise to the Creole ladies for their many amiable qualities, impartiality forbids me to suppress what is highly to their discredit; I mean, their disdaining to suckle their own helpless offspring! They give them up to a Negroe or Mulatto wet nurse, without reflecting that her blood may be corrupted, or considering the influence which the milk may have with respect to the disposition, as well as health, of their little ones. This shameful and savage custom they borrowed from England; and, finding it relieve them from a little trouble, it has gained their general sanction. How barbarous the usage, which, to purchase a respite from that endearing employment so agreeable to the humanity of their sex, so consonant to the laws of nature, at once so honourable and delightful to a real parent, thus sacrifices the well-being of a child! Notwithstanding every precaution they take to examine the nurse of their choice, it is a million to one but the harbours in her blood the feeds of many terrible distempers. There is scarcely one of these nurses who is not a common prostitute, or at least who has not commerce with more than one man; or who has not some latent taint of the veneral distemper, or *scrofa*, either hereditary, or acquired, and ill-cured.

[...]

Another misfortune is, the constant intercourse from their birth with Negroe domestics, whose drawling, dissonant gibberish they insensibly adopt, and with it no small tincture of their aukward carriage and vulgar manners; all which they do not easily get rid of, even after an English education, unless sent away extremely young.

---

5   He later adds that 'there are no men, nor orders of men, in Great-Britain, possessed of more disinterested charity, philanthropy, and clemency, than the Creole gentleman of this island' and that 'his authority over them [the slaves] is like an antient patriarch', vol. 2, pp. 269, 271.

A planter of this island, who had several daughters, being apprehensive of these consequences, sent to England, and procured a tutoress for them. After her arrival, they were never suffered to converse with the Blacks. In short, he used all his vigilance to preserve their language and manners from this infection. He succeeded happily in the design; and these young ladies proved some of the most agreeable and well-behaved in the island: nor could it be distinguished from their accent, but they had been brought up at some genteel boarding-school in England; insomuch that they were frequently asked, by strangers, how long they had resided in that kingdom. Until a proper seminary can be established, every master of a family here might pursue the like method, at least with his daughters, who are generally kept more at home than boys. But a mother, who has been trained in the accustomed mode among a herd of Negroe-domestics, adopts the same plan, for the most part, with her own children, having no idea of the impropriety of it, because she does not discern those singularities, in speech or deportment, which are so apt to strike the ears and eyes of well-educated persons on a first introduction to them.

The ladies, however, who live in and about the towns, being often in company with Europeans, and others brought up in Great Britain, copy imperceptibly their manners and address; and become better qualified to fill the honourable station of a wife, and to head their table with grace and propriety. Those, who have been bred up entirely in the sequestered country parts, and had no opportunity of forming themselves either by example or tuition, are truly to be pitied. We may see, in some of these places, a very fine young woman aukwardly dangling her arms with the air of a Negro-servant, lolling almost the whole day upon beds or settees, her head muffled up with two or three handkerchiefs, her dress loose, and without stays. At noon, we find her employed in gobbling pepper-pot, seated on the floor, with her sable hand-maids around her. In the afternoon, she takes her *siesto* as usual; while two of these damsels refresh her face with the gentle breathings of the fan; and a third provokes the drowsy powers of Morpheus by delicious scratchings on the sole of either foot. When she rouzes from slumber, her speech is whining, languid, and childish. When arrived at maturer years, the consciousness of her ignorance makes her abscond from the sight or conversation of every rational creature. Her ideas are narrowed to the ordinary subjects that pass before her, the business of the plantation, the tittle-tattle of the parish; the tricks, superstitions, diversions, and profligate discourses, of black servants, equally illiterate and unpolished.

Who is there, that does not sincerely deplore the lot of this unhappy *tramontane*, and blame the inattention of the legislature to that important article, Education! To this defect we must attribute all that cruel ridicule and sarcasm, so frequently lavished upon these unfortunate females by others of their sex, who, having experienced the blessings of a regular course of instruction at school, are too ostentatiously fond of holding in derision what they ought to look upon with candour and concern. What ornaments to society might not these neglected women have proved, if they could have received the same degree of liberal polish! On the other hand, deprived thus of the means of culture and refinement, ill-furnished as they are with capacity for undertaking the province of managing domestic concerns, uninformed of what pertains to œconomy, order, and decency; how unfit are they to be the companions of sensible men, or the patterns of imitation to their daughters! How incapable of regulating their manners, enlightening their understanding, or improving their morals! Can the wisdom of legislature be more usefully applied, than to the attainment of these ends; which, by making the women more desirable partners in marriage, would render the island more populous, and residence in it more eligible; which would banish ignorance from the rising generation, restrain numbers from seeking these improvements, at the hazard of life, in other countries; and from unnaturally reviling a place which they would love and prefer, if they could enjoy in it that necessary culture, without which life and property lose their relish to those who are born, not only to inherit, but to adorn, a fortune.

[...]

[From 'Negroes']⁶

In general, they are void of genius, and seem almost incapable of making any progress in civility or science. They have no plan or system of morality among them. Their barbarity to their children debases their nature even below that of brutes. They have no moral sensations; no taste but for women; gormondizing, and drinking to excess; no wish but to be idle. Their children, from their tenderest years, are suffered to deliver themselves up to all that nature suggests to them. Their houses are miserable cabbins. They conceive no pleasure from the most beautiful parts of their country, preferring the more sterile. Their roads, as they call them, are mere sheep-paths, twice as long as they need be, and almost impassable. Their country in most parts is one continued wilderness, beset with briars and thorns. They use neither carriages, nor beasts of burthen. They are represented by all authors as the vilest of the human kind, to which they have little more pretension of resemblance than what arises from their exterior form.

In so vast a continent as that of Afric, and in so great a variety of climates and provinces, we might expect to find a proportionable diversity among the inhabitants, in regard to their qualifications of body and mind; strength, agility, industry, and dexterity, on the one hand; ingenuity, learning, arts, and sciences, on the other. But, on the contrary, a general uniformity runs through all these various regions of people; so that, if any difference be found, it is only in degrees of the same qualities; and, what is more strange,

---

⁶ From vol. 2, pp. 353–4, 371–2, 383.

those of the worst kind; it being a common known proverb, that all people on the globe have some good as well as ill qualities, except the Africans. Whatever great personages this country might anciently have produced, and concerning whom we have no information, they are now every where degenerated into a brutish, ignorant, idle, crafty, treacherous, bloody, thievish, mistrustful, and superstitious people, even in those states where we might expect to find them more polished, humane, docile, and industrious. It is doubtful, whether we ought to ascribe any superior qualities to the more ancient Africans; for we find them represented by the Greek and Roman authors under the most odious and despicable character; as proud, lazy, deceitful, thievish, addicted to all kinds of lust, and ready to promote them in others, incestuous, savage, cruel, and vindictive, devourers of human flesh, and quaffers of human blood, inconstant, base, and cowardly, devoted to all sorts of superstition; and, in short, to every vice that came their way, or within their reach.

[...]

The Negroe race (consisting of varieties) will then appear rising progressively in the scale of intellect, the further they mount above the ourang-outang and brute creation. The system of man will seem more consistent, and the measure of it more compleat, and analogous to the harmony and order that are visible in every other line of the world's stupendous fabric. Nor is this conclusion degrading to human nature, while it tends to exalt our idea of the infinite perfections of the Diety; for how vast is the distance between inert matter, and matter endued with thought and reason!

[...]

In short, their corporeal sensations are in general of the grossest frame; their sight is acute, but not correct; they will rarely miss a standing object, but they have no notion of shooting birds on the wing, nor can they project a straight line, nor lay any substance square with another. Their hearing is remarkably quick; their faculties of smell and taste are truly bestial, nor less so their commerce with the other sex; in these acts they are libidinous and shameless as monkies, or baboons. The equally hot temperament of their women has given probability to the charge of their admitting these animals frequently to their embrace. An example of this intercourse once happened, I think, in England;[7] and if lust can prompt to such excesses in that northern

---

[7] 'It is said the lady conceived by her paramour, which gave occasion to the Stat.25 Hen. VIII. which was purposely extended to women, as well as men' [Long's note]. This law, passed in 1533, made 'buggery committed with mankind or beast' punishable by death.

region, and in despight of all the checks which national politeness and refined sentiments impose, how freely may it not operate in the more genial soil of Afric, that parent of every thing that is monstrous in nature, where these creatures are frequent and familiar; where the passions rage without any controul; and the retired wilderness presents opportunity to gratify them without fear of detection!

Frances Burney to Mr Crisp, 1 December 1774

Frances, or Fanny, Burney (1752–1840) is best known for her first novel, *Evelina*, published in 1778. Among her other novels were *Cecilia* (1782) and *Camilla* (1796), and her published diaries and letters offer a lively window on late eighteenth- and early nineteenth-century life. In this letter to her father (who was staying at the home of his friend Samuel Crisp) Fanny describes the visit to the Burney's home of Omai. Her brother, Captain James Burney ('Jem'), had sailed with Cook on the second expedition to the Pacific, during which they had met Omai who was brought back to England in 1774 aboard the expedition's sister vessel *Adventure*. Omai (*c.*1753–79) – or Mai to his family – was from Raiatea, in the Society Islands, and born into a rank of society second only to the sacred chiefs. He was exiled in Tahiti after his island was invaded by neighbouring warriors. When he arrived in England he was introduced to the leading figures of the day – including Samuel Johnson and the Earl of Sandwich (First Lord of the Admiralty) – and presented to George III. He was tutored in the social niceties by Dr Daniel Solander and Sir Joseph Banks (with whom he stayed until he was given his own house), was taken to concerts, assemblies and plays, and had his portrait painted by Sir Joshua Reynolds. He was taken back in 1776 on Cook's third mission.

In her letter Fanny Burney praises Omai as an example of a natural man. Indeed, the figure of the noble savage chimed well with the culture of sensibility of the latter half of the eighteenth century which commended natural benevolence over the artificiality of civility (even though Burney seems impressed by his manners). Recording another meeting with him in her diary, however, her idealisation of Omai is tested when he is asked to perform a Tahitian song: 'so queer, wild, strange a *rumbling of sounds* never did I before hear; & very contentedly can I go to the Grave if I Never do again. His *song* is the only thing that is *savage* belonging to him.'[1]

---

[1]   Text from MS Egerton 3694. I have not reproduced the portions of the MS which have been overscored: for full textual details see Lars E. Triode, ed., *The Early Journal and Letters of Fanny Burney, vol. II 1774–1777* (Clarendon Press, 1990). Diary entry 14 December 1775, p. 196.

My dear Daddy, …

My Brother went last Monday to the play of Isabella at Drury Lane, he sat in one of the Upper Boxes, from whence he spied Omai and Mr. Banks[2]—Upon which, he crossed over to speak to his friend. Omai received him with a hearty shake of the Hand, and made room for him by his side. Jem asked Mr. Banks when he could see him to Dinner? Mr. B. said that he believed he was engaged every Day till the holydays, which he was to spend at Hinchinbrook. However on Tuesday night, very late, there came a note which I will write down. It was directed to my Brother.—Omai presents his Compts. to Mr Burney, and if it is agreeable and convenient to him, he will do himself the Honour of Dining with Mr. Burney to-morrow, but if it is not so, Omai will wait upon Mr. Burney some other Time that shall suit him better. Omai begs to have an answer, and that if he is to come, begs Mr. Burney to fetch him.

Early on Wednesday morning, Jem called at Mr. Banks, with my father's Compts. to him, and to Dr. Solander,[3] and begging their company also. But they were engaged at the Royal Society.

Mr. Strange and Mr. Hayes, at their own motion, came to Dinner to meet our Guest. We did not Dine till 4. But Omai came at 2, and Mr. Banks and Dr. Solander brought him, in order to make a short visit to my father. They were all just come from the House of Lords, where they had taken Omai to hear the King make his speech from the Throne.

For my part, I had been confined up stairs for 3 days—however, I was much better, and obtained leave to come down, though very much wrapt up, and *quite a figure*. But I did not chuse to appear till Mr. Banks and Dr. Solander were gone. I found Omai seated on the Great Chair, and my Brother next to him, and talking Otaheite as fast as possible. You cannot imagine how fluently and easily Jem speaks it. Mama and Susy and Charlotte were opposite. As soon as there was a *cessation* of talk, Jem Introduced me, and told him I was another sister. He rose, and made a very fine Bow and then seated himself again. But when Jem went on, and told him I was not well, he again directly rose, and muttering something of the *Fire*, in a very polite *manner*, without *speech* insisting upon my taking his seat,—and he *would* not be refused. He then drew his chair next to mine, and looking at me with an expression of pity said 'very well to-*morrow-morrow?*'—I imagine he meant I *hope* you will be very well in *two or 3 morrows*—and when I shook my head, he said *'no? O very bad!'*

When Mr. Strange and Mr. Hayes were Introduced to him, he paid his Compliments with great politeness to them, which he has found a method of doing without *words*.

---

2   *Mr Banks*: Sir Joseph Banks (1744–1820), botanist on the first expedition, and president of the Royal Society from 1778.

3   *Dr Solander*: Daniel Carl Solander (1732–82), Swedish naturalist who accompanied Cook on the first voyage to the Pacific aboard *Endeavour*.

As he had been to Court, he was very fine. He had on a suit of Manchester velvet, lined with white satten, a *Bag*, lace Ruffles, and a very handsome sword which the King had given to him. He is tall and very well made, much Darker than I expected to see him, but has a pleasing Countenance.

He makes *remarkably* good Bows—not for *him*, but for *anybody*, however long under a Dancing Master's care. Indeed he seems to shame Education, for his manners are so extremely graceful, and he is so polite, attentive, and easy, that you would have thought he came from some foreign Court.[4] You will think that I speak in a *high style*; but I assure you there was but one opinion about him.

At Dinner I had the pleasure of sitting next to him, as my Cold kept me near the Fire. The moment he was helped, he presented his plate to me, which, when I declined, he had not the *over shot* politeness to offer *all round*, as I have seen some people do, but took it quietly again. He eat heartily and committed not the slightest blunder at Table, neither did he do anything *awkwardly* or *ungainly*. He found by the turn of the Conversation, and some wry faces, that a Joint of Beef was not roasted enough, and therefore when he was helped, he took some pains to assure mama that he liked it, and said two or three Times—'*very dood*—, very *dood*.' It is very odd, but true, that he can pronounce the *th*, as in *thank you*, and the *w*, as in *well*, and yet cannot say *G*, which he uses a *d* for. But I now recollect, that in the beginning of a word, as *George*, he *can*, pronounce it.

He took a good deal of Notice of Dick,[5] yet was not quite so well pleased with him as I had expected him to be.

During Dinner, he called for some Drink. The man, not understanding what he would have, brought the Porter. We saw that he was wrong. However, Omai was too well bred to send it back. He took it in his Hand, and the man then brought him the small Beer;—he laughed, and said—'Two!'—however, he sent off the *small* Beer, as the *worse* of the *two*. Another time he called for *port wine*. And when the Bread was Handed, he took two Bits, and laughed and said '*one—two.—*'

He even observed *my abstinence*, which I think you would have laughed at, for he turned to me with some surprize, when Dinner was almost over, and said '*no* wine?'

Mr. Hayes asked him, through Jem, how he liked the King and his Speech. He had the politeness to try to answer in English and *to* Mr. Hayes—and said '*very well, King George!*'

After Dinner, mama gave the King for a toast. He made a Bow, and said '*Thank you, madam*', and then *tost off* '*King George!*'

---

4   *foreign Court*: the French, in particular, were renowned for their attention to manners and
     polite behaviour.
5   *Dick*: Richard Burney, Fanny's half-brother.

He told Jem that he had an Engagement at 6 o'clock, to go with Dr. Solander to see no less than twelve Ladies.—Jem translated this to us— he understands enough of English to find out when he is talked of, in general, and so he did now, and he laughed heartily, and began to Count, with his Fingers, in order to be understood—'1. 2. 3. 4. 5. 6. 7. 8. 9. 10.—*twelve— woman!*' said he.

When Mr. Banks and Dr. Solander went away, he said to them *Good-bye— good-bye.*

He never looked at his Dress, though it was on for the first time. Indeed he appears to be a perfectly rational and intelligent man, with an understanding far superior to the common race of *us cultivated gentry.* He could not else have borne so well the way of Life into which he is thrown, without some practice.

When the man brought him the *two* Beers, I forgot to mention that in returning them, one hit against the other, and occasioned a little sprinkling. He was *shocked* extremely—indeed I was afraid for his fine Cloaths, and would have pin'd up the wet table cloth, to prevent its hurting them—but he would not permit me; and, by his *manner* seem'd to *intreat* me not to trouble myself!—however, he had thought enough to spread his Napkin wider over his knee.

Before 6, the Coach came. Our man said 'Mr. Omai's servant.' He heard it at once, and answered *'very well.'* He kept his seat about 5 minutes after, and then rose and got his Hat and sword. My father happening to be talking to Mr. Strange, Omai stood still, neither chusing to interrupt him, nor to make his Compliments to any body else first. When he was disengaged, Omai went up to him, and made an exceeding fine Bow—the same to mama— then separately to every one in the company, and then went out with Jem to his Coach.

He must certainly possess an uncommon share of observation and attention. I assure you every body was delighted with him. I only wished I could have spoke his Language. Lord Sandwich has actually studied it so as to make himself understood in it. His *Hands* are very much *tattooed*, but his face is not at all. He is *by no means* handsome, though I like his *Countenance.*

The Conversation of our house has turned ever since upon Mr. *Stanhope*[6] and *Omai*—the first with all the advantage Lord Chesterfield's Instructions,[7] brought up at a great School, Introduced at 15 to a Court, taught all possible accomplishments from an Infant, and having all the care, expence, labour and benefit of the best Education that any man can receive,—proved after

---

[6] *Mr. Stanhope*: Philip Stanhope, illegitimate son of Philip Dormer Stanhope, fourth Earl of Chesterfield (1694–1773).

[7] *Chesterfield's instructions*: the fourth earl of Chesterfield's *Letters*, written to his son and published in 1774, were (in)famous for their rather worldly advice on gentlemen's manners and etiquette.

it all a meer *pedantic Booby;*—the second with no Tutor but Nature, changes after he is grown up, his Dress, his way of Life, his Diet, his Country and his friends;—and appears in a *new world* like a man who had all his life studied *the Graces*, and attended with unremitting application and diligence to form his manners, and to render his appearance and behaviour *politely easy*, and thoroughly *well bred!* I think this shews how much more *Nature* can do without *art*, than *art* with all her refinement unassisted by *Nature*.

If I have been too *prolix*, you must excuse me, because it is wholly owing to the great curiosity I have heard you express for whatever concerns Omai. My father desires his love to you, and says that if you will but come to Town, as soon as Omai returns from Hinchinbrooke, he will promise you that you shall still have a meeting with him.

> Adieu, my dear Sir,
> I beg you to believe me
> Your ever affectionate
> and obliged
>   F. BURNEY.

Edmund Burke, from *The Speech of Edmund Burke, Esq., on Moving his Resolutions for Conciliation with the Colonies, March 22, 1775*

Born in Dublin, Edmund Burke (1729–97) became renowned for his encyclopaedic knowledge of imperial affairs and his flair for passionate eloquence. His most famous early work, *A Philosophical Enquiry into the Sublime and Beautiful* (1757), however, concerned aesthetics. Later, mobilising the language of sensibility allied to a conservative political outlook, he was to decry the revolutionary movement in France in his *Reflections on the French Revolution* (1790). He was allied to the Whig party under Lord Rockingham, and elected MP for Wendover in 1766 at a point in British politics when relations with America were beginning to show cracks. His intercessions in the debates concerning British imperial authority display a view of the British empire as truly worldwide, encompassing the West-Indies, America, Ireland and India (see his *Speech on Fox's India Bill*). Although never reducible to a single principle or theory, his arguments generally sought to uphold British parliamentary sovereignty, but to reconcile and temper this authority with a benevolent and humane attitude to its colonies.

His *Speech ... for Conciliation* raises urgent questions as to the nature of the British empire and the identity of its colonists in America. In the extracts below, Burke attempts to account for the 'American' character, while also emphasising a shared set of seemingly English values – such as 'liberty' – that link colonist and homeland. In this, he attempted to grapple with the crucial and perhaps intractable problem of synthesising liberty with the governance of a large empire. Burke worried, as many others did, that the insistence on colonial compliance would undermine the value of liberty at home: obedience could not be forced at the expense of this touch-stone of Englishness.[1]

In this Character of the Americans, a love of Freedom is the predominating feature, which marks and distinguishes the whole: and as an ardent is always a jealous affection, your Colonies become suspicious, restive, and untractable, whenever they see the least attempt to wrest from them by force, or shuffle from them by chicane, what they think the only advantage worth living for. This fierce spirit of Liberty is stronger in the English Colonies probably than in any other people of the earth; and this from a great variety of powerful causes; which, to understand the true temper of their minds, and the direction which this spirit takes, it will not be amiss to lay open somewhat more largely.

First, the people of the Colonies are descendants of Englishmen. England, Sir, is a nation, which still I hope respects, and formerly adored her free-dom. The Colonists emigrated from you, when this part of your character was most predominant; and they took this bias and direction the moment they parted from your hands. They are therefore not only devoted to Liberty, but to Liberty according to English ideas, and on English princi-ples. Abstract Liberty, like other mere abstractions, is not to be found. Liberty inheres in some sensible object; and every nation has formed to itself some favourite point, which by way of eminence becomes the crite-rion of their happiness. It happened, you know, Sir, that the great contests for freedom in this country were from the earliest times chiefly upon the question of Taxing. Most of the contests in the ancient commonwealths turned primarily on the right of election of magistrates; or on the balance among the several orders of the state. The question of money was not with them so immediate. But in England it was otherwise. On this point of Taxes the ablest pens, and most eloquent tongues have been exercised; the great-est spirits have acted and suffered. In order to give the fullest satisfaction concerning the importance of this point, it was not only necessary for those who in argument defended the excellence of the English constitution, to insist on this privilege of granting money as a dry point of fact, and to prove, that the right had been acknowledged in ancient parchments, and

---

[1]   Text from pp. 15–20, 23, 60–2.

blind usages, to reside in a certain body called an House of Commons. They went much further; they attempted to prove, and they succeeded, that in theory it ought to be so, from the particular nature of a House of Commons, as an immediate representative of the people; whether the old records had delivered this oracle or not. They took infinite pains to inculcate, as a fundamental principle, that, in all monarchies, the people must in effect themselves mediately or immediately possess the power of granting their own money, or no shadow of liberty could subsist. The Colonies draw from you, as with their life-blood, these ideas and principles. Their love of Liberty, as with you, fixed and attached on this specific point of taxing. Liberty might be safe, or might be endangered in twenty other particulars, without their being much pleased or alarmed. Here they felt its pulse; and as they found that beat, they thought themselves sick or sound. I do not say whether they were right or wrong in applying your general arguments to their own case. It is not easy indeed to make a monopoly of theorems and corollaries. The fact is, that they did thus apply those general arguments; and your mode of governing them, whether through lenity or indolence, through wisdom or mistake, confirmed them in the imagination, that they, as well as you, had an interest in these common principles.

They were further confirmed in this pleasing error by the form of their provincial legislative assemblies. Their governments are popular in a high degree; some are merely popular; in all, the popular representative is the most weighty; and this share of the people in their ordinary government never fails to inspire them with lofty sentiments, and with a strong aversion from whatever tends to deprive them of their chief importance.

If anything were wanting to this necessary operation of the form of government, Religion would have given it a complete effect. Religion, always a principle of energy, in this new people, is no way worn out or impaired; and their mode of professing it is also one main cause of this free spirit. The people are protestants; and of that kind, which is the most adverse to all implicit submission of mind and opinion. This is a persuasion not only favourable to liberty, but built upon it. I do not think, Sir, that the reason of this averseness in the dissenting churches from all that looks like absolute Government is so much to be sought in their religious tenets, as in their history. Every one knows, that the Roman Catholick religion is at least coeval with most of the governments where it prevails; that it has generally gone hand in hand with them; and received great favour and every kind of support from authority. The Church of England too was formed from her cradle under the nursing care of regular Government. But the dissenting interests have sprung up in direct opposition to all the ordinary powers of the world; and could justify that opposition only on a strong claim to natural Liberty. Their very existence depended on the powerful and unremitted assertion of that claim. All protestantism, even the most cold and passive, is a sort of dissent. But the religion most prevalent in our Northern Colonies is a refinement on the principle of resistance; it is the dissidence of dissent; and the protestantism of the protestant religion. This religion, under a variety of denominations, agreeing in nothing but in the communion of the spirit of liberty, is predominant in most of the Northern provinces; where the Church of England, notwithstanding its legal rights, is in reality no more than a sort of private sect, not composing most probably the tenth of the people. The Colonists left England when this spirit was high; and in the emigrants was the highest of all:[2] and even that stream of foreigners, which has been constantly flowing into these Colonies, has, for the greatest part, been composed of dissenters from the establishments of their several countries, and have brought with them a temper and character far from alien to that of the people with whom they mixed.

Sir, I can perceive by their manner, that some Gentlemen object to the latitude of this description; because in the Southern Colonies the Church of England forms a large body, and has a regular establishment. It is certainly true. There is however a circumstance attending these Colonies, which in my opinion, fully counterbalances this difference, and makes the spirit of liberty still more high and haughty than in those to the Northward. It is that in Virginia and the Carolinas, they have a vast multitude of slaves. Where this is the case in any part of the world, those who are free, are by far the most proud and jealous of their freedom. Freedom is to them not only an enjoyment, but a kind of rank and privilege. Not seeing there, that freedom, as in countries where it is a common blessing, and as broad and general as the air, may be united with much abject toil, with great misery, with all the exterior of servitude, Liberty looks amongst them, like something that is more noble and liberal. I do not mean, Sir, to commend the superior morality of this sentiment, which has at least as much pride as virtue in it; but I cannot alter the nature of man. The fact is so; and these people of the Southern Colonies are much more strongly, and with a higher and more stubborn spirit, attached to Liberty than those to the Northward. Such were all the ancient commonwealths; such were our Gothick ancestors; such in our days were the Poles; and such will be all masters of slaves, who are not slaves themselves. In such a people the haughtiness of domination combines with the spirit of freedom, fortifies it, and renders it invincible.

Permit me, Sir, to add another circumstance in our Colonies, which contributes no mean part towards the growth and effect of this untractable spirit. I mean their education. In no country perhaps in the world is the law so general a study. The profession itself is numerous and powerful; and in most provinces it takes the lead. The greater number of the Deputies sent to

---

[2]   *The Colonists ... all*: Non-conformist, or dissenting, religions were persecuted most harshly during the seventeenth-century. Religious migration to America is satirised in Joseph Peart's *A Continuation of Hudibras*.

the Congress were Lawyers. But all who read, and most do read, endeavour to obtain some smattering in that science. I have been told by an eminent Bookseller, that in no branch of his business, after tracts of popular devotion, were so many books as those on the Law exported to the Plantations. The Colonists have now fallen into the way of printing them for their own use. I hear that they have sold nearly as many of Blackstone's Commentaries in America as in England.[3] General Gage[4] marks out this disposition very particularly in a letter on your table. He states, that all the people in his government are lawyers, or smatterers in law; and that in Boston they have been enabled, by successful chicane, wholly to evade many parts of one of your capital penal constitutions. The smartness of debate will say, that this knowledge ought to teach them more clearly the rights of legislature, their obligations to obedience, and the penalties of rebellion. All this is mighty well. But my[5] honourable and learned friend on the floor, who condescends to mark what I say for animadversion, will disdain that ground. He has heard as well as I, that when great honours and great emoluments do not win over this knowledge to the service of the state, it is a formidable adversary to government. If the spirit be not tamed and broken by these happy methods, it is stubborn and litigious. *Abeunt studia in mores.*[6] This study renders men acute, inquisitive, dexterous, prompt in attack, ready in defence, full of resources. In other countries, the people, more simple and of a less mercurial cast, judge of an ill principle in government only by an actual grievance; here they anticipate the evil, and judge of the pressure of the grievance by the badness of the principle. They augur misgovernment at a distance; and snuff the approach of tyranny in every tainted breeze.

The last cause of this disobedient spirit in the Colonies is hardly less powerful than the rest, as it is not merely moral, but laid deep in the natural constitution of things. Three thousand miles of ocean lie between you and them. No contrivance can prevent the effect of this distance, in weakening Government. Seas roll, and months pass, between the order and the execution; and the want of a speedy explanation of a single point is enough to defeat an whole system. You have, indeed, winged ministers of vengeance,[7] who carry your bolts in their pounces to the remotest verge of the sea.

---

3   *Blackstone's Commentaries*: Sir William Blackstone (1723–80). His *Commentaries on the Laws of England* (1765–69) was the most influential and authoritative treatise on the law.

4   *Gage*: General Thomas Gage (1721–87), Commander-in-Chief of British forces in America from 1763–72. In 1774 he was Governor of Massachusetts. In April (the month after this speech) he sent forces against colonists and the battle of Lexington effectively started the War of American Independence.

5   'The Attorney General' [Burke's note].

6   *Abeunt studia in mores*: 'Passions become characteristics'. Ovid (43BC–17AD), *Heriodes*, XV.

7   *ministers of vengeance*: 'But see the angry victor hath recalled/His ministers of vengeance and pursuit'. John Milton, *Paradise Lost* (1667), 1: lines 169–70. Satan, thrown down in Hell, is referring to God's army of angels.

But there a power steps in, that limits the arrogance of raging passions and furious elements, and says, 'So far shalt thou go, and no farther.' Who are you, that should fret and rage, and bite the chains of Nature?—Nothing worse happens to you, than does to all Nations, who have extensive Empire; and it happens in all the forms into which Empire can be thrown. In large bodies, the circulation of power must be less vigorous at the extremities. Nature has said it. The Turk cannot govern Ægypt, and Arabia, and Curdistan, as he governs Thrace; nor has he the same dominion in Crimea and Algiers, which he has at Brusa and Smyrna. Despotism itself is obliged to truck and huckster. The Sultan gets such obedience as he can. He governs with a loose rein, that he may govern at all; and the whole of the force and vigour of his authority in his centre, is derived from a prudent relaxation in all his borders. Spain, in her provinces, is, perhaps, not so well obeyed, as you are in yours. She complies, too; she submits; she watches times. This is the immutable condition; the eternal Law, of extensive and detached Empire.

[...]

In effect, we suffer as much at home, by this loosening of all ties, and this concussion of all established opinions, as we do abroad. For, in order to prove, that the Americans have no right to their Liberties, we are every day endeavouring to subvert the maxims, which preserve the whole Spirit of our own. To prove that the Americans ought not to be free, we are obliged to depreciate the value of Freedom itself; and we never seem to gain a paltry advantage over them in debate, without attacking some of those principles, or deriding some of those feelings, for which our ancestors have shed their blood.

[...]

But to clear up my ideas on this subject—a revenue from America transmitted hither—do not delude yourselves—you can never receive it— No, not a shilling. We have experience that from remote countries it is not to be expected. If, when you attempted to extract revenue from Bengal, you were obliged to return in loan what you had taken in imposition; what can you expect from North America? for certainly, if ever there was a country qualified to produce wealth, it is India; or an institution fit for the transmission, it is the East-India company. America has none of these aptitudes. If America gives you taxable objects, on which you lay your duties here, and gives you, at the same time, a surplus by a foreign sale of her commodities to pay the duties on these objects which you tax at home, she has performed her part to the British revenue. But with regard to her own internal establishments; she may, I doubt not she will, contribute in moderation. I say in moderation; for she ought not to be permitted to exhaust herself. She ought to be reserved to a war; the weight of which, with the enemies that we are most likely to have, must be considerable in her quarter of the globe.[8] There she may serve you, and serve you essentially.

For that service, for all service, whether of revenue, trade, or empire, my trust is in her interest in the British constitution. My hold of the Colonies is in the close affection which grows from common names, from kindred blood, from similar privileges, and equal protection. These are ties, which, though light as air, are as strong as links of iron. Let the Colonies always keep the idea of their civil rights associated with your Government; — they will cling and grapple to you; and no force under heaven will be of power to tear them from their allegiance. But let it be once understood, that your Government may be one thing, and their Privileges another; that these two things may exist without any mutual relation; the cement is gone; the cohesion is loosened; and every thing hastens to decay and dissolution. As long as you have the wisdom to keep the sovereign authority of this country as the sanctuary of liberty, the sacred temple consecrated to our common faith, wherever the chosen race and sons of England worship freedom, they will turn their faces towards you. The more they multiply, the more friends you will have; the more ardently they love liberty, the more perfect will be their obedience. Slavery they can have any where. It is a weed that grows in every soil. They may have it from Spain, they may have it from Prussia. But until you become lost to all feeling of your true interest and your natural dignity, freedom they can have from none but you. This is the commodity of price, of which you have the monopoly. This is the true act of navigation,[9] which binds to you the commerce of the Colonies, and through them secures to you the wealth of the world. Deny them this participation of freedom, and you break that sole bond, which originally made, and must still preserve, the unity of the Empire. Do not entertain so weak an imagination, as that your registers and your bonds, your affidavits and your sufferances, your cockets and your clearances,[10] are what form the great securities of your commerce. Do not dream that your letters of office, and your instructions, and your suspending clauses, are the things that hold together the great contexture of this mysterious whole. These things do not make your government. Dead instruments, passive tools as they are, it is the spirit of the English communion that gives all their life and efficacy to them. It is the spirit of the English constitution, which, infused through the mighty mass, pervades, feeds, unites, invigorates, vivifies, every part of the Empire, even down to the minutest member.

---

[8]   *enemies ... globe*: France and Spain.

[9]   *Act of Navigation*: statutes passed in 1650 and 1651 (and re-enacted in 1660) ensured that all colonial trade was to be shipped via England or another English colony, and only by English shipping, and that the English colonies could only buy English goods.

[10] *affidavit ... clearances*: 'affidavits' are a type of bond; 'sufferances' are licences to unload a cargo at a specific port; a 'cocket' is a certificate of payment of a duty; 'clearance' is the clearing of a cheque.

Is it not the same virtue which does everything for us here in England? Do you imagine then, that it is the land-tax act which raises your revenue? that it is the annual vote in the committee of supply, which gives you your army? or that it is the Mutiny Bill which inspires it with bravery and discipline? No! surely no! It is the love of the people; it is their attachment to their government from the sense of the deep stake they have in such a glorious institution, which gives you your army and your navy, and infuses into both that liberal obedience, without which your army would be a base rabble, and your navy nothing but rotten timber.

All this, I know well enough, will sound wild and chimerical to the profane herd of those vulgar and mechanical politicians, who have no place among us; a sort of people who think that nothing exists but what is gross and material; and who therefore, far from being qualified to be directors of the great movement of Empire, are not fit to turn a wheel in the machine. But to men truly initiated and rightly taught, these ruling and master principles, which, in the opinion of such men as I have mentioned, have no substantial existence, are in truth every thing, and all in all. Magnanimity in politicks is not seldom the truest wisdom; and a great Empire and little minds go ill together. If we are conscious of our situation, and glow with zeal to fill our place as becomes our station and ourselves, we ought to auspicate all our public proceedings on America, with the old warning of the church, *Sursum corda!*[11] We ought to elevate our minds to the greatness of that trust to which the order of Providence has called us. By adverting to the dignity of this high calling, our ancestors have turned a savage wilderness into a glorious Empire; and have made the most extensive, and the only honourable conquests; not by destroying, but by promoting the wealth, the number, the happiness, of the human race. Let us get an American revenue as we have got an American empire. English privileges have made it all that it is; English privileges alone will make it all it can be.

Adam Smith, from *An Inquiry into the Nature and Causes of the Wealth of Nations* (1776)

Adam Smith (1723–90) was a native of Scotland. His major works, the *Theory of Moral Sentiments* (1759) and *An Inquiry into the Nature and Causes of the Wealth of*

---

11   *Sursum corda!*: 'Lift up your hearts!'

Nations (1776), set him at the centre of the Scottish Enlightenment. *Wealth of Nations* is generally thought to have originated the study of economics as a separate scientific field of inquiry: its argument against monopolies has led to its reputation as the catalyst for economic free trade. Smith's discussion of the economics of colonialism and imperial governance did not, however, form part of his original thinking. On the eve of its completion, in 1773, Smith went to London and was caught up in the furore over the looming crisis with America. In two sections added subsequently, Smith dismantled what he saw as a dangerous illusion propagated by mercantile monopolists, who had argued that America was a wellspring of vast wealth for the mother country and rightly supported by the British monopoly of American trade. Smith's attack against these arguments led to the conclusion, in his most famous phrase, that the empire was a project only 'fit for a nation that is governed by shop-keepers'.[1] He advocated either a Union with America in which they had rights equal to Britain to trade and tax, or that all the territories of the empire should be subject to taxation. Both ideas he rejected as unlikely or at least highly speculative. The extract below is his trenchant conclusion to the whole work.[2]

The last war, which was undertaken altogether on account of the colonies, cost Great Britain, it has already been observed, upwards of ninety millions. The Spanish war of 1739 was principally undertaken on their account; in which, and in the French war that was the consequence of it, Great Britain spent upwards of forty millions, a great part of which ought justly to be charged to the colonies. In those two wars the colonies cost Great Britain much more than double the sum which the national debt amounted to before the commencement of the first of them. Had it not been for those wars that debt might, and probably would by this time have been compleatly paid; and had it not been for the colonies, the former of those wars might not, and the latter certainly would not have been undertaken. It was because the colonies were supposed to be provinces of the British empire, that this expence was laid out upon them. But countries, which contribute neither revenue nor military force towards the support of the empire, cannot be considered as provinces. They may perhaps be considered as appendages, as a sort of splendid and showy equipage of the empire. But if the empire can no longer support the expence of keeping up this equipage, it ought certainly to lay it down; and if it cannot raise its revenue in proportion to its expence, it ought, at least, to accommodate its expence to its revenue. If the colonies, notwithstanding their refusal to submit British taxes, are still to be considered as provinces of the British empire, their defence in some future war may cost Great Britain as great an expence as it ever has done in any former war. The rulers of Great Britain have for more than a century past amused the people with the imagination that they possessed a great empire on the west side of the Atlantic. This empire,

---

[1]   'Of Colonies', vol. 2, p. 221.
[2]   Text from 'Of public Debts', vol. 2, pp. 586–7.

however, has hitherto existed imagination only. It has hitherto been, not an empire, but the project of the empire; not a gold mine, but the project of a gold mine; a project which has cost, which continues to cost, and which if pursued in the same way it has been hitherto, is likely to cost immense expence, without being likely to bring any profit; for the effects of the monopoly of the colony trade, it has been shewn, are, to the great body of the people, mere loss instead of profit. It is surely now time that our rulers should either realize this golden dream, in which they have been indulging themselves, perhaps, as well as the people; or, that they should awake from it themselves, and endeavour to awaken the people. If the project cannot be compleated, it ought to be given up. If any of the provinces of the British empire cannot be made to contribute towards the support of the whole empire, it is surely time that Great Britain should free herself from the expence of defending those provinces in time of war, and of supporting any part of their civil or military establishments in time of peace, and endeavour to accommodate her future views and designs to the real mediocrity of her circumstances.

Janet Schaw, from *Journal of a Lady of Quality: Being the Narrative of a Journey from Scotland to the West Indies, North Carolina, and Portugal, in the years 1774 to 1776*

Janet Schaw (c.1737–c.1801) was from Edinburgh, and this journey through Britain's Atlantic colonies was taken while accompanying her brother, Alexander, who was to take up a customs post at St. Christopher in the West Indies. She sailed from the Firth of Forth on October 1774, landing in Antigua in December, and sailed on to America in February 1775. She left America in November and arrived in Lisbon in December 1775. The Scots were deeply involved in colonial settlement and governance and the military overseas in the eighteenth century, and her journey took her through a network of Scottish connections within the British empire: her other brother, Robert, owned the plantation in North Carolina 'Schawfield', which he bought in 1772–73.

The first two extracts concern her visit to the West Indian island of Antigua and the Martin plantation, and the last three extracts depict her visit to North Carolina, on mainland America. While Schaw may be accused of being blind to the nature of slavery in her paean to Colonel Martin's benevolent paternalism, her praise of the white inhabitants of Antigua does not stop her from voicing the common criticism of the sexual promiscuity of the Creole men, or from noting the obsessive care the women take to preserve their white pallor. In contrast to the relatively cultivated men of Antigua, when it comes to the colonials of North Carolina the men seem as uncivilised as the savage and poorly cultivated land around them. Written in the early days of the War of American Independence, and written from a Loyalist stance, the comparison of these two British colonies offer a timely contrast: one seemingly in blooming prosperity, the other in a disastrous state of health.[1]

[Antigua]

I shall say nothing of many other places, as I long to bring you acquainted with the most delightful character I have ever yet met with, that of Coll. Martin, the loved and revered father of Antigua, to whom it owes a thousand advantages, and whose age is yet daily employed to render it more improved and happy.[2] This is one of the oldest families on the Island, has for many generations enjoyed great power and riches, of which they have made the best use, living on their Estates, which are cultivated to the height by a large troop of healthy Negroes, who cheerfully perform the labour imposed on them by a kind and beneficent Master, not a harsh and unreasonable Tyrant. Well fed, well supported, they appear the subjects of a good prince, not the slaves of a planter. The effect of this kindness is a daily increase of riches by the slaves born to him on his own plantation. He told me he had not bought in a slave for upwards of twenty years, and that he had the morning of our arrival got the return of the state of his plantations, on which there were no less than fifty two wenches who were pregnant. These slaves, born on the spot and used to the Climate, are by far the most valuable, and seldom take these disorders, by which such numbers are lost that many hundreds are forced yearly to be brought into the Island.[3]

---

[1] Text from *Journal of a Lady of Quality*, eds, Evangeline Walker Andrews and Charles McLean Andrews (Yale University Press,1921), pp. 103–6, 111–15, 141, 153–62, 189–93.

[2] *Coll. Martin*: Colonel Samuel Martin (*c*.1690–1776), owner of the 'Green Castle' plantation. He was author of *An Essay on Plantership* (Antigua, 1750).

[3] This picture of slavery should be tempered by Schaw's later comment on the use of the whip: 'I will do the Creoles the justice to say, they would be as averse to it as we are, could it be avoided, which has often been tried to no purpose. When one comes to be better acquainted with the nature of the Negroes, the horrour of it must wear off. It is the suffering of the human mind that constitutes the greatest misery of punishment, but with them it is merely corporeal. As to the brutes it inflicts no wound on their mind, whose Natures seem made to bear it, and whose sufferings are not attended with shame or pain beyond the present moment' (p. 127).

On our arrival we found the venerable man seated in his piazza to receive us; he held out his hands to us, having lost the power of his legs, and embracing us with the embraces of a fond father, 'You are welcome,' said he, 'to little Antigua, and most heartily welcome to me. My habitation has not looked so gay this long time.' Then turning to Mr. Halliday[4] who had brought us his invitation, 'How shall I thank you, my good friend,' said he, 'for procuring me this happiness, in persuading these ladies to come to an old man. Old, did I say? I retract the word: Eighty five that can be sensible of beauty, is as young as twenty five that can be no more.' There was gallantry for you. We now had fruit, sangarie[5] and beverage brought us, not by slaves; it is a maxim of his that no slave can render that acceptable Service he wishes from those immediately about himself; and for that reason has made them free, and the alacrity with which they serve him, and the love they bear him, shew he is not wrong. His table was well served in every thing; good order and cheerfulness reigned in his house. You would have thought the servants were inspired with an instinctive knowledge of your wishes, for you had scarcely occasion to ask them. His conversation was pleasant, entertaining and instructive, his manners not merely polite but amiable in a high degree. It was impossible not to love him. I never resisted it; but gave him my heart without hesitation, for which I hope you will not blame me, nor was Fanny less taken than myself with this charming old man.

He told us that in compliance with the wishes of his children, he had resided in England for several years, 'but tho' they kept me in a greenhouse,' said he, 'and took every method to defend me from the cold, I was so absolute an exotick, that all could not do, and I found myself daily giving way, amidst all their tenderness and care; and had I stayed much longer,' continued he, smiling, 'I had actually by this time become an old man. I have had, Madam,' said he turning to me, 'twenty three children, and tho' but a small number remain, they are such as may raise the pride of any father. One of my sons you will know if you go to Carolina, he is governor there; another, my eldest, you know by character at least.'[6] This I did and much admired that character. He wishes to have his dear little Antigua independent; he regrets the many Articles she is forced to trust to foreign aid, and the patriot is even now setting an example, and by turning many

---

4   *Mr. Halliday*: Mr. John Halliday was another Scottish connection: though born on Antigua, he was from an old Scottish family. He owned seven plantations around the West-Indies, and was the Customs Collector for the islands from 1759–77.

5   *Sangarie*: or sangaree, 'a cold drink of diluted and spiced wine' OED.

6   *one of my sons … at least*: the former is Josiah Martin (1737–86), Governor of North Carolina 1771–75, with British forces, 1775–81. The eldest son, whose character Schaw 'admired', is Samuel Martin, half-brother to Josiah, and famous for his duel with John Wilkes (1727–97), a radical MP and a supporter of American rights.

of the plantations into grass, he allows them to rest and recover the strength they have lost, by too many crops of sugar, and by this means is able to rear cattle which he has done with great success. I never saw finer cows, nor more thriving calves, than I saw feeding in his lawns, and his wagons are already drawn by oxen of his own rearing.

[…]

As I am now about to leave them, you, no doubt, will expect me, to give my opinion as fully on the Inhabitants, as I have done on their Island and manners, but I am afraid you will suspect me of partiality, and were I to speak of Individuals, perhaps you might have reason, but as to the characters in general I can promise to write without prejudice, and if I only tell truth, they have nothing to fear from my pen. I think the men the most agreeable creatures I ever met with, frank, open, generous, and I dare say brave; even in advanced life they retain the Vivacity and Spirit of Youth; they are in general handsome, and all of them have that sort of air, that will ever attend a man of fashion. Their address is at once soft and manly; they have a kind of gallantry in their manner, which exceeds mere politeness, and in some countries, we know, would be easily mistaken for something more interesting than civility, yet you must not suppose this the politeness of French manners, merely words of course. No, what they say, they really mean; their whole intention is to make you happy, and this they endeavour to do without any other view or motive than what they are prompted to by the natural goodness of their own natures. In short, my friend, the woman that *brings a heart here* will have little sensibility if she carry it away.

I hear you ask me, if there is no alloy to this fine character, no reverse to this beautiful picture. Alas! my friend, tho' children of the Sun, they are mortals, and as such must have their share of failings, the most conspicuous of which is, the indulgence they give themselves in their licentious and even unnatural amours, which appears too plainly from the crouds of Mullatoes, which you meet in the streets, houses and indeed every where; a crime that seems to have gained sanction from custom, tho' attended with the greatest inconveniences not only to Individuals, but to the publick in general. The young black wenches lay themselves out for white lovers, in which they are but too successful. This prevents their marrying with their natural mates, and hence a spurious and degenerate breed, neither so fit for the field, nor indeed any work, as the true bred Negro. Besides these wenches become licentious and insolent past all bearing, and as even a mulattoe child interrupts their pleasures and is troublesome, they have certain herbs and medicines, that free them from such an incumbrance, but which seldom fails to cut short their own lives, as well as that of their offspring. By this many of them perish every year. I would have gladly drawn a veil over this part of a character, which in everything else is most estimable.

As to the women, they are in general the most amiable creatures in the world, and either I have been remarkably fortunate in my acquaintance, or they are more than commonly sensible, even those who have never been off the Island are amazingly intelligent and able to converse with you on any subject. They make excellent wives, fond attentive mothers and the best house wives I have ever met with. Those of the first fortune and fashion keep their own keys and look after every thing within doors; the domestick Economy is entirely left to them; as the husband finds enough to do abroad. A fine house, an elegant table, handsome carriage, and a croud of mullatoe servants are what they all seem very fond of. The sun appears to affect the sexes very differently. While the men are gay, luxurious and amorous, the women are modest, genteel, reserved and temperate. This last virtue they have indeed in the extreme; they drink nothing stronger in general than Sherbet,[7] and never eat above one or two things at table, and these the lightest and plainest. The truth is, I can observe no indulgence they allow themselves in, not so much as in scandal, and if I stay long in this country, I will lose the very idea of that innocent amusement; for since I resided amongst them, I have never heard one woman say a wrong thing of another. This is so unnatural, that I suppose you will (good naturedly) call it cunning; but if it is so, it is the most commendable cunning I ever met with, as nothing can give them a better appearance in the eyes of a stranger.

As we became better acquainted, their reserve wore off, and I now find them most agreeable companions. Jealousy is a passion with which they are entirely unacquainted, and a jealous wife would be here a most ridiculous character indeed. Let me conclude this by assuring you, that I never admired my own sex more than in these amiable Creoles.[8] Their Sentiments are just and virtuous; in religion they are serious without ostentation, and perform every duty with pleasure from no other motive but the consciousness of doing right. In their persons they are very genteel, rather too thin till past thirty, after that they grow plump and look much the better for it. Their features are in general high and very regular, they have charming eyes, fine teeth, and the greatest quantity of hair I ever saw, which they dress with taste, and wear a great deal of powder. In short, they want only colour to be termed beautiful, but the sun who bestows such rich taints on every other flower, gives none to his lovely daughters; the tincture of whose skin is as pure as the lily, and as pale. Yet this I am convinced is owing to the way in which they live, entirely excluded from proper air and exercise. From childhood they never suffer the sun to have a peep at them, and to prevent him are covered with masks and bonnets, that absolutely makes them look as if they were stewed. Fanny who just now is blooming as a new blown rose,

---

7   *Sherbet*: 'a cooling drink made of sweetened and diluted fruit juice' OED.
8   *Creole*: anyone born in the West-Indies, but here Schaw means the white planters born on the islands.

was prevailed on to wear a mask, while we were on our Tour, which in a week changed her colour, and if she had persevered I am sure a few months would have made her as pale as any of them.[9] As to your humble Servant, I have always set my face to the weather; wherever I have been, I hope you have no quarrel at brown beauty.

[…]

[North Carolina]

But tho' I may say of this place what I formerly did of the West India Islands, that nature holds out to them every thing that can contribute to conveniency, or tempt to luxury, yet the inhabitants[10] resist both, and if they can raise as much corn and pork, as to subsist them in the most slovenly manner, they ask no more; and as a very small proportion of their time serves for that purpose, the rest is spent in sauntering thro' the woods with a gun or sitting under a rustick shade, drinking New England rum made into grog, the most shocking liquor you can imagine. By this manner of living, their blood is spoil'd and rendered thin beyond all proportion, so that it is constantly on the fret like bad small beer, and hence the constant slow fevers that wear down their constitutions, relax their nerves and infeeble the whole frame. Their appearance is in every respect the reverse of that which gives the idea of strength and vigor, and for which the British peasantry are so remarkable. They are tall and lean, with short waists and long limbs, sallow complexions and languid eyes, when not inflamed by spirits. Their feet are flat, their joints loose and their walk uneven. These I speak of are only the peasantry of this country, as hitherto I have seen nothing else, but I make no doubt when I come to see the better sort, they will be far from this description. For tho' there is a most disgusting equality, yet I hope to find an American Gentleman a very different creature from an American clown. Heaven forefend else.

[…]

[Schawfield]

After I put my last packet into a safe hand, I left Wilmingtown and returned to Schawfield by water, which is a most delightful method of travelling thro' this Noble country, which indeed owes more favours to its God and

---

[9]   *pale*: this attention to skin complexion is underlined later when Schaw meets Lady Isabella Hamilton, who 'had standing by her a little Mulatto girl not above five years old, whom she retains as a pet. This brown beauty was dressed out like an infant sultana, and is a fine contrast to the delicate complexion of her lady' (p. 124).

[10]   *inhabitants*: that is, of North Carolina.

king than perhaps any other in the known world and is equally ungrateful to both, to the God who created and bestowed them and to the king whose indulgent kindness has done every thing to render them of the greatest utility to the owners. Well may the following text from the prophets be applied to this people, and with very little alteration may be addressed to them. 'My beloved has a vineyard in a very pleasant land, he Dig'd it, he planted it, he hedged it round, and built a winepress in the midst thereof, but when he looked for grapes, they brought forth wild grapes. Judge I pray you between me and my vineyard, what could I do more for it than I have done, yet when I looked for grapes, behold it brought forth only wild grapes. Go to, I will tell you what I will do to my vineyard, I will take away the fence thereof, I will break down the wine press in the midst thereof, and I will leave it as I found it a habitation to wolves and bears.'[11] Such is the fate it deserves, but both its God and its king are merciful. May they be inspired to seek it before it be too late.

Nothing can be finer than the banks of this river; a thousand beauties both of the flowery and sylvan tribe hang over it and are reflected from it with additional lustre. But they spend their beauties on the desert air, and the pines that wave behind the shore with a solemn gravity seem to lament that they too exist to no purpose, tho' capable of being rendered both useful and agreeable. For those noble trees that might adorn the palaces of kings are left to the stroke of the thunder, or to the annihilating hand of time, and against whom the hard Sentence (tho' innocent of the crime) may be pronounced, why cumber ye the ground? As that is all that can be said of them in their present state that they cover many hundred, nay thousand acres of the finest ground in the universe, and give shelter to every hurtful and obnoxious animal, tho' their site is a most convenient situation both for trading towns and plantations. This north west branch is said to be navigable for Ships of 400 tons burthen for above two hundred miles up, and the banks so constituted by nature that they seem formed for harbours, and what adds in a most particular manner to this convenience is, that quite across from one branch to the other, and indeed thro' the whole country are innumerable creeks that communicate with the main branches of the river and every tide receive a sufficient depth of water for boats of the largest size and even for small Vessels, so that every thing is water-borne at a small charge and with great safety and ease.

But these uncommon advantages are almost entirely neglected. In the course of sixteen miles which is the distance between these places and the town, there is but one plantation, and the condition it is in shows, if not the poverty, at least the indolence of its owner. My brother indeed is in some degree an exception to this reflection. Indolent he is not; his industry is visible in every thing round him, yet he also is culpable in adhering to the

---

[11]   *My beloved … bears*: a paraphrase of Isaiah, ch. 5 (especially verses 1–5).

prejudices of this part of the world, and in using only the American methods of cultivating his plantation. Had he followed the style of an East Lothian farmer, with the same attention and care, it would now have been an Estate worth double what it is. Yet he has done more in the time he has had it than any of his Neighbours, and even in their slow way, his industry has brought it to a wonderful length. He left Britain while he was a boy, and was many years in trade before he turned planter, and had lost the remembrance of what he had indeed little opportunity of studying, I mean farming. His brother easily convinced him of the superiority of our manner of carrying on our agriculture, but Mrs Schaw was shocked at the mention of our manuring the ground, and declared she never would eat corn that grew thro' dirt. Indeed she is so rooted an American, that she detests every thing that is European, yet she is a most excellent wife and a fond mother. Her dairy and her garden show her industry, tho' even there she is an American. However he has no cause to complain. Her person is agreeable, and if she would pay it a little more attention, it would be lovely. She is connected with the best people in the country, and, I hope, will have interest enough to prevent her husband being ruined for not joining in a cause he so much disapproves.

I have just mentioned a garden, and will tell you, that this at Schawfield is the only thing deserving the name I have seen in this country, and laid out with some taste. I could not help smiling however at the appearance of a soil, that seemed to me no better than dead sand, proposed for a garden. But a few weeks have convinced me that I judged very falsely, for the quickness of the vegetation is absolutely astonishing. Nature to whose care every thing is left does a vast deal; but I remember to have read, tho' I forget where, that Adam when he was turned out of paradise was allowed to carry seeds with him of those fruits he had been suffered to eat of when there, but found on trial that the curse had extended even to them; for they were harsh and very unpalatable, far different from what he had eat there in his happy state. Our poor father,[12] who from his infancy had been used to live well, like those of his descendents, was the more sensible of the change, and he wept bitterly before his beneficent Creator, who once more had pity on him, and the compassionate Angel again descended to give him comfort and relief. 'Adam,' began the heavenly messenger, 'the sentence is passed, it is irrevocable; the ground has been cursed for your sake, and thorns and briers it must bring forth, and you must eat your bread with the sweat of your brow, yet the curse does not extend to your labours, and it yet depends on your own choice to live in plenty or in penury. Patience and industry will get the better of every difficulty, and the ground will bear thistles only while your indolence permits it. The fruits also will be harsh while you

---

12   *father*: in other words, Adam. What follows is a commentary on Genesis, 3: 17–19. See also Locke.

allow them to remain in a state of uncultivated nature; because man is allowed no enjoyment without labour; and the hand of industry improves even the choicest gifts of heaven.' Adam bowed in grateful acknowledgement, and his heavenly instructor led him forth to the field, and soon taught him that God had given him power over the inanimate as well as the animate part of the creation, and that not only every beast and every bird was under his command, but that he had power over the whole vegetable world; and he soon proved that the hand of industry could make the rose bloom, where nature had only planted the thistle, and saw the fig-tree blossom, where lately the wild bramble was all its boast. He taught him that not only the harsh sourness of the crab was corrected, but the taste and flavour of the peach improven; by the art of in-grafting and budding the pear became more luscious, and even the nectarine juice was poor and insipid without this assistance. Adam had no prejudices to combat, he gave the credit due to his heavenly instructor, and soon saw a new Eden flourish in the desert from his labours, and eat fruit little inferior to those he had left, rendered indeed even superior to his taste by being the reward of his honest Industry.

[...]

[Wilmingtown]

Good heavens! What a scene this town is: Surely you folks at home have adopted the old maxim of King Charles: 'Make friends of your foes, leave friends to shift for themselves.'

We came down in the morning in time for the review, which the heat made as terrible to the spectators as to the soldiers, or what you please to call them. They had certainly fainted under it, had not the constant draughts of grog supported them. Their exercise was that of bush-fighting, but it appeared so confused and so perfectly different from anything I ever saw, I cannot say whether they performed it well or not; but this I know that they were heated with rum till capable of committing the most shocking outrages. We stood in the balcony of Doctor Cobham's house and they were reviewed on a field mostly covered with what are called here scrubby oaks, which are only a little better than brushwood. They at last however assembled on the plain field, and I must really laugh while I recollect their figures: 2000 men in their shirts and trousers, preceded by a very ill beat-drum and a fiddler, who was also in his shirt with a long sword and a cue at his hair, who played with all his might. They made indeed a most unmartial appearance. But the worst figure there can shoot from behind a bush and kill even a General Wolfe.[13]

---

[13]   *Wolfe*: General James Wolfe (1727–59), lauded for leading successful attacks against the French in North America during the Seven Years War (1756–63).

Before the review was over, I heard a cry of tar and feather. I was ready to faint at the idea of this dreadful operation. I would have gladly quitted the balcony, but was so much afraid the Victim was one of my friends, that I was not able to move; and he indeed proved to be one, tho' in a humble station. For it was Mr Neilson's poor English groom. You can hardly conceive what I felt when I saw him dragged forward, poor devil, frighted out of his wits. However at the request of some of the officers, who had been Neilson's friends, his punishment was changed into that of mounting on a table and begging pardon for having smiled at the regiment. He was then drummed and fiddled out of the town, with a strict prohibition of ever being seen in it again.

One might have expected, that tho' I had been imprudent all my life, the present occasion might have inspired me with some degree of caution, and yet I can tell you I had almost incurred the poor groom's fate from my own folly. Several of the officers came up to dine, amongst others Coll: Howe,[14] who with less ceremony than might have been expected from his general politeness stept into an apartment adjoining the hall, and took up a book I had been reading, which he brought open in his hand into the company. I was piqued at his freedom, and reproved him with a half compliment to his general good breeding. He owned his fault and with much gallantry promised to submit to whatever punishment I would inflict. You shall only, said I, read aloud a few pages which I will point out, and I am sure you will do Shakespear justice. He bowed and took the book, but no sooner observed that I had turned up for him, that part of Henry the fourth, where Falstaff describes his company, than he coloured like Scarlet.[15] I saw he made the application instantly; however he read it thro', tho' not with the vivacity he generally speaks; however he recovered himself and coming close up to me, whispered, you will certainly get yourself tarred and feathered; shall I apply to be the executioner? I am going to seal this up. Adieu.

I closed my last packet at Doctor Cobham's after the review, and as I had hoped to hear of some method of getting it sent to you, stayed, tho' Miss Rutherfurd was obliged to go home. As soon as she was gone, I went into the town, the entry of which I found closed up by a detachment of the soldiers; but as the officer immediately made way for me, I took no further notice of it, but advanced to the middle of the street, where I found a number of the first people in town standing together, who (to use Milton's

---

14   *Howe*: Colonel Robert Howe. The dangerous relations between the branches of her family are clear here: her brother Robert has married a pro-American, and Howe is a relative of this sister-in-law.

15   *that part ... company*: William Shakespeare, *Henry the Fourth; Part One* (first performed 1597). Possibly the scene in which Sir John Falstaff, together with Prince Henry and other accomplices, has planned to rob rich pilgrims on the way to Canterbury. Falstaff, although a knight, is a boisterous carouser and reprobate, and in his speech curses his fellow thieves as rogues and villains (I.ii.1–30).

phrase) seemed much impassioned.[16] As most of them were my acquaintances, I stopped to speak to them, but they with one voice begged me for heaven's sake to get off the street, making me observe they were prisoners, adding that every avenue of the town was shut up, and that in all human probability some scene would be acted very unfit for me to witness. I could not take the friendly advice, for I became unable to move and absolutely petrified with horror.

Observing however an officer with whom I had just dined, I beckoned him to me. He came, but with no very agreeable look, and on my asking him what was the matter, he presented a paper he had folded in his hand. If you will persuade them to sign this they are at liberty, said he, but till then must remain under this guard, as they must suffer the penalties they have justly incurred. 'And we will suffer every thing,' replied one of them, 'before we abjure our king, our country and our principles.' 'This, Ladies," said he turning to me, who was now joined by several Ladies, "is what they call their Test,[17] but by what authority this Gentleman forces it on us, we are yet to learn.' 'There is my Authority,' pointing to the Soldiers with the most insolent air, 'dispute it, if you can.' Oh Britannia, what are you doing, while your true obedient sons are thus insulted by their unlawful brethren; are they also forgot by their natural parents?

We, the Ladies, adjourned to the house of a Lady, who lived in his street, and whose husband was indeed at home, but secretly shut up with some ambassadors from the back settlements on their way to the Governor[18] to offer their service, provided he could let them have arms and ammunition, but above all such commissions as might empower them to raise men by proper authority. This I was presently told tho' in the midst of enemies, but the Loyal party are all as one family. Various reasons induced me to stay all Night in the house I was then at, tho' it could afford me no resting place. I wished to know the fate of the poor men who were in such present jeopardy, and besides hoped that I should get word to my brother, or send your packet by the Gentlemen who were going to the man-of-war. In the last I have succeeded, and they are so good as to promise to get it safely there to my brother or the Governor who would not fail to send it by first opportunity to Britain. Indeed it is very dangerous to keep letters by me, for whatever noise general warrants made in the mouths of your sons of faction at home, their friends and fellow rebels use it with less ceremony that ever it was practised in Britain, at any period.

Rebels, this is the first time I have ventured that word, more than in thought.

---

[16]   *impassioned*: John Milton: 'The tempter all impassioned thus began'. Satan, as the serpent, is tempting Eve. *Paradise Lost* (1667), 9: line 678.

[17]   *test*: house-owners of the town are being asked to sign the Continental Association, in other words to declare their allegiance to the American revolutionary cause.

[18]   *the Governor*: Josiah Martin (son of Samuel Martin in Antigua).

Jemima Kindersley, from
Letters from the Island of Teneriffe, Brazil, the Cape of Good Hope, and the East Indies (1777)

Jemima Kindersley (c.1741–1809), was described by her son as from humble beginnings but self-educated. Around 1762, she married Nathaniel Kindersley, and in 1764 he took up the post as Captain in the East India Company's artillery. She and her one-year old son accompanied him to Bengal, where she stayed until ill health drove her back to England in 1769; he died in Calcutta later the same year. Her letters cover the journey from Tenerife, in the Canary Islands, in June 1764, through their three month stay in Brazil. The next letters are from the Cape of Good Hope, where they stayed from November 1764 to March 1765; they finally arrived in India in June 1765. She arrived at a significant point in British-Indian history: the years 1764–65 saw the British achieve an unrivalled control over the Bengal region.

Kindersley's letters from what was then the furthest outpost of the English in Bengal reproduce many of the dominant stereotypes of the Oriental – passive, indolent, effeminate, tyrannical, crafty – but she is hesitant to racialise difference, preferring to look to cultural differences such as the nature of government. To many in the eighteenth century, the treatment of women in other societies was a measure of civilisation, and Kindersley's disparaging views of *sati*, and of women's social and political exclusion are highly revealing. In 1781, her translation of Antione Léonard Thomas's *An Essay on the Character, the Manners, and the Understanding of Women* was published: her own appended essays offer a fascinating gloss on her discussion of women in India. Reflecting on the attention lavished upon Indian women, she concludes:

This extreme uxoriousness of the men, is what gives the women their natural power over them; and the knowledge of this power, has caused the men to establish laws and customs, to prevent in some measure its effects. These laws prevent the women from having any share in government, debar them from entering the mosques, from holding any lands, or enjoying any fortune independent from their husbands or parents, and, in short, give their husbands an absolute authority over them.[1]

---

[1] *An Essay on the Character, the Manners, and the Understanding of Women,* 'Essay 1', pp. 221–2.

Letter XVIII

Pondicherry, June 1765.

The ship we came in stopped at Nagapatam, a Dutch settlement on the coast of Coromandel;[2] this first specimen I had of India rather surprised than pleased me; I could not be reconciled to the vast numbers of black people who flocked to the shore on my first arrival; although I must acknowledge, that they were so far from being terrible in their appearance, that at first sight I believed them all to be women, from the effeminacy both of their persons and dress, the long white jemmers[3] and turbands appear so truly feminine to strangers. But the almost stark-nakedness of the lowest class is still more disgusting.

[...]

Letter XXXI

Allahabád, July 1767.

The *Hindoo* women we can know little of, as none but the very lowest are visible; they are almost in their infancy married by the care of their parents to some of their own cast. Every *Hindoo* is obliged to marry once: and polygamy is allowed, but there is generally one wife who is held as superior to the rest. The women have no education given them, they live retired in the *zanannahs*,[4] and amuse themselves with each other, smoking the *hooker*, bathing, and seeing their servants dance.

There is one well-known circumstance relative to these women, which is the most extraordinary and astonishing custom in the world; I mean their burning themselves with the dead bodies of their husbands: this custom is not at present so frequent as formerly, they cannot burn without permission from the Nabób of the province, and it is much to be hoped, that the English will in future prevent those Nabóbs we are in alliance with, from giving any such permission, but there has been within a very short time at least one instance.

I have endeavoured to find out what could give rise (if you'll permit me the expression) to such a barbarous exertion of virtue; but it is difficult to find out the cause of institutions of so ancient a date, therefore I do not depend on either of the following reasons, although they have each their advocates, who insist strongly that their opinion is the right one.

The first is, that it was so common for women to poison their husbands, that this institution was necessary to prevent it.

---

2   *Coromandel*: in the Carnatic region, on the south-east coast of India.
3   *jemmers*: pyjamas; loose trousers tied around at the waist and worn by both men and women.
4   *zanannahs*: or zenana; the harem, or womens' quarters.

The other is, that the *Brahmins*,[5] to promote their own interest, first persuaded the women that it was for the everlasting good of their families; that their souls would not enter into any grovelling insects, but animate a cow, or some such noble animal, and that their term of purgation would be shortened, and they would have the fewer transmigrations to go through, before they become pure enough to be received by the Almighty in Heaven.

Whatever may be the cause, it is however certain, that the *Brahmins* greatly encourage this practice, and that they receive great benefits from it; for the woman, when she is brought out to sacrifice herself, is dressed with all her jewels, which are often of considerable value; when the pile is prepared, and the woman has taken leave of her friends, she throws all her ornaments from her, which the priests take for themselves.

It is said, that the strict rule of *casts* is on this occasion sometimes dispensed with; and the daughter of a mother who has burned may be married to a man of higher rank.

I cannot myself subscribe to the first opinion of the cause of this custom, because they have many of them more than one wife, and only one is permitted the honour of burning.

No people in the world have stricter notions of the honour of their women, particularly those of the higher *casts*. If any one has an improper connexion, such a woman has not only lost her *cast*, but it is an indelible stain upon the honour of her family: and in case of an elopement, it has been known that the girl has been pursued and recovered by her parents, who have put her immediately to death, to expiate, by her blood, part of the disgrace she has brought upon them.

Nevertheless, the retirement of the women does not appear to be part of the religion, or caused by the jealousy of the men, so much as an idea of delicacy and dignity, in concealing themselves from vulgar eyes.

Letter XXXII

Allahabád, July 1767.

The tribe of *Hindoos* the English have most connexion with, and are obliged to put most confidence in, are in the third great division, called *Banians* who are a kind of merchants, or rather brokers in every kind of merchandize. Every European both civil and military, who has either trade, or troops under him to pay, is obliged to have one of them in his service, who is sort of steward: one of them is likewise necessary at the head of every family, to hire and pay the servants, and purchase whatever is wanting, for nothing can be bought or sold without them.

They are exceedingly indolent; crafty, and artful to an astonishing degree; and shew in all their dealings the most despicable low cunning, which

---

[5]   *Brahmins*: the Hindu priestly caste, at the top of the caste hierarchy.

makes them not to be depended upon for any thing: they have not only a secret premium out of whatever they pay to servants, trades-people &c. but keep them out of their money long after the master supposes they have been paid.

They are the most tedious people in the world, for besides the holidays, which they will on no account break through, they have a method of putting everything off till to-morrow: when it is found out, as it often is, that they have told an untruth, they have no shame for it, but immediately tell another and another; nothing can hurry them, nothing can discompose or put them out of countenance, nothing can make them angry; provided their gains are sure, the master may fret to find his fussiness go on slowly, may abuse them for want of honesty, may argue with them for their ingratitude, may convict them of falshood and double-dealing, it signifies nothing; the same mild and placid countenance remains, without the least symptom of fear, anger, or shame.

Those who are concerned with us usually speak pretty tolerable English; they are many of them worth large sums of money, and frequently lend a great deal to their masters, mostly at the interest of nine or ten per cent.

By being in the service of an English gentleman, particularly if he has any considerable rank or employment in the company's service, they have great advantages, not only from all his concerns, out of which they have a profit, but it enables them to carry on their own with the greater security; besides their wages, which, according to their master's situation and their own importance, is from a hundred to ten *rupees* a month, they are many of them of consequence amongst their own people, keep a palenqueen,[6] horses, and a number of servants.

Those who act in that capacity to a Governor or Commander in Chief, pretend to a superior rank, and take the title of *Duan* instead of *Banian*.

Letter XXXIII

Allahabád, July 1767.

The temples of the *Hindoos* are called *pagodas*, they are generally square high buildings of brick or stone, but with very little taste. In the Decan and Carnatic are[7] many of these *pagodas*; but in Bengal and up the Ganges very few, except in the province of Benaras.[8] I must observe in favour of the *Hindoos*, that, in spite of the absurdity and unmeaningness of most of their ceremonies and customs, their strict observation of them does them honor.

---

6   *palenqueen*: palanquin, a covered chair carried by two or four men.
7   *Decan … Carnatic*: southern India.
8   *Bengal … Benaras*: Bengal, a large region which formed part of East India, is now part of modern Bangladesh; Benaras, or Benares, is on the river Ganges to the west of Bengal.

To sum up their general character in few words, they are gentle, patient, temperate, regular in their lives, charitable, and strict observers of their religious ceremonies. They are superstitious, effeminate, avaritious, and crafty; deceitful and dishonest in their dealings, void of every principle of honor, generosity, or gratitude. Gain is the predominant principle; and as a part of their gains bestowed in gifts to their priests, or charities to the poor, will procure their pardon, they can cheat without fearing the anger of their gods.

But for the *Brahmins*, to whom alone all their learning is confined, it is a circumstance not much to their credit; that while all other nations, those in Europe particularly, have been making constant improvements and new discoveries in science, they have contented themselves with that which has been handed down to them from their forefathers; and still less, that they have made so ill a use of their learning; and, instead of informing those whose *casts* forbid them to enquire into the laws and religion, in such plain and simple truths as might tend to virtue and happiness, they have encumbered them with forms, and filled their heads with stories, which can tend to no other purpose but to raise their own importance.

[...]

Letter XXXVIII

Allahabád, August 1767.

... The English put the prince in possession of this province,[9] placed him on the throne, and proclaimed him Emperor by the title of *Shaw Allum;*[10] the revenues of his province, and a certain annual sum paid to him by the company out of the revenues of Bengal, amount to be about thirty *lacks* of *rupees* yearly, which is equal to 370,000£. this is the whole he has to support the rank of an Emperor, in a country where money is not of one quarter the value it is in Europe.

We are now in alliance with both this prince, and *Sujah Dowlah*, who has the title of *Vizier*; but the apprehension the king is in of his *Vizier* (who is at this time the most formidable Nabób in Hindostán, active, enterprising, deceitful, and unprincipled, bound by no laws divine or human, which can interfere with his interest; supple to the greatest meanness to those he fears; a tyrant in power; in short, a true oriental *Great Man*) makes the King

---

9   *province*: the city Allahabad and the province surrounding it. After the defeat of Sujah Dowlah, the nabob of Oudh, in 1765 Robert Clive took up the post of governor-general of Bengal and installed Shah Alam II as emperor. In turn, Alam granted to the East India Company the *diwani* – the post of Treasurer – and so the right to raise taxes, for the provinces of Bengal, Bihar and Orissa, in return for an annual tribute.

10   'His father being now dead'. [Kindersley's note].

desirous of having an army of English always near him; he has given up his fort and palace of Allahábád to accommodate them with quarters, and pays the extra allowance called *batta*, which is given to the army when out of the provinces.[11] He resides now with his court and *zanannah*, and several children, in a few bungalows, a short distance from the fort on the banks of the Jumna, a dwelling very unworthy of the imperial dignity; where he keeps up a shabby fort of grandeur and parade, and has a few seapoys[12] in his own pay, just sufficient to attend him when he appears abroad, not at most a battalion; they are cloathed after the English custom, but are ill-disciplined, and as ill-paid.

This Mogul is one of the darkest of the Musselmen, of a grave deportment bordering upon sadness: of an indolent and inactive life; supposed to be the consequence of repeated disappointments, which have at last left him, perhaps, without even the hope of ever recovering the possession of his empire, or even being seated on the throne of his ancestors at Delhi.

His chief amusement is in smoking his *hooker*, bathing according to the Mahomedan custom, and his *harram*[13] in which he passeth the greatest part of his time: when he goes out, which is but seldom, it is with his whole court, himself generally upon an elephant: he sometimes goes upon the river of an evening, which is a pleasing sight; the boats, which are excessively pretty, are illuminated; and the music, though always barbarous, sounds to advantage upon the water.

[...]

Letter XLI

Allahábád, August 1767.

As the Mahomedans are all Predestinarians, added to the faith they have that whoever is slain in battle goes immediately into paradise, one should expect to find them excellent soldiers. This was undoubtedly the intention of their prophet, who was a martial genius, and founded his empire by conquest.

When the Mogul Tartars first conquered Hindostan,[14] they are said to have been a hardy, warlike, active race of people: who carried their conquests through the land with irresistible valor; though most likely that the effeminacy of the people they had to oppose them, helped as much to promote their reputation and coquest, as their own courage.

---

[11]   *provinces*: 'The provinces of Bengal, Bahar, and Oriza. The company's troops, who are beyond these three provinces, have an additional daily allowance' [Kindersley's note]. Bahar, or Bihar, is West of Bengal; Orissa was on the eastern coast, south of Bengal.

[12]   *seapoys*: or sepoys, were Indian soldiers, mostly under British command.

[13]   'Seraglio' [Kindersley's note].

[14]   *conquered Hindustan*: in the sixteenth century.

It is a common and just observation, that the nature of this climate is such as to enervate every person who resides in it, and to render the most active after a time indolent; this disposition increases, and every generation becomes more and more slothful, which seems to account for the present degeneracy of the Mahomedans of Hindostan.

Nothing can more justly show their present military and political force than the progress of the British arms, since the English, in comparison of the black people, are but as a handful of men.

Not but there are still influences of the seapoys, under the command of British officers fighting with the greatest bravery; but under black people, they want that continual attention to discipline, which is as necessary as courage. This general depravity and indolence is the cause, that if one man in a century arises, possessed of common abilities, a daring spirit, resolution and activity; let him be even of the lowest rank in life, he is certain to carry all before him, and become a great man; when his endeavors once meet with success he is looked upon as invincible, and neighboring powers, who oppose him while they think they dare, on his success will join him, till his army becomes immense; but should ever a reverse of fortune happen, he is deserted at the time he stands most in need of assistance – One of these sort of adventures is Hyder Alli,[15] now so formidable in the Decan.

[...]

Letter XLV

Allahabád, August 1767.

I fear that my account of the government and people of Hindustán must appear uncharitable, or you may think, that, with the true spirit of an Englishwoman, I condemn whatever is contrary to the customs of my own country.

[...]

I will not pretend to determine (on a point which has been often urged) whether black people are whether black people are by nature inferior in understanding to white; who can judge of it here, where the nature of the government checks the growth of every virtue? Where property is not secure, what incitement is there to industry? Where knowledge is of no use, who will resign his indolence and ease in endeavors to obtain it?

---

[15] *Hyder Alli*: Haidar Ali Khan, Sultan of Mysore in the south-west of India. He waged a damaging war against the British at Madras at the time of these letters; later his son Tipu Sultan posed a formidable threat to British influence and control in the south until the 1790s.

In such a government can we wonder, that the general characteristic of the inhabitants should be stupidity and low cunning?

[...]

Letter LIII

September 1767.

It gives me much pleasure that I am now able to give you some account of the Oriental ladies, which would never have been in my power had I remained at Calcutta.

I was lately, with much ceremony, introduced into a great *Mussulman's Zanannah*; a favour which they are not very fond of granting to Europeans. The great man's wives were seated on cushions, cross-legged, as is the custom of the country; the rest of the numerous attendants of females were sitting on the carpet, or standing round.

Even the handsomest of the Mahomedan women have very disagreeable complexions; and the fairest amongst them may rather be called more yellow than more white; but they are admired in proportion as they are distant from black: a beauty much esteemed in them is the long-cut eye, and long eye-brows, which most of them have naturally; but the female infants have sometimes the skin at the corner of their eyes cut, to increase their length, and give them more room to play: it must be acknowledged, that there is often a wantonness in the rolling of their eyes; but, exclusive of that, many of the Eastern women have so much beauty in their fine long black eyes, eye-brows, and long black eye-lashes, that if they were set off by a fine red and white complexion they would be incomparable.

They are generally small persons, and delicately made; crookedness is a defect unknown amongst them; and it is said that their black skins have a most delicate softness.

The dress, which is not, as in Europe, continually altering to what is called the fashion, but unchangeable, consists of a pair of long straight drawers, of silk, or gold or silver stuff; a sort of gown, called a jemden, mostly of very fine muslin, worked with thread, or gold, or silver; the jemden has very long straight sleeves down to the wrists; and the waist so short that it scarcely reaches below the arms; the skirt is plaited very full, and hangs down upon the ground. It is an exceeding light dress, and scarcely a covering: but the climate requires every thing which contributes to coolness, beside, they are never seen but by one man: their long black hair is parted on the forehead, combed smooth, and hangs down behind: they generally throw a piece of shawl, or silver gauze, over them, which is a sort of vail or cloak.

The jewels they wear are mostly superb; their necks are ornamented with long rows of pearls, mixed with rubies, emeralds, &c.; which jewels are often rough, and holes bolted through them, to string as the pearls: they have likewise jewels set as ornaments for their necks, arms, &c.; the workmanship is always clumsy, and the jewels a mixture of bad and good: besides, they mostly spoil their diamonds, by cutting them in flat pieces before they are set; their ear-rings are generally a bunch of loose pearl, which are very ornamental: they wear rings on their fingers and toes; but it is mostly the lowest *casts* of women who have rings in their noses.

The Eastern ladies are not strangers to arts which embellish the person; they wash their hair and eye-brows with a leaf which makes them of a perfect black; and use a black powder, which, with a knife, they convey into their eyes; it rests upon the lower eye-lash; and is said, to give life to the eye; they stain the nails of their fingers and toes with red, and paint the palms of their hands and bottoms of their feet.

Their chief employment is bathing, smoaking the hooker, and seeing the girls dance, while others play upon a sort of drum; for no man is admitted within the walls of the *Zanannah*; whatever cannot be performed by the girls, is the business of eunuchs.

Whenever the ladies go out of the *Zanannah*, which is very rare, they are in covered carriages, called *hackries*, drawn by bullocks, with close curtains all round; or else in covered *doolies*, something like a chair, carried by men; so that it is impossible for them to be seen; and it is necessary they should guard against it, for the jealousy of the *Mussulmen* exceeds all bounds; and a woman's being seen by any stranger, particularly an infidel, might cost her no less a penalty than her life.

Confinement cannot be reckoned a misfortune to these women, as they have always been accustomed to it; and besides would be degraded to a level with the lowest people were they to appear in public. Many of them have been married, by the care of their parents, even in their infancy; and the others have mostly been purchased when very young, and brought up in the *Zanannahs*; so that they can know little more of the world than what they see around them.

If a man has ever so many favorites and women, they live together in the *Zanannah*; but sometimes not without jealousy and strife between themselves.

Amongst the Nabóbs and other great people, there is always one woman who takes place of the rest, is dressed with more magnificence, treated with greater respect, and is called the *Bigum*.[16] But it is difficult to determine what it is which entitles them to this pre-eminence. Sometimes it is the first wife, but oftener the mother of the first male child.

As the Mahomedan principles do not allow women any share in religion, so of course they have no public share in government, or any other, except the influence of a beautiful face over an ignorant and voluptuous prince.

---

[16] *Bigum*: Begum, an Indian Muslim noblewoman.

These poor women, not only are never seen, but, if possible, they are never named out of the *Zanannah*: a Mahomedan never speaks of his wives; and it is thought a very great affront and indelicacy to enquire after them.

The *Zanannahs* of the people of condition have spacious apartments, and gardens with bath and jet d'eaus; but the buildings are heavy and in bad taste: the women enjoy the cool air in the evenings on the terraces; and notwithstanding their aversion to exercise, they sometimes amuse themselves with swinging in the gardens.

The Indian women have often children at twelve years of age; and by the time they are turned of twenty are thought old women; and are really so in point of beauty; for after fifteen their complexions grow every year darker: the climate, as it hastens their maturity, likewise hastens their decline.

The boys, as well as girls, are kept in the *Zanannah* while they continue young, not however without sometimes going out.

James Cook, from *A Voyage Towards the South Pole and Round the World* (1777)

James Cook (1728–79), the son of a rural labourer, was eventually hailed as the prototype of the enlightened explorer. After his indentured service to Whitby ship-owners, he joined the Navy in 1755. Cook assiduously applied himself to the intricacies of navigation, and between 1759 and 1767 he was appointed to various surveying operations around St. Lawrence and Newfoundland. In 1768 Cook was commissioned as lieutenant aboard the *Endeavour* to voyage to Tahiti to observe the transit of Venus. The success of this encouraged the admiralty to put together a second expedition to search for the unknown continent in the southern hemisphere. Cook was made commander of this mission and took with him the German scientist Johann Reinhold Foster and his son George Forster, and the artist William Hodges. The two ships – *Resolution* (Cook's ship) and *Adventure* – sailed in 1772 and reached New Zealand in March 1773. Cook's third and last voyage (1776–79) was to discover a passage around the north coast of America linking the Pacific and the Atlantic: it was during a stop-over at Hawaii that he was killed in a skirmish with the islanders.

A Voyage Towards the South Pole and Round the World, written with the help of Dr John Douglas, Canon of Windsor, is Cook's account of the second expedition. While New Zealand functioned as a base, a large part of the time was spent revisiting Tahiti and the Society Islands, and mapping the Tonga group, Easter island, the New Hebrides and New Caledonia. As in the first expedition, contact with non-Europeans generated debate about the nature of indigenous customs and society.

The first extract concerns the infamous proof of Maori cannibalism. In November 1773, at Queen Charlotte's Sound, his crew found the remains of a boat crew from the *Adventure* which had been massacred there. Cook offers the subsequent scene in the spirit of an impartial and scientific inquiry but this must be weighed against its tendency to inspire a kind of cultural voyeurism. It also reveals contemporary debates concerning the stages of civilisation, the power of custom (in our words, culture) and the benefical effect of international contact. The second extract demonstrates the potential for cultural misunderstanding – in this case, concerning sexual practices and masculinity.[1]

[November 1773. Queen Charlotte Sound, New Zealand]

Calm or light airs from the North, all day, on the 23d, hindered us from putting to sea as intended. In the afternoon, some of the officers went on shore to amuse themselves among the natives, where they saw the head and bowels of a youth, who had lately been killed, lying on the beach; and the heart stuck on a forked stick, which was fixed to the head of one of the largest canoes. One of the gentlemen bought the head, and brought it on board, where a piece of the flesh was broiled and eaten by one of the natives, before all the officers, and most of the men. I was on shore at this time, but soon after returning on board, was informed of the above circumstances; and found the quarter-deck crowded with the natives, and the mangled head, or rather part of it, (for the under jaw and lip were wanting) lying on the tasseral. The scull had been broken on the left side, just above the temples; and the remains of the face had all the appearance of a youth under twenty.

The sight of the head, and the relation of the above circumstances, struck me with horror, and filled my mind with indignation against these cannibals. Curiosity, however, got the better of my indignation, especially when I considered that it would avail but little, and being desirous of becoming an eye-witness of a fact which many doubted, I ordered a piece of the flesh to be broiled and brought to the quarter-deck, where one of these cannibals eat it with surprising avidity. This had such an effect on some of our people as to make them sick. Oedidee[2] (who came on board with me) was so affected with the sight as to become perfectly motionless, and seemed as if metamorphosed into the statue of Horror. It is utterly impossible for art to describe that passion with half the force that it appeared in his countenance. When rouzed from this state by some of us, he burst into tears; continued to weep and scold by turns; told them they were vile men; and that he neither was, nor would be any longer their friend. He even would not suffer them to touch him; he used the same language to one of the gentlemen who cut

1   Text from vol. 1, pp. 243–46; vol. 2, pp. 65–7.
2   *Oedidee*: or Odiddy (also known as Mahine), from Bora-Bora in the Society Isles, the same group as Tahiti. He was taken on board the *Resolution* at Raiatea.

off the flesh; and refused to accept, or even touch, the knife with which it was done. Such was Oedidee's indignation against the vile custom; and worthy of imitation by every rational being.

I was not able to find out the reason for their undertaking this expedition; all I could understand for certain was, that they went from hence into Admiralty Bay (the next inlet to the West)[3] and there fought with their enemies, many of whom they killed. They counted to me fifty; a number which exceeded probability, as they were not more, if so many, themselves. I think I understood them clearly, that this youth was killed there; and not brought away prisoner, and afterwards killed. Nor could I learn that they had brought away any more than this one, which increased the improbability of their having killed so many. We had also reason to think that they did not come off without loss; for a young woman was seen, more than once, to cut herself, as is the custom when they lose a friend or relation.

That the New Zealanders are cannibals, can now no longer be doubted. The account given of this in my former voyage, being partly founded on circumstances, was, as I afterwards understood, discredited by many persons. Few consider what a savage man is in his natural state, and even after he is, in some degree, civilised. The New Zealanders are certainly in some state of civilization; their behaviour to us was manly and mild, shewing, on all occasions, a readiness to oblige. They have some arts among them which they execute with great judgment, and unwearied patience; they are far less addicted to thieving than the other islanders of the South Sea; and, I believe, those in the same tribe, or such as are at peace one with another, are strictly honest among themselves. This custom of eating their enemies slain in battle (for I firmly believe they eat the flesh of no others) has, undoubtedly, been handed down to them from the earliest times; and we know it is not an easy matter to wean a nation from their ancient customs, let them be ever so inhuman and savage; especially if that nation has no manner of connexion or commerce with strangers. For it is by this that the greatest part of the human race has been civilized; an advantage which the New Zealanders, from their situation, never had. An intercourse with foreigners would reform their manners, and polish their savage minds. Or, were they more united under a settled form of government, they would have fewer enemies, consequently this custom would be less in use, and might in time be in a manner forgotten. At present, they have but little idea of treating others as themselves would *wish* to be treated, but treat them as they *expect* to be treated. If I remember right, one of the arguments they made use of to Tupia,[4] who frequently expostulated with them against this custom, was,

---

3	*Admiralty Bay*: on the North Eastern end of the south island of New Zealand.
4	*Tupia*: Tupaia, high chief (*arii*) and priest of Raiatea. He was taken aboard the *Endeavour* in the first voyage, but as he died in 1770, Cook is obviously remembering a conversation from this first voyage.

that there could be no harm in killing and eating the man who would do the same by them, if it was in his power. For, said they, 'can there be any harm in eating our enemies, whom we have killed in battle? Would not those very enemies have done the same to us?' I have often seen them listen to Tupia with great attention; but I never found his arguments have any weight with them, or that, with all his rhetoric, he could persuade any one of them that this custom was wrong. And when Oedidee, and several of our people, shewed their abhorrence of it, they only laughed at them.

Among many reasons which I have heard assigned for the prevalence of this horrid custom, the want of animal food has been one; but how far this is deducible either from facts or circumstances, I shall leave those to find out who advanced it. In every part of New Zealand where I have been, fish was in such plenty, that the natives generally caught as much as served both themselves and us. They have also plenty of dogs; nor is there any want of wild-fowl, which they know very well how to kill. So that neither this, nor the want of food of any kind, can, in my opinion, be the reason. But, whatever it may be, I think it was but too evident, that they have a great liking for this kind of food.

[...]

[14 August 1774. Island of Tana, or Vanuatu, New Hebrides]

Before this excursion some of us had been of opinion, that these people were addicted to an unnatural passion, because they had endeavoured to entice some of our men into the woods; and, in particular, I was told, that one who had the care of Mr. Forster's plant bag, had been, once or twice, attempted. As the carrying of bundles, &c. is the office of the women in this country, it had occurred to me, and I was not singular in this, that the natives might mistake him, and some others, for women. My conjecture was fully verified this day. For this man, who was one of the party, and carried the bag as usual, following me down the hill, by the words which I understood of the conversation of the natives, and by their actions, I was well assured that they considered him as a female; till, by some means, they discovered their mistake, on which they cried out, *Erramange! Erramange!* It's a man! It's a man! The thing was so palpable that everyone was obliged to acknowledge, that they had before mistaken his sex; and that, after they were undeceived, they seemed not to have the least notion of what we had suspected. This circumstance will shew how liable we are to form wrong conjectures of things, among people whose language we are ignorant of. Had it not been for this discovery, I make no doubt that these people would have been charged with this vile custom.

Joseph Peart, from
A Continuation of Hudibras in Two Cantos. Written in the Time of the Unhappy Contest between Great Britain and America, in 1777 and 1778 (1778)

Nothing is known about the author of this timely and witty adaptation of *Hudibras* other than that he was a solicitor. The three-part mock-romantic poem by Samuel Butler concerning the adventures of the Don Quixote-like Sir Hudibras, a Presbyterian 'Knight' (the first two parts were published in 1663), was an allusive and highly sceptical satire on the hypocrisy and prejudice exemplified by narrow-minded religious and political beliefs that Butler saw all around him. Most important for this adaptation, however, was its satire on Non-conformist and Dissenting religions, and the politics of the English Civil War and the Commonwealth period. Out of these materials Peart has constructed an elaborate continuation in which Sir Hudibras is aligned with the dissenters who fomented the Civil war and who plan to emigrate to the American colonies to sow the seeds of future rebellion there. Peart uses another important allusion, John Milton's *Paradise Lost* (1667), when he has Hudibras echo the speeches of Satan after the rebellion in Heaven and his plans to overthrow Eden. To many Britons the war with the colonies presaged another paradise lost.

> When Hudribras's cause of Dudgeon,
> Had scarcely got one foot to budge'on,
> But all the presbyters were routed,
> Or by the royal party scouted,
> When ev'ry church and hall resounded,   5
> With curses on fanatic roundhead,
> When holy cropt ears were despis'd,
> And large full bottoms only priz'd;
> Sir Hudibras and many more,
> That fought upon religion's score,   10
> Conven'd a Presbyterian meeting,
> (They dare not fit the open street in,
> But could improve their arts and wiles
> Beneath the covert of pantiles:)

There the desponding congregation, 15
No longer doom'd to rule the nation,
The knight address'd, by way of preacher,
Or rather as politic teacher.—
But first assist me mirthful muse!
To tell as other poets use, 20
The names of those who took their places
And shew'd their hypocritic faces;
First, Prynn appear'd,[1] and tho' I fear
He had not any ears to hear,
Since fate had cruelly bereft'em, 25
And on a lofty pulpit left'em,
Yet he'd a tongue in whole condition,
And hands to write and spread sedition.
Bastwick in self-same plight came next,
And with the like misfortune vext; 30
With him his dear companion Burton,[2]
With this ear whole—and that a hurt one.
Next follow'd a long train of those,
Who genealogists suppose,
Descend from men averse to marry, 35
From John, from Tom, from Will and Harry,
Their children being such-a-one's-son,
As Will's son, Harry's son and John's son,
And to descend to Grandson from son,
We shant omit the name of Tom's son;[3] 40
A mighty name by fate intended,
When their ill-fortune should be mended,

---

[1] *Prynne*: William Prynne (1600–69), Puritan pamphleteer and barrister and an outspoken critic of Charles I. He was sentenced to imprisonment, a fine, and to have his ears cut off. Peart seems unaware of, or to ignore, the fact that he later spoke in favour of the rights of Charles II.

[2] *Bastwick … Burton*: John Bastwick (1593–1654) was fined and imprisoned for writing controversial puritanical pamphlets; he was also leader of a Parliamentarian army unit. Henry Burton (1578–1648), highly critical of bishops under Charles I, was fined, imprisoned and also had his ears cut off. He became an Independent MP under the Commonwealth.

[3] *Will's son … Tom's son*: Rowland Wilson MP (1613–50), Commonwealth sheriff; Thomas Harrison MP (1606–60), was one of the signatories to the execution warrant for Charles I. 'John's son' may be either Francis Johnson (1562–1618) a Presbyterian separatist or George Johnson (1564–1605), a Puritan separatist who sailed for America. George Thomson MP (1607–68), later conspired against the Restoration. The 'mighty name by fate' might be the poet James Thomson (1700–48), who became Secretary of the Briefs (overseeing church charity appeals) in 1733 under his patron, the well-respected statesman Charles Talbot (1685–1737). Thomson's other patron was George Lyttelton MP (1709–73), and who opposed the repeal of the Stamp Act.

(For oft to good from ill she varies)
To grace the best of secretaries.—
Then crowded in, at least by dozens,   45
The sons, the brother's and the cousens,
Of those who late their monarch tried,
And got the name of Regicide.
Nor shall the muse forget to notice,
The names of *Adams, Hancock, Otis,*   50
With more for pride of heart to rankle in,
As *Cushing, Silas Deane,* and *Franklin,*[4]
Whose sage descendants we shall see,
Shine forth in the next century,
Proving their wishes to inherit   55
That discontented factious spirit,
Disguis'd with hypocritic zeal,
I'th' name of love of common weal,
That principle republican,
Or levelling 'twixt man and man,   60
That shone so bright in their ancestors,
Th' above-mention'd dissenting Nestors,[5]
Who thus destroy'd subordination,
And of all laws depriv'd the nation,
Of all the ancient laws o'th' land,   65
But what their rigid wills command;
Until the friends o'th' constitution,
Had gain'd sufficient resolution;
Then at the death of that sly Hector,[6]
Stil'd, England's commonwealth protector,   70
They rose with courage stout and hearty,
Upon the drooping, headless party;

---

[4] *Adams … Franklin*: Samuel Adams (1722–1803), was a vehement and radical critic of
British policy and taxation in the colonies, and together with John Hancock (1737–93) was
a signatory to the Declaration of Independence in 1776. James Otis (1725–83) was an ener-
getic activist and writer on behalf of the colonists' grievances against British taxation in the
1760s. William Cushing (1732–1810) was a high-ranking judge in the American courts of
the 1770s. Benjamin Franklin (1706–90), the inventor and experimenter, was the leading
spokesperson for the American colonists' rights in Britain in the 1760s and early 70s, and
was also a signatory to the Declaration. Franklin and Silas Deane (1732–89) were instrumental in obtaining a treaty of commerce and alliance with France in 1778.

[5] *Nestor*: in Greek mythology, the elder statesman who was a fund of sound advice to the
Greeks in their war against Troy; he was also known for his long stories recounting his
own glorious past.

[6] *Hector*: in mythology, the greatest of Trojan warriors renowned for his strength. Here, the
ironic allusion is to Cromwell.

Again brought home their lawful lord,[7]
Their laws and liberties restor'd,
And brought the puritannic crew,   75
To that desponding point of view,
In which we see them at the meeting,
When Hudibras had giv'n them greeting.
And as that greatest of all bards,[8]
Whose mem'ry same so well rewards,   80
Such fine descriptive lines has giv'n,
Of Satan that was newly driv'n,
Out of the Heav'n of Heav'ns to dwell,
In regions of despair and Hell,
Where after he a-while had laid,   85
Quite stunn'd, astonish'd and dismay'd,
He rose—and his new realms survey'd:
And having for himself regretted,
As well as those he had abetted,
The fatal loss they had sustain'd,   90
And such a dismal change obtain'd;
He call'd his brother devils round him,
Who felt some joy that they had found him;
And soon advis'd them, tho' ambition
Had lost its aim,—to sow sedition;   95
By guile, by fraud, and close design,
The works of God to undermine,
And well-designing men to lead,
To vice, to folly and misdeed.

So Hudibras in imitation;   100
Or what some call an instigation,
Of that designing prince of fiends,
In self-same way address'd his friends:—[9]
'Brethren, in meaning! strict dissenters!
Since fate and fortune prove tormentors,   105
(Tho' for some time—we play'd our part
With matchless skill—and fraudful art,
And prov'd the strife not then inglorious,
When king and peers bow'd down before us,)
Yet in the end th'event was dire,   110

---

7   *lawful lord*: Charles II, crowned in 1660.
8   *that greatest of all bards*: John Milton. The poem is *Paradise Lost* (1667), in particular, books 1
     and 2 where Satan and his fellow angels, having been consigned to hell for their rebellion
     against God, bemoan their fate and plot the downfall of humankind in Eden.
9   Lines 104–47 echo *Paradise Lost*, 1: lines 622–56.

Of that no better proof require
Than the great length of ev'ry face,
I see affected with disgrace:
But who could think the king bereft
Of crown,—had got so many left,   115
To aid his cause instead of ours,
Or even to withstand our pow'rs?
Or who could yet believe or fear,
That such close hypocrites as we are,
Could fail to work upon the people,   120
And beat down king again and steeple?
But since this Charles,[10] restor'd again,
Securely has begun his reign,
Upheld therein beyond dispute,
By ancient usage and repute: 125
Since him 'tis own'd we find a Tartar in,
And may dread hanging, drawing, quart'ring,
If we should dare again by force,
T'oppose or interrupt his course;
Our better part remains as yet,   130
By which we may advantage get,
By fraud conceal'd and guile unnoted,
Our int'rest may be yet promoted;
By that perhaps we may obtain,
What force might venture at in vain: 135
At length our enemies may know,
Those who by fighting overthrow,
Yet overcome but half their foe.—
More realms than one may be possest,
I see one rising in the West.   140
Which Charles in infant state supplies,
By name of English Colonies,
With all their wants can well demand,
Transported from this fruitful land,
And shews them equal care and love,   145
To that his English subjects prove:
Thither let us repair and fix,
With natives and with transports mix,
Bend low to him who gave us quarter,
And pray for privilege and charter,   150
Raising by slow degrees our numbers,

---

[10]   *Charles*: the Restoration of the monarchy and the Stuart line in 1660 with Charles II
        (1630–85).

And nursing hate, that never slumbers:
Until our sons—or children's sons,
Increas'd like Vandals, Goths or Huns,[11]
May throw their long dependence off,   155
And at Old England laugh and scoff;
Pretending to forget the tye,
They gain'd their situation by.—
Then those possessed of no estate, or
Expectance,—shall claim rights of nature,   160
Insist that all men are born free,
And have a right to liberty:
Some meaning liberty of taking,
Part of what fortune made mistake in,
Bestowing blindly upon others,   165
Less worthy than themselves and brothers.
Some meaning liberty of living,
By law protected—without giving,
Or being made to give or grant,
One penny to the nation's want,[12]   170
To pay th'expences of that state,
Under whose influence they grew great.
Most meaning liberty of using
The name—all order to confuse in,
Thus anarchy and mischief brewing,   175
And rising on the realm's undoing.
But whatsoever their reason may be,
By '*Crede quod habes et habe,*'[13]
By fools they may be understood,
To act on grounds and reasons good;   180
Make them believe they have a reason,
That war against the king's no treason.—
No rogue that e'er was hang'd at Tyburn,
(Whether a vulgar wretch or high-born)
Suppose him to have common sense,   185
But for his crime finds some pretence:
To rob—necessity compels him;

---

[11] *Vandals, Goths or Huns*: Germanic (Vandal and Goth) and Asiatic (Hun) tribes that devastated Europe between the third and fifth centuries.

[12] *one penny*: a reference to the Stamp Act, a taxation on the colonies thought necessary to defer the huge costs of the war against France in America during the Seven Year's War (1756–63). It proved unenforceable and was repealed in 1766 (see also lines 213–40). See also Wheatley, n. 3, and Freeth, n. 4.

[13] *Crede quod habes et habe*: 'believe what you have, and have it'; in other words, a form of self-justification.

To ravish,—heat of blood impels him;
To murder and assassination,—
Abuse is ample provocation;   190
To smuggle and defraud the crown,—
Keeps prices of provisions down;
To riot and to break the windows,
And frighten all the maids within doors,
Is love of liberty for ever,—   195
Divides the stupid from the clever,
And shews to all who mark it well,
How much a patriot may excell,
(One of true fire—a hearty blade)
Those heavy plodders in their trade,   200
Who aim to pay,—to whom they're debtors,
And leave the nation to their betters;
So guided by this happy notion,
Our sons beyond th'Atlantic Ocean,
Taught the sweet poison to imbibe,   205
By some of the abovesaid tribe;
(Who 'stead of hanging on a string,
Not doom'd by destiny to swing,
But by a better fortune courted,
May have the luck to be transported,)   210
This boasted privilege may claim,
Of giving things another name.—
For instance should the English people,
(Who to our tiles prefer a steeple)[14]
Having the strongest efforts made,   215
To guard their Colonies in trade;
And prov'd their ardour to advance
Against the force of Spain and France;
Laying out millions of their own,
For distant subjects of the throne,   220
(The British throne, whose rights to guard
To some may seem its own reward,)
Should they, my friends!—observe—I say,
Be doom'd to conquer in the fray,
And by their loss of gold and blood,   225
Work out to our descendants—good:
Yet, if these future Englishmen,
Should ask one shilling for their ten,

---

[14]   *tiles … steeple*: Non-conformist chapels as against Anglican churches.

To be by law repaid, by those
Who have been guarded from their foes, 230
And thus preserv'd from low subjection,
To hostile arms—by their protection.
Nay, should they ask them for a penny,
Our children (scarce excepting any)
Shall rise, and to a man refuse, 235
To pay for what they will not chuse;
Calling—(as prov'd by our tradition)
A claim like this, an imposition,
A cruel plan,—in freedom's spite,
Of forcing people to do right. 240

[…]

In this confusion of affairs,
Fortune shall smile upon our heirs,
They shall be first in the promotion
Of civil war, and strange commotion, 310
Rising therein to new made pow'rs.
Such as of late were some of ours,
The new republic then shall mend on't,
And bear the stile of independant;
Tradesmen of ev'ry occupation, 315
Shall then be lords of a new nation,
Members of Congress,—by the fates,
Doom'd to be rulers of the states.
Lawyers and their attendant bums,
Shall turn their parchment into drums, 320
Instead of bags, long briefs and deeds,
Shall think of banners—neighing steeds,
Swords, gun-powder and cannon shot,
To send poor Englishmen to pot.—
Some gen'rals too of matchless skill, 325
Shall rise from brothers of the quill,
And ruin'd men, releas'd from duns,
Shall live by rifle barrell'd guns,
With which from trees or broken wall,
They'll aim the death devoting ball, 330
At men of highest rank 'mong those,
To whom they'll give the name of foes.—
And though such dastardly behaviour,
May be detested by the braver,
As bitt'rest enemies are right in, 335

The fair and honest mode of fighting:
To rifle men, all honour's laws
Give way, in such a noble cause,
They'll think the only way to war well,
Is first to kill with rifle barrel,   340
And when the victim is laid low,
They'll rifle then his pockets too.—
Let then my friends your hopes be great,
Of what is promis'd us by fate,
And quick prepare to emigrate.   345
When settled on the destin'd shore,
Ponder my sayings o'er and o'er,
Train up your sons in detestation,
And hate unchang'd of th'English nation;
Prepare them by dissembling well,   350
To hope the days which I foretell;
When time is ripen'd for the task,
Sudden to throw away the mask,
And aim with steady resolution,
Again to change the constitution.'—   355

Thus spoke the knight, and free consent,
From ear to ear, in murmurs went.
Not one of all the num'rous party,
But in the plan was strong and hearty.
The meeting ended, thus approving,   360
They soon were busied in removing;
Some sail'd to Massachuset's Bay,
And some to Pennsylvania;
Some settled on Virginia's Strand,
And other's fix'd in Maryland;   365
In Jersey some begun their work,
Others were seated in New York;
A few were left in England's realm,
To watch the guiders of the helm,
By letters here, and thither going,   370
To tell what each of them were doing.

Anna Seward, from
An Elegy on Captain Cook
(1780)

Anna Seward (1742–1809) was known as 'the Swan of Lichfield' and her poetry was initially circulated among a coterie of friends that included Erasmus Darwin (grandfather of Charles). She gained fame through her elegy to Cook in 1780. She contributed to arguments on poetry in the press, and published *Llangollen Vale, with Other Poems* in 1796, and *Original Sonnets* in 1799.

In 1779, on his third voyage, Captain James Cook was at the island of Hawaii. During a fracas to retrieve a stolen boat, Cook – always strict when it came to policing the infractions of indigenes – came to take King Kalani'opu'u hostage, but the Englishmen and the islanders came to blows, and Cook was stabbed to death. His death caused an outpouring of national grief, and Seward's poem is an example of the apotheosis of Cook by numerous writers who celebrated him as a explorer motivated by enlightened ideals of cultural contact – signalled in her poem by the voyage's presiding spirit, 'HUMANITY'. Seward's poem, however, is also interesting for the extremely ambivalent portrayals of the Pacific peoples.

> Sorrowing, the Nine[1] beneath yon blasted yew
> Shed the bright drops of Pity's holy dew;
> Mute are their tuneful tongues, extinct their fires;
> Yet not in silence sleep their silver lyres;
> To the bleak gale they vibrate sad and slow,
> In deep accordance to a Nation's woe.   5
>
>   Ye, who ere while for COOK'S illustrious brow
> Pluck'd the green laurel, and the oaken bough,
> Hung the gay garlands on the trophied oars,
> And pour'd his fame along a thousand shores,
> Strike the death-bell!—weave the sacred verse,   10
> And strew the cypress o'er his honor'd hearse;
> In sad procession wander round the shrine,
> And weep him mortal, whom ye sung divine!
>
>   Say first, what Pow'r inspired his dauntless breast
> With scorn of danger, and inglorious rest,   15

---

[1]   *Nine*: the Nine Muses, daughters of Zeus and Mnemosyne: Calliope (muse of epic poetry and eloquence and inspiration), Clio (history), Erato (erotic poetry), Euterpe (Dionysian music, joy and pleasure), Melpomene (tragedy), Polyhymnia (lyric poetry), Terpsichore (dancing and dramatic chorus), Thalia (comic and pastoral poetry), Urania (astrology, heavens, wisdom).

To quit imperial London's gorgeous plains,
Where, rob'd in thousand tints, bright Pleasure reigns;
In cups of summer-ice her nectar pours,
And twines, 'mid wint'ry snows, her roseate bow'rs?
Where Beauty moves with undulating grace,   20
Calls the sweet blush to wanton o'er her face,
On each fond Youth her soft artillery tries,
Aims her light smile, and rolls her frolic eyes?

    What Pow'r inspir'd his dauntless breast to brave   25
The scorch'd Equator, and th' Antarctic wave?
Climes, where fierce suns in cloudless ardors shine,
And pour the dazzling deluge round the Line;
The realms of frost, where icy mountains rise,
'Mid the pale summer of the polar skies?—   30
IT WAS HUMANITY!—on coasts unknown,
The shiv'ring natives of the frozen zone,
And the swart Indian, as he faintly strays
'Where Cancer reddens in the solar blaze,'[2]
She bade him seek;—on each inclement shore   35
Plant the rich seeds of her exhaustless store;
Unite the savage hearts, and hostile hands,
In the firm compact of her gentle bands;
Strew her soft comforts o'er the barren plain,
Sing her sweet lays, and consecrate her fane.[3]   40

[…]

    Now leads HUMANITY the destin'd way,
Where all the Loves in Otaheite stray.[4]
To bid the Arts disclose their wond'rous pow'rs,   165
To bid the virtues consecrate the bow'rs,
She gives her Hero to its blooming plain.—
Now has he wander'd, has he bled in vain!
His lips persuasive charm th' uncultur'd youth,
Teach Wisdom's lore, and point the path of Truth.   170
See![5] chasten'd love in softer glances flows,
See! with new fires parental duty glows.

---

2   *Where Cancer … blaze*: in other words, at the height of the summer solstice. From
    James Thomson, 'Summer' (first published 1727), *The Seasons* (1746), line 44.
3   *fane*: temple.
4   *Otaheite*: Tahiti.
5   '*Chasten'd love*: Captain Cook observes, in his second voyage, that the women of Otaheite
    were grown more modest, and that the barbarous practice of destroying their children was
    lessened' [Seward's note].

Thou smiling Eden of the southern wave,
Could not, alas! thy grateful wishes save
That angel-goodness, which has bless'd thy plain? —   175
Ah! vain thy gratitude, thy wishes vain!
On a far distant, and remorseless shore,[6]
Where human fiends their dire libations pour;
Where treachery, hov'ring o'er the blasted heath,
Poises with ghastly smile the darts of death,   180
Pierc'd by their venom'd points, your favorite bleeds,
And on his limbs the lust of hunger feeds!

    Thus when, of old, the Muse-born Orpheus[7] bore
Fair Arts and Virtues to the Thracian shore;
Struck with sweet energy the warbling wire,   185
And pour'd persuasion from th' immortal lyre;
As soften'd brutes, the waving woods among,
Bow'd their meek heads, and listen'd to the song;
Near, and more near, with rage and tumult loud,
Round the bold bard th' inebriate maniacs crowd—   190
Red on th' ungrateful soil his life-blood swims,
And Fiends and Furies tear his quiv'ring limbs!

    Gay Eden of the south, thy tribute pay,
And raise, in pomp of woe, thy COOK's[8] Morai!
Bid mild Omiah[9] bring his choicest stores,   195
The juicy fruits, and the luxuriant flow'rs;
Bring the bright plumes, that drink the torrid ray,
And strew each lavish spoil on COOK's Morai!

    Come, Oberea, hapless fair-one![10] come,
With piercing shrieks bewail thy Hero's doom!—   200
She comes!—she gazes round with dire survey!—
Oh! fly the mourner on her frantic way.

---

[6] *shore*: Hawaii is never directly mentioned.

[7] *Orpheus*: in Greek legend, Orpheus was the son of Apollo by the Muse Calliope, celebrated as a gifted musician and poet. He died when the Maenads (women followers of Dionysus gripped in a cultish frenzy) tore him limb from limb.

[8] 'Morai—The Morai is a kind of funeral altar, which the people of Otaheite raise to the memory of their deceased friends. They bring to it a daily tribute of fruits, flowers, and the plumage of birds. The chief mourner wanders around it in a state of apparent distraction, shrieking furiously, and striking at intervals a shark's tooth into her head. All people fly her, as she aims at wounding not only herself, but others' [Seward's note]. Cook's remains were buried in Kealakekua bay, Hawaii.

[9] *Omiah*: Omai, prince of Raiatea, Society Islands. Cook met him on his second expedition, and Omai was brought to England in 1774 (see headnote to Frances Burney to Mr. Crisp).

[10] *Oberea*: Purea, Queen of Tahiti. For this ritual, see Hawkesworth.

See! see! the pointed ivory wounds that head,
Where late the Loves impurpled roses spread;
Now stain'd with gore, her raven-tresses flow,   205
In ruthless negligence of mad'ning woe;
Loud she laments!—and long the Nymph shall stray
With wild unequal step round COOK's Morai!

    But ah!—aloft on Albion's rocky steep,
That frowns incumbent o'er the boiling deep,   210
Solicitous, and sad, a softer form
Eyes the lone flood, and deprecates the storm.—
Ill-fated matron![11]—for, alas! in vain
Thy eager glances wander o'er the main!—
'Tis the vex'd billows, that insurgent rave,   215
Their white foam silvers yonder distant wave,
'Tis not his sails!—thy husband comes no more!
His bones now whiten an accursed shore!—
Retire,—for hark! the sea-gull shrieking soars,
The lurid atmosphere portentous low'rs;   220
Night's sullen spirit groans in ev'ry gale,
And o'er the waters draws the darkling veil,
Sighs in thy hair, and chills thy throbbing breast—
Go, wretched mourner!—weep thy griefs to rest!

    Yet, tho' through life is lost each fond delight,   225
Tho' set thy earthly sun in dreary night,
Oh! raise thy thoughts to yonder starry plain,
And own thy sorrow selfish, weak, and vain;
Since, while Britannia, to his virtues just,[12]
Twines the bright wreath, and rears th' immortal bust;   230
While on each wind of heav'n his fame shall rise,
In endless incense to the smiling skies;
THE ATTENDANT POWER, that bade his sails expand,
And waft her blessings to each barren land,
Now raptur'd bears him to th' immortal plains,   235
Where Mercy hails him with congenial strains;
Where soars, on Joy's white plume, his spirit free,
And angels choir him, while he waits for THEE.

---

[11]   *matron*: Cook's wife, Elizabeth Cook née Batts (1740–1835).
[12]   *Since … just*: while Britannia is just to Cook's virtues.

John Freeth

John Freeth (1731–1808) was a landlord of a Birmingham tavern and coffee-house, who hosted various meetings of the radical thinkers of Birmingham from the 1770s. He was also a writer of ballads from around 1760: his first praised the release of radical MP John Wilkes in 1763. He published a number of song collections, but his most recurrent was *The Political Songster* which first appeared in 1766, after which it went through many different editions with additional material until 1798. Although a large amount of his output was political, a portion of it included light-hearted commentaries on beer, Birmingham, fashion and sports. While often fiercely patriotic when it came to war, his poems on the American war are rueful reflections on the dominant concerns and images of the relationship between America and Britain.

American Contest (1780)[1]

Mother England's own child, a fine lusty grown lass,
Who for size through the world for a woman might pass,
To her neighbours, in violent anger, complains,
That her dame is preparing to load her with chains.

The daughter is able to earn her own bread,   5
And long on plain diet has decently fed;
On her true ancient rights will admit no controul,
For freedom she loves as she loves her own soul.

Her high pamper'd matron, to luxury prone,
In folly and fashion extravagant grown,   10
Pretended she'd got an old reck'ning to pay,
And could wipe off the score, if her daughter drank tea.[2]

By the invoice the girl at an instant could see,
If she took to the goods, a hard bargain 'twould be;
So as soon as the cargo was brought to the key,   15
In a passionate air toss'd it into the sea.

At this insolent freak the old lady was stir'd,
She gave her command, and revenge was the word;
Resolv'd, if she still disregarded her call,
To force down the poison with powder and ball.   20

---

[1]   From, *The Warwickshire Medley: or, Convivial Songster, Being a Collection of Original Songs, Political, Humourous and Satyrical* (1780), pp. 1–3.

[2]   *tea*: in response to the near-bankruptcy of the East India Company in 1772, Parliament passed the Tea Act which sought to direct unsold tea to America: it was accompanied by a tax. The result was the 'Boston Tea Party' in 1773 where colonists dressed as American Indians tipped large amounts of imported tea into the harbour.

You impudent hussy, you termagant jade,
When a powerful foe did your suburbs invade,
Were not my best blood and my treasure expended,
And were not your settlements nobly defended.

In the most corrupt kingdom the world ever knew,   25
Do not wonder, in peace, why fresh taxes ensue;
And you, spite of threats, by St. Stephen,[3] I swear,
From this time a part of such burthens shall bear.

But say, is it more than your duty to nourish
The brat which has caus'd your whole empire to flourish?   30
And if, cries the lass, cruel measures are sought,
Tis twenty to one but you cut your own throat.

My trade you restrain, of my produce you share;
But don't pick my pocket, for that I can't bear;
To serve you in want I exerted my power,   35
The late war will prove it, what would you have more?

Years ago the same maxim you meant to pursue,
Ill judg'd was the deed, and oppression your view;
When forgetting the parent, you storm'd like a brute,
And but for *Will. Pitt* I'd been *stamp'd* under foot.[4]   40

As ravenous creatures surrounding the throne
Increase ev'ry year, something fresh must be done;
England long has been fleec'd, the Hibernians drain'd,
And supplies from America must be obtain'd.

Taxation's a burthen destructive of trade,   45
A plague worse than ever did Egypt invade,
And England will ever the folly deplore,
Till she takes up a spunge, and wipes off the whole score.

Derry down, &c.

Bunker Hill, or the Soldier's Lamentation (1780)[5]

I am a jolly soldier,
    Enlisted years ago,

---

3   *St. Stephen*: see Davenant, n. 2.
4   *Will … foot*: William Pitt, First Earl of Chatham (1708–78), secretary of state. He was
     opposed to the high-handed tactics with the colonists and spoke against the Stamp Act,
     which was repealed in 1766. See also Wheatley, n. 3.
5   From, *The Warwickshire Medley*, pp. 18–20. The battle of Bunker Hill, Boston, was the site of
     the first major clash of the War of American Independence. In 17 June 1775, the British
     successfully stormed the hill but at the cost of frighteningly high casualties.

To serve my king and country,
    Against the common foe.
But when across th' Atlantic   5
    My orders were to go,
I griev'd to think that English hearts,
    Should draw their swords on those
Who fought and conquer'd by their side,
    When Frenchmen were their foes.   10

In drubbing French and Spaniards,
    A soldier takes delight,
But troops coop'd up in Boston,
    Are in so sad a plight,
That many think their stomachs more   15
    Inclin'd to eat than fight,
And like us would be loth to stir;
    For ev'ry vet'ran knows,
We fought and conquer'd side by side,
    When Frenchmen were our foes.   20

'Twas on the seventeenth of June,
    I can't forget the day,
The flower of our army
    For Charles Town sail'd away.
The town was soon in ashes laid,   25
    When bombs began to play:
But oh! the cruel scene to paint,
    It makes my blood run chill,
Pray heaven grant I never more,
    My climb up Bunker's Hill.   30

America to frighten,
    The tools of power strove,
But ministers are cheated,
    Their schemes abortive prove.
The men they told us would not fight,   35
    Are to the combat drove,
And to our gallant officers,
    It prov'd a bitter pill,
For numbers dropt before they reach'd
    The top of Bunker's Hill.   40

I would not be amaz'd to hear
    Wolfe's ghost[6] had left the shades,

---

[6] *Wolfe's ghost*: General James Wolfe (1727–59), lauded for leading successful attacks against the French in North America during the Seven Years War (1756–63).

To check that shameful bloody work,
    Which England's crown degrades.
The lads who scorn to turn their backs,   45
    On Gallia's[7] best brigades,
Undaunted stood but frankly own,
    They better had lain still,
Than such a dear-bought victory gain,
    As that of Bunker's Hill.   50

Did they who bloody measures crave,
    Our toil and danger share,
Not one to face the Rifle-Men,
    A second time would dare.
Ye Britons who your country love,   55
    Be this your ardent pray'r:
To Britain and her colonies,
    May peace be soon restor'd,
And knaves of high and low degree,
    Be *destin'd to the cord*.   60

The Contest (1782)[8]

When luxury reign'd, the *court-panders* obtain'd,
    Rewards for no services done;
Hopes of still greater sway, caus'd a FATHER to lay
    An extra demand on his SON.

Such a plan to uphold, he by many was told,   5
    Would soon his own fortune impair;
BRITANNIA in tears, whisper'd this in his ears,
    Yet all could not make him forbear.

After words had arose, he proceeded to blows,
    And being with power replete,   10
Made oath to his friends, that he'd never shake hands,
    Till the YOUTH was laid down at his feet.

The GALLIC COCK crew, when his sabre he drew,
    And, anxious to cherish the fire,
At their wounds and their stings, kept clapping his wings,   15
    Better pastime he could not desire.

This treacherous foe, to give a bye blow,
    Will all opportunities take;

---

[7] *Gallia*: France.
[8] From *Modern Songs, on Various Subjects* (1782), pp. 16–17.

Time has been that MONSIEUR, would have trembled with fear,
    If the LION his mane did but shake.   20

Savage Monsters let loose, did their scalping knives use,
    The *Indians* their *tomahawks* threw;[9]
Every effort was try'd, *German Butchers*[10] employ'd,
    Yet nothing the business would do.

After millions expended, and no good intended,   25
    Oh! think how it humbled their pride;
When touch'd to the quick, his ADVISERS turn'd sick,
    Chang'd colour, recanted and cry'd.

False friends by his side, the STATE RUDDER to guide,
    Are dangerous leaders to trust;   30
Yet strange as it seems, he those best esteems,
    Who his property injure the most.

Few minds, 'tis well known, to maturity grown,
    Imperious commands can endure;
And terms better made, might the PARENT have had,   35
    Than conquest can ever ensure.

Then come, smiling PEACE,[11] cause discord to cease,
    And all be united and free;
Thy welcome approach, is solicited much,
    Grant soon we the BLESSING may see.   40

Ignatius Sancho, from *The Letters of the Late Ignatius Sancho, An African* (1782)

Ignatius Sancho (*c.*1729–80) was born on a slave ship on the middle passage from
Africa to the Americas. He was baptised in the Spanish colonies in the North of

---

[9]   *Savage ... threw*: Edmund Burke, in his 'Speech on the Use of Indians' (1778), was
     outraged by the recruitment of North American Indians by British forces.
[10] *German Butchers*: sections of the British forces were made up of German mercenaries.
[11] PEACE: peace negotiations started in 1782 a finished with the Peace of Versailles in 1783.

South America, and, aged two, was taken to England and given as a present to three sisters in Greenwich. Eventually he was taken under the wing of the Dowager Duchess of Montagu and made valet to the Duke, her son, who would help him set up a grocery store in Westminster with his wife, Anne (another ex-slave). Sancho was also a musician, the first Afro-Briton to have his correspondence published, as well as the first art critic, and the only Afro-British voter in the eighteenth century. His correspondence was edited and published by Francis Crewe, one of Sancho's correspondents, in 1782.

Sancho's *Letters* was prefaced by a short 'Life' by Joseph Jekyll which concludes with the resounding comment that 'he who surveys the extent of intellect to which Ignatius Sancho had attained by self-education, will perhaps conclude, that the perfection of reasoning faculties does not depend on a peculiar conformation of the skull or the colour of a common integument'.[1] Sancho's idiosyncratic style owes a heavy debt to the novelist Laurence Sterne: the copious use of the dash, which conveys a breathless sincerity, taps into contemporary sentimental modes that espouse the display of fine and humane feelings. Yet, like Sterne, Sancho combines this with a deft use of irony – how are we to read his declaration that 'I am only a lodger'? As a free black man living at the centre of the British empire, Sancho's identity in these letters is interesting. He condemns slavery, yet is a vociferous supporter of the British empire's claims on America and disparages Catholic rioters with an ironic reference to 'liberty'; and while he censures a friend's son's racism in India, in the same letter he imagines a beneficial empire of trade that Thomson would have applauded. This selection includes his letter to Sterne, a letter to his friend's son Jack Wingrave, one on the American War of Independence, and finally a letter describing the anti-Catholic 'Gordon riots'.

**LETTER XXXV,
TO MR. STERNE.[2]**

July, [1766].

REVEREND SIR,
It would be an insult on your humanity (or perhaps look like it) to apologize for the liberty I am taking.—I am one of those people whom the vulgar and illiberal call '*Negurs*.'—The first part of my life was rather unlucky, as I was placed in a family who judged ignorance the best and only security for obedience.—A little reading and writing I got by unwearied application.— The latter part of my life has been—thro' God's blessing, truly fortunate, having spent it in the service of one of the best families in the kingdom.— My chief pleasure has been books.—Philanthropy I adore.—How very much, good Sir, am I (amongst millions) indebted to you for the character of your amiable uncle Toby!—I declare, I would walk ten miles in the

---

[1]   Jekyll, 'The Life of Ignatius Sancho', *Letters*, xv–xvi. For the annotation of Sancho's correspondence, my debts are to the scholarship of Vincent Carretta.

[2]   MR. STERNE: Laurence Sterne (1713–68) novelist and clergyman. This letter is from volume I where it is incorrectly dated as 1776.

dog-days, to shake hands with the honest corporal.[3]—Your Sermons have touch'd me to the heart, and I hope have amended it, which brings me to the point.—In your tenth discourse, page seventy-eight, in the second volume—is this very affecting passage—'Consider how great a part of our species—in all ages down to this—have been trod under the feet of cruel and capricious tyrants, who would neither hear their cries, nor pity their distresses.—Consider slavery—what it is—how bitter a draught—and how many millions are made to drink it!'[4]—Of all my favorite authors, not one has drawn a tear in favour of my miserable black brethren—excepting yourself, and the humane author of Sir George Ellison.[5]—I think you will forgive me;—I am sure you will applaud me for beseeching you to give one half hour's attention to slavery, as it is at this day practised in our West Indies.—That subject, handled in your striking manner, would ease the yoke (perhaps) of many—but if only of one—Gracious God!—what a feast to a benevolent heart!—and, sure I am, you are an epicurean in acts of charity.—You, who are universally read, and as universally admired—you could not fail—Dear Sir, think in me you behold the uplifted hands of thousands of my brother Moors.—Grief (you pathetically observe) is eloquent;—figure to yourself their attitudes; hear their supplicating addresses!—alas!—you cannot refuse.—Humanity must comply—in which hope I beg permission to subscribe myself,

Reverend, Sir, &c.
I. SANCHO

[...]

LETTER I.
TO MR. J[ACK] W[INGRAV]E.[6]

1778.

Your good father insists on my scribbling a sheet of absurdities, and gives me a notable reason for it, that is, 'Jack will be pleased with it.'—Now be it known to you—I have a respect both for father and son—yea for the whole family,

---

3   *Uncle Toby ... corporal*: in Sterne's *Tristram Shandy* (1759–67), Uncle Toby and Corporal Trim (both retired from service) pity the victims of slavery and the effects of inequality; vol. IX, ch. VI.

4   *Consider ... drink it!*: the quotation (with minor changes) is from Sterne's *The Sermons of Mr. Yorick* (1760–69), Sermon X, 'Job's Account of the Shortness and Troubles of Life, Considered'. Mr. Yorick is the benevolent parson from *Tristram Shandy*.

5   *Ellison*: the novel *The History of Sir George Ellison* (1766) by Sarah Scott (1720–95), concerned the actions of its eponymous hero. Ellison is a man of sentimental feeling, and re-orders his Jamaican plantation along more benevolent lines (though never abolishes slavery itself).

6   *MR. J[ACK] W[INGRAV]E*: this is the son of Sancho's friend John Wingrave (a London bookbinder and bookseller), who is working in India. The following letters are from volume II.

who are every soul (that I have the honour or pleasure to know anything of) tinctured—and leavened with all the obsolete goodness of old times—so that a man runs some hazard in being seen in the W[ingrav]e's society of being biased to Christianity.—I never see your poor Father—but his eyes betray his feelings—for the hopeful youth in India—a tear of joy dancing upon the lids— is a plaudit not to be equalled this side death!—See the effects of right-doing, my worthy friend—continue in the tract of rectitude—and despise poor paltry Europeans—titled—Nabobs.—Read your Bible—as day follows night, God's blessings follow virtue—honour—and riches bring up the rear—and the end is peace.—Courage, my boy—I have done preaching.—Old folks love to seem wise—and if you are silly enough to correspond with grey hairs—take the consequence.—I have had the pleasure of reading most of your letters, through the kindness of your father.—Youth is naturally prone to vanity— such is the weakness of Human Nature, that pride has a fortress in the best of hearts—I know no person that possesses a better than Johnny W[ingrav]e— but although flattery is poison to youth, yet truth obliges me to confess that your correspondence betrays no symptom of vanity—but teems with truths of an honest affection—which merits praise—and commands esteem.

In some one of your letters which I do not recollect—you speak (with honest indignation) of the treachery and chicanery of the Natives.[7]—My good friend, you should remember from whom they learnt those vices:— the first christian visitors found them a simple, harmless people—but the cursed avidity for wealth urged these first visitors (and all the succeeding ones) to such acts of deception—and even wanton cruelty—that the poor ignorant Natives soon learnt to turn the knavish—and diabolical arts which they too soon imbibed—upon their teachers.

I am sorry to observe that the practice of your country (which as a resident I love—and for its freedom—and for the many blessings I enjoy in it—shall ever have my warmest wishes—prayers—and blessings); I say it is with reluctance, that I must observe your country's conduct has been uniformly wicked in the East—West-Indies—and even on the coast of Guinea.—The grand object of English navigators—indeed of all christian navigators—is money—money—money—for which I do not pretend to blame them— Commerce was meant by the goodness of the Deity to diffuse the various goods of the earth into every part — to unite mankind in the blessed chains of brotherly love—society—and mutual dependence:—the enlightened

---

7   'Extracts of two letters from Mr. W[ingrav]e to his Father, dated Bombay, 1776 and 1777. "1776. I have introduced myself to Mr G—, who behaved very friendly in giving me some advice, which was very necessary, as the inhabitants, who are chiefly Blacks, are a set of canting, deceitful people, and of whom one must have great caution." "1777. I am now thoroughly convinced, that the account which Mr G— gave me of the natives of this coun- try is just and true, that they are a set of deceitful people, and have not such a word as Gratitude in their language, neither do they know what it is—and as to their dealings in trade, they are like unto Jews."' [original note].

Christian should diffuse the riches of the Gospel of peace—with the commodities of his respective land—Commerce attended with strict honesty—and with Religion for its companion—would be a blessing to every shore it touched at.—In Africa, the poor wretched natives—blessed with the most fertile and luxuriant soil—are rendered so much the more miserable for what Providence meant as a blessing:—the Christians' abominable traffic for slaves—and the horrid cruelty and treachery of the petty Kings—encouraged by their Christian customers—who carry them strong liquors—to enflame their national madness—and powder—and bad fire-arms—to furnish them with the hellish means of killing and kidnapping.—But enough—it is a subject that sours my blood—and I am sure will not please the friendly bent of your social affections.—I mentioned these only to guard my friend against being too hasty in condemning the knavery of a people who bad as they may be—possibly—were made worse—by their Christian visitors.—Make human nature thy study—wherever thou residest—whatever the religion—or the complexion—study their hearts.—Simplicity, kindness, and charity be thy guide—with these even Savages will respect you—and God will bless you!

[...]

LETTER XXXVIII.
TO MR. R[USH].[8]

September 7, 1779.

DEAR FRIEND,
We are all in the wrong—a *little*.—Admiral Barrington is arrived from the West-India station—and brings the pleasant news—that d'Estaigne fell in with five of our ships of the line—with the best part of his fleet.[9] We fought like Englishmen—unsupported by the rest:—they fought till they were quite dismasted—and almost wrecked;—and at last gave the French enough of it—and got away all, though in plight—bad enough:—but the consequence was, the immediate capture of the Grenadas.—Add to this—Sir Charles Hardy is put into Portsmouth, or Gosport;[10]—and although forty odd strong in line of battle ships—is obliged to give up the sovereignty of the channel to the enemy—L[or]d S[andwic]h is gone to Portsmouth, to be a witness of England's disgrace—and his own shame.[11]—In faith, my friend, the present time is rather *comique*.—Ireland almost in as

---

8 *MR. R[USH]*: Roger Rush, a former fellow servant.

9 *Barrington ... d'Estaigne*: Samuel Barrington (1729–1800), commander-in chief in the West-Indies in 1778. He was replaced by John Byron (1723–86), who has just lost a battle to the French, commanded by Jean Baptiste Charles Henri Hector, comte d'Estaing (1729–74).

10 *Hardy*: Sir Charles Hardy (?1716–80) was commander in the English channel.

11 *Sandwich*: John Montagu, Fourth Earl of Sandwich, (1718–92), first Lord of the Admiralty (1748–51, 1771–82).

true a state of rebellion as America.—Admirals uarrelling in the West-Indies—and at home admirals that do not chuse to fight.—The British empire mouldering away in the West—annihilated in the North—Gibraltar going—and England fast asleep.—what says Mr. B[rowne] to all this?[12]—he is a ministerialist:—for my part it's nothing to me—as I am only a lodger—and hardly that.—Give my love and respect to the ladies—and best compliments to all the gentlemen with respects to Mr. And Mrs. I[reland].

Give me a line to know how you all do—the post is going—only time to say God bless you.—I remain

Yours affectionate,

I. SANCHO.

[...]

LETTER LXVII.
TO J[OHN] S[PINK], ESQ.[13]

Charles Street, June 6, 1780.

DEAR AND MOST RESPECTED SIR,

In the midst of the most cruel and ridiculous confusion—I am now set down to give you a very imperfect sketch of the maddest people—that the maddest times were ever plagued with.—The public prints have informed you (without doubt) of last Friday's transactions;—the insanity of L[or]d G[eorge] G[ordon][14] and the worse than Negro barbarity of the populace;—the burnings and devastations of each night—you will also see in the prints:—This day, by consent, was set apart for the farther consideration of the wished-for repeal;—the people (who had their proper cue from his lordship) assembled by ten o'clock in the morning.—Lord N[orth],[15] who had been up in council at home till four in the morning, got to the house before eleven, just a quarter of an hour before the associators reached Palace-yard:—but, I should tell you, in council there was a deputation from all parties;—the S[helburne][16] party were for prosecuting L[or]d G[eorge], and leaving him at large;—the At[torne]y G[enera]l laughed at the idea,

---

12   *Mr. Browne*: this may be Charles Browne, steward of Sir Charles Bunbury.
13   *J[OHN] S[PINK], ESQ*: John Spink (1729–94), friend of Sancho's and a draper and banker.
14   *Gordon*: Lord George Gordon MP (1751–93) vehemently opposed the Roman Catholic Relief Act, which offered a small measure of toleration for Catholics, but which was deeply resented by many in Protestant England. In 1780 his political protest soon turned into an anarchic riot as the working-class populace of London broke windows, burned down the homes and chapels of Catholics, and finally set free the inmates of Newgate, London's main prison. After five days of the 'Gordon riots', nearly a thousand people had died before the army finally brought order. Gordon was unsuccessfully tried for treason.
15   *Lord North*: Frederick, Lord North (1732–92), Prime Minister 1770–82.
16   *Shelburne*: William Petty, Second earl of Shelburne (1737–1805) statesman.

and declared it was doing just nothing;—the M[inistr]y were for his expulsion, and so dropping him gently into insignificancy;—that was thought wrong, as he would still be industrious in mischief;—the R[ockingha]m party,[17] I should suppose, you will think counselled best, which is, this day to expel him the house—commit him to the Tower—and then prosecute him at leisure—by which means he will lose the opportunity of getting a seat in the next parliament—and have decent leisure to repent him of the heavy evils he has occasioned.—There is at this present moment at least a hundred thousand poor, miserable, ragged rabble, from twelve to sixty years of age, with blue cockades in their hats[18]—besides half as many women and children—all parading the streets—the bridge—the park—ready for any and every mischief.—Gracious God! what's the matter now? I was obliged to leave off—the shouts of the mob—the horrid clashing of swords—and the clutter of a multitude in swiftest motion—drew me to the door—when every one in the street was employed in shutting up shop.—It is now just five o'clock—the ballad—singers are exhausting their musical talents—with the downfall of Popery, S[andwic]h, and N[ort]h.—Lord S[andwic]h narrowly escaped with life about an hour since;—the mob seized his chariot going to the house, broke his glasses, and, in struggling to get his lordship out, they somehow have cut his face;—the guards flew to his assistance—the light-horse scowered the road, got his chariot, escorted him from the coffee-house, where he had fled for protection, to his carriage, and guarded him bleeding very fast home. This—this — is liberty! genuine British liberty!—This instant about two thousand liberty boys are swearing and swaggering by with large sticks—thus armed in hopes of meeting with the Irish chairmen and labourers—all the guards are out—and all the horse;—the poor fellows are just worn out for want of rest—having been on duty ever since Friday.—Thank heaven, it rains; may it increase, so as to send these deluded wretches safe to their homes, their families, and wives! About two this afternoon, a large party took it into their heads to visit the King and Queen, and entered the Park for that purpose—but found the guard too numerous to be forced, and after some useless attempts gave it up.—It is reported, the house will either be prorogued, or parliament dissolved, this evening—as it is in vain to think of attending any business while this anarchy lasts.

I cannot but felicitate you, my good friend, upon the happy distance you are placed from our scene of confusion.—May foul Discord and her cursed train never nearer approach your blessed abode! Tell Mrs. S[pink], her good heart would ache, did she see the anxiety, the woe, in the faces of mothers,

---

17   *Rockingham*: Charles Wentworth, Marquis of Rockingham (1730–82), leader of the opposition party to North.

18   *blue cockades*: Protestants wore these as a sign of their opposition to those who supported the Catholic Relief act.

wives, and sweethearts, each equally anxious for the object of their wishes, the beloved of their hearts. Mrs. Sancho and self both cordially join in love and gratitude, and every good wish—crowned with the peace of God, which passeth all understanding, &c.

I am, dear Sir,

Yours ever by inclination,

IGN. SANCHO

Postscript

The Sardinian ambassador offered 500 guineas to the rabble, to save a painting of our Saviour from the flames, and 1000 guineas not to destroy an exceeding fine organ: the gentry told him, they would burn him if they could get at him, and destroyed the picture and organ directly.[19]—I am not sorry I was born in Afric.—I shall tire you, I fear—and, if I cannot get a frank, make you pay dear for bad news.[20]—There is about a thousand mad men, armed with clubs, bludgeons, and crows, just now set off for Newgate, to liberate, they say, their honest comrades.—I wish they do not some of them lose their lives of liberty before morning. It is thought by many who discern deeply, that there is more at the bottom of this business than merely the repeal of an act—which has as yet produced no bad consequences, and perhaps never might.—I am forced to own, that I am for an universal toleration. Let us convert by our example, and conquer by our meekness and brotherly love!

Eight o'clock. Lord G[eorge] G[ordon] has this moment announced to my Lords the mob—that the act shall be repealed this evening:—upon this, they gave a hundred cheers—took the horses from his hackney-coach—and rolled him full jollily away:—they are huzzaing now ready to crack their throats

Huzzah.

Edmund Burke, from
Mr. Burke's Speech ... on
Mr. Fox's East India Bill (1784)

Charles James Fox's bill of 1783 was one of a series of bills from the 1760s onwards that attempted to increase the British government's intervention in the East India

---

[19]   *The Sardinian ... directly*: the rioting mob destroyed the Catholic chapel of Vittorio Amedeo Sallier de la Tour (1726–1800), the Sardinian ambassador.

[20]   *frank ... news*: the receiver paid for letters unless 'franked' by an MP or Lord.

Company's operations after concerns of corruption. The bill was unsuccessful and the rather more conservative India Act was passed by William Pitt in 1784. Burke was a fierce critic of the East India Company and his speech on this bill came from a knowledge of Indian culture and affairs that was unmatched in Parliament. His fear was that the misrule and greed of the Company in India would corrupt the traditional values of British liberty and virtuous commerce. Burke's speech, given in December 1783, focused on the company factor, the 'nabob', as responsible for overturning the proper order of relations between the Company and its agents, and therefore between the British government and India: a disruption that would spread out into the social fabric of Britain itself. Burke's rhetorical manipulation of his audience is clear in the portrayal of the dignity of Indian culture and civilisation (even if this is in the past) and provides a point of contrast to the depredations of the Company's agents who are 'birds of prey'. Yet at the same time, Burke is arguing for a less 'crude' and more pervasive and lasting imperial management of India.[1]

The population of this great empire[2] is not easy to be calculated. When the countries, of which it is composed, came into our possession, they were all eminently peopled, and eminently productive; though at that time considerably declined from their antient prosperity. But, since they are come into our hands!—! However if we take the period of our estimate immediately before the utter desolation of the Carnatic,[3] and if we allow for the havoc which our government had even then made in these regions, we cannot, in my opinion, rate the population at much less than thirty millions of souls; more than four times the number of persons in the island of Great Britain.

My next enquiry to that of the number, is the quality and description of the inhabitants. This multitude of men does not consist of an abject and barbarous populace; much less of gangs of savages, like the Guaranies and Chiquitos, who wander on the waste borders of the river of Amazons, or the Plate; but a people for ages civilized and cultivated; cultivated by all the arts of polished life, whilst we were yet in the woods. There, have been (and still the skeletons remain) princes once of great dignity, authority, and opulence. There, are to be found the chiefs of tribes and nations. There is to be found an antient and venerable priesthood, the depository of their laws, learning, and history, the guides of the people whilst living, and their consolation in death; a nobility of great antiquity and renown; a multitude of cities, not exceeded in population and trade by those of the first class in Europe; merchants and bankers, individual houses of whom have once vied in capital with the Bank of England; whose credit had often supported a tottering state, and preserved their governments in the midst of war and

---

[1]   From *Mr. Burke's Speech, on 1st December 1783, Upon the Question for the Speaker's Leaving the Chair, in Order for the House to Resolve Itself into a Committee on Mr. Fox's East India Bill,* pp. 13–15, 31–3, 85.

[2]   *empire*: that is, India.

[3]   *Carnatic*: a region in the South Eastern coast of India.

desolation; millions of ingenious manufacturers and mechanicks; millions of the most diligent, and not the least intelligent, tillers of the earth. Here are to be found almost all the religions professed by men, the Bramincal, the Mussulmen, the Eastern and the Western Christian.[4]

If I were to take the whole aggregate of our possessions there, I should compare it, as the nearest parallel I can find, with the empire of Germany. Our immediate possessions I should compare with the Austrian dominions, and they would not suffer in the comparison. The Nabob of Oude might stand for the King of Prussia; the Nabob of Arcot I would compare, as superior in territory, and equal in revenue, to the Elector of Saxony.[5] Cheyt Sing, the Rajah of Benares, might well rank with the prince of Hesse at least; and the Rajah of Tanjore (though hardly equal in extent of dominion, superior in revenue) to the Elector of Bavaria.[6] The Polygars and the northern Zemindars,[7] and other great chiefs, might well class with the rest of the Princes, Dukes, Counts, Marquisses, and Bishops in the empire; all of whom I mention to honour, and surely without disparagement to any or all of those most respectable princes and grandees.

All this vast mass, composed of so many orders and classes of men, is again infinitely diversified by manners, by religion, by hereditary employment, through all their possible combinations. This renders the handling of India a matter in an high degree critical and delicate. But oh! it has been handled rudely indeed. Even some of the reformers seem to have forgot that they had any thing to do but to regulate the tenants of a manor, or the shopkeepers of the next county town.

It is an empire of this extent, of this complicated nature, of this dignity and importance, that I have compared to Germany, and the German government; not for an exact resemblance, but as a sort of a middle term, by which India might be approximated to our understandings, and if possible to our feelings; in order to awaken something of sympathy for the unfortunate natives, of which I am afraid we are not perfectly susceptible, whilst we look at this very remote object through a false and cloudy medium.

[...]

Our conquest there, after twenty years, is as crude as it was the first day. The natives scarcely know what it is to see the grey head of an Englishman.

---

4   *Bramincal ... Western Christian*: the Brahminical caste of Hinduism; Islam; and the Eastern, or Greek Orthodox Church, which separated from the Western, or Roman Church in the ninth century.

5   *nabob of Oude ... nabob of Arcot*: Oude is a region in the North of India; Arcot is in the Carnatic.

6   *Cheyt Singh ... rajah of Tanjore*: Cheyt Singh was rajah of Benares, in the North-east of India; Tanjore was another city in the Carnatic.

7   *Polygars ... Zemindars*: Polygars were minor rulers on the Malabar coast, west India. Zamindars were revenue-collecting landholders in the North Eastern coast of India.

Young men (boys almost) govern there, without society, and without sympathy with the natives. They have no more social habits with the people, than if they still resided in England; nor indeed any species of intercourse but that which is necessary to making a sudden fortune, with a view to a remote settlement. Animated with all the avarice of age, and all the impetuosity of youth, they roll in one after another; wave after wave; and there is nothing before the eyes of the natives but an endless, hopeless prospect of new flights of birds of prey and passage, with appetites continually renewing for a food that is continually wasting. Every rupee of profit made by an Englishman is lost for ever to India. With us are no retributory superstitions, by which a foundation of charity compensates, through ages, to the poor, for the rapine and injustice of a day. With us no pride erects stately monuments which repair the mischiefs which pride had produced, and which adorn a country out of its own spoils. England has erected no churches, no hospitals,[8] no palaces, no schools; England has built no bridges, made no high roads, cut no navigations, dug out no reservoirs. Every other conqueror of every other description has left some monument, either of state or beneficence, behind him. Were we to be driven out of India this day, nothing would remain, to tell that it had been possessed, during the inglorious period of our dominion, by any thing better than the ouran-outang or the tiger.

There is nothing in the boys we send to India worse than the boys whom we are whipping at school, or that we see trailing a pike, or bending over a desk at home. But as English youth in India drink the intoxicating draught of authority and dominion before their heads are able to bear it, and as they are full grown in fortune long before they are ripe in principle, neither nature nor reason have any opportunity to exert themselves for remedy of the excesses of their premature power. The consequences of their conduct, which in good minds, (and many of theirs are probably such) might pro- duce penitence or amendment, are unable to pursue the rapidity of their flight. Their prey is lodged in England; and the cries of India are given to seas and winds, to be blown about, in every breaking up of the monsoon, over a remote and unhearing ocean. In India all the vices operate by which sudden fortune is acquired; in England are often displayed, by the same persons, the virtues which dispense hereditary wealth. Arrived in England, the destroyers of the nobility and gentry of a whole kingdom will find the best company in this nation, at a board of elegance and hospitality. Here the manufacturer and husbandman will bless the just and punctual hand, that in India has torn the cloth from the loom, or wrested the scanty portion of rice and salt from the peasant of Bengal, or wrung from him the very opium in which he forgot his oppressions and his oppressor. They marry into your families; they enter into your senate; they ease your estates by loans; they raise their value by demand; they cherish and protect your relations which

---

8   'The paltry foundation at Calcutta is scarcely worth naming as an exception' [Burke's note].

lie heavy on your patronage; and there is scarcely an house in the kingdom that does not feel some concern and interest that makes all reform of our eastern government appear officious and disgusting; and, on the whole, a most discouraging attempt. In such an attempt you hurt those who are able to return kindness or to resent injury. If you succeed, you save those who cannot so much as give you thanks. All these things shew the difficulty of the work we have on hand: but they shew its necessity too. Our Indian government is in its best state a grievance. It is necessary that the correctives should be uncommonly vigorous; and the work of men sanguine, warm, and even impassioned in the cause. But it is an arduous thing to plead against abuses of a power which originates from your own country, and affects those whom we are used to consider as strangers.

[…]

The vote is not to protect the stock, but the stock is bought to acquire the vote; and the end of the vote is to cover and support, against justice, some man of power who has made an obnoxious fortune in India; or to maintain in power those who are actually employing it in the acquisition of such a fortune; and to avail themselves in return of his patronage, that he may shower the spoils of the East, "barbaric pearl and gold,"[9] on them, their families, and dependents. So that all the relations of the Company are not only changed, but inverted. The servants in India are not appointed by the Directors, but the Directors are chosen by them. The trade is carried on with their capitals. To them the revenues of the country are mortgaged. The seat of the supreme power is in Calcutta.

---

[9]   *barbaric pearl and gold*: from John Milton, *Paradise Lost* (1667), 2: 4, where Satan's throne in Hell is described. Burke's cause for concern is the manipulation of the company's directors: Burke argued that the interest on the stock in the company that directors were required to hold was virtually worthless compared to the profits that were capable of being made from India. What they were worth, however, was the price of a vote on the General Court, the meeting of stockholders.

Quobna Ottobah Cugoano, from *Thoughts and Sentiments on the Evil and Wicked Traffic of the Slavery and Commerce of the Human Species* (1787)

Quobna Ottobah Cugoano (usually known as Ottobah Cugoano) was born around 1757 on the coast of what is now Ghana. He was kidnapped into slavery at about the age of thirteen and taken to Grenada. Eventually he was brought to England in 1772 and set free. He was advised to be baptised in order not to be re-enslaved and took the name John Stuart. Cugoano wrote *Thoughts and Sentiments* while working in London as a servant to the artist Richard Cosway, and it was there that he also became friends with the ex-slave Olaudah Equiano (who would rise to fame with his autobiography *The Interesting Narrative of the Life of Olaudah Equiano* in 1789). After this, we have no record of Cugoano's subsequent life, or when or how he died. Cuguano's *Thoughts and Sentiments* was the first work by an African that explicitly called for the outright abolition of the slave trade and for the freeing of the slaves. In the extracts below, his re-appropriation of the key tropes of cultural difference in the eighteenth century – liberty, complexion, commerce – reveal an attempt to undermine racialised identity and to synthesise Christianity and imperialism.[1]

No necessity, or any situation of men, however poor, pitiful and wretched they may be, can warrant them to rob others, or oblige them to become thieves, because they are poor, miserable and wretched: But the robbers of men, the kidnappers, ensnarers and slave-holders, who take away the common rights and privileges of others to support and enrich themselves, are universally those pitiful and detestable wretches; for the ensnaring of others, and taking away their liberty by slavery and oppression, is the worst kind of robbery, as most opposite to every precept and injunction of the Divine Law, and contrary to that command which enjoins that *all men should love their neighbours as themselves,*[2] and *that they should do unto others, as they would that men should do to them.*[3] As to any other laws that slave-holders may make among themselves, as respecting slaves, they can be of no better kind, nor give them any better character, than what is implied in the common report—that there may be some honesty among thieves. This may seem a harsh comparison, but the parallel is so coincident that, I must

---

[1] Text from pp. 4–5, 143–4.
[2] *all men … themselves*: Matthew, 19.19.
[3] *that … them*: Matthew, 7.12.

say, I can find no other way of expressing my Thoughts and Sentiments, without making use of some harsh words and comparisons against the carriers on of such abandoned wickedness. But, in this little undertaking, I must humbly hope the impartial reader will excuse such defects as may arise from want of better education; and as to the resentment of those who can lay their cruel lash upon the backs of thousands, for a thousand times less crimes than writing against their enormous wickedness and brutal avarice, is what I may be sure to meet with.

However, it cannot but be very discouraging to a man of my complexion in such an attempt as this, to meet with the evil aspersions of some men, who say, 'That an African is not entitled to any competent degree of knowledge, or capable of imbibing any sentiments of probity; and that nature designed him for some inferior link in the chain,[4] fitted only to be a slave.' But when I meet with those who make no scruple to deal with the human species, as with the beasts of the earth, I must think them not only brutish, but wicked and base; and that their aspersions are insidious and false: And if such men can boast of greater degrees of knowledge, than any African is entitled to, I shall let them enjoy all the advantages of it unenvied, as I fear it consists only in a greater share of infidelity, and that of a blacker kind than only skin deep. And if their complexion be not what I may suppose, it is at least the nearest in resemblance to an infernal hue. A good man will neither speak nor do as a bad man will; but if a man is bad, it makes no difference whether he be a black or a white devil.

[...]

To put an end to the wickedness of slavery and merchandizing of men, and to prevent murder, extirpation and dissolution, is what every righteous nation ought to seek after; and to endeavour to diffuse knowledge and instruction to all the heathen nations wherever they can, is the grand duty of all Christian men. But while the horrible traffic of slavery is admitted and practiced, there can be but little hope of any good proposals meeting with success anywhere; for the abandoned carriers of it on have spread the poison of their iniquity wherever they come, at home and abroad. Were the iniquitous laws in support of it, and the whole of that oppression and injustice abolished, and the righteous laws of Christianity, equity, justice and humanity established in the room thereof, multitudes of nations would flock to the standard of truth, and instead of revolting away, they would count it their greatest happiness to be under the protection and jurisdiction of a righteous government. And in that respect, *in the multitude of the people is the King's honour; but in the want of people, is the destruction of the Prince.*[5]

---

4   *chain*: the 'Great Chain of Being', where existence was ordered as a gradated hierarchy from God, down through humankind, and through the animals. Some, like Edward Long, deemed Africans not far removed from apes.

5   *in the multitude … Prince*: Proverbs, 14.28.

We would wish to have the grandeur and fame of the British empire to extend far and wide; and the glory and honor of God to be promoted by it, and the interest of Christianity set forth among all the nations wherever its influence and power can extend; but not to be supported by the insidious pirates, depredators, murderers and slave-holders. And as it might diffuse knowledge and instruction to others, that it might receive a tribute of reward from all its territories, forts and garrisons, without being oppressive to any. But contrary to this the wickedness of many of the White People who keep slaves, and contrary to all the laws and duties of Christianity which the Scriptures teach, they have in general endeavoured to keep the Black People in total ignorance as much as they can, which must be a great dishonor to any Christian government, and injurious to the safety and happiness of rulers.

CODA: John Freeth, *Botany Bay* (1790)

Botany Bay (discovered and annexed by Cook on his first expedition) was identified by the expedition's botanist Joseph Banks as particularly fertile ground for colonisation. By 1786 schemes for transporting convicts there were being noisily debated, and in January 1788 the first convicts arrived. It is now difficult to reconstruct the strategy or motives behind this colonisation, but Freeth acutely grasps the mood as the British empire turns away from its losses and looks to another potential new Eden.[1]

> Away with all whimsical bubbles of air,
> Which only excite a momentary stare;
> Attention to plans of utility pay,
> Weigh anchor and steer towards BOTANY BAY.
>
> Let no one think much of a trifling expence,   5
> Who knows what may happen a hundred years hence;
> The loss of America what can repay?
> New colonies seek for at BOTANY BAY.
>
> O'er Neptune's domain how extensive the scope!
> Of quickly returning how distant the hope!   10
> The CAPE must be doubled, and then bear away,
> Two thousand good leagues to reach BOTANY BAY.

---

[1]   From *The Political Songster or, a Touch on the Times* (6th edn, 1790), pp. 124–5.

Of those *precious* souls which for nobody care,
It seems a large cargo the kingdom can spare;
To ship a few hundreds off make no delay,   15
They cannot too soon go to BOTANY BAY.
They go of an island to take special charge,
Much warmer than Britain, and ten times as large;
No Custom-house duty, no freightage to pay,
And tax-free they'll live when at BOTANY BAY.   20

This garden of Eden, this new promis'd land,
The time to set sail for is almost at hand;
Ye worst of land-lubbers, made ready for sea,
There's room for you all about BOTANY BAY.

As scores of each sex to this place must proceed,   25
In twenty years time—only think of the breed;
Major Semple, should Fortune much kindness display,[2]
May live to be king over BOTANY BAY.

For a general good, make a general sweep,
The beauty of life is good order to keep;   30
With night-prowling hateful disturbers away,
And send the whole tribe into BOTANY BAY.

Ye chiefs who go out on this naval exploit,
The work to accomplish, and set matters right;
To IRELAND be kind, call at CORK on your way,   35
And take a few WHITE BOYS to BOTANY BAY.[3]

Commercial arrangements give prospect of joy,
Fair and firm may be kept ev'ry national tie;
And mutual confidence those who betray,
Be sent to the bottom of BOTANY BAY.   40

---

[2]   *Major Semple*: a notorious adventurer who was sentenced to transportation.
[3]   *WHITE BOYS*: Irish nationalists.

Bibliography and Further Reading

While some attempt has been made to list further eighteenth-century texts under certain issues or geographical area in the name of clarity, they of course engage with issues across these headings. It should also be understood that this is a selective and indicative bibliography and far from exhaustive.

EMPIRE AND IDENTITY

On defining 'empire' and conceptualising eighteenth-century imperialism, the following have been influential: Richard Koebner, *Empire* (Cambridge University Press, 1961); C.A. Bayly, *Imperial Meridian: The British Empire and the World, 1780–1830* (Longman, 1989); Anthony Pagden, *Lords of all the World: Ideologies of Empire in Spain, Britain and France c.1500–c.1800* (Yale University Press, 1995); Kathleen Wilson, *The Sense of the People: Politics, Culture and Imperialism in England, 1715–1785* (Cambridge University Press, 1995); David Armitage, *The Ideological Origins of the British Empire* (Cambridge University Press, 2000); Linda Colley, *Captives: Britain, Empire and the World 1600–1850* (Jonathan Cape, 2002). See also the essays in Nicholas Canny, ed., *Oxford History of the British Empire, vol. I: The Origins of Empire: British Overseas Enterprise to the Close of the Seventeenth Century* (Oxford University Press, 1998); P.J. Marshall, ed., *Oxford History of the British Empire, vol. II: The Eighteenth Century* (Oxford University Press, 1998) [hereafter *OHBE II*]. For two sides of the debate over the analysis of empire in the eighteenth century, see Robert W. Winks, ed., *Oxford History of the British Empire, vol. V: Historiography* (Oxford University Press, 1999); Kathleen Wilson, ed., *A New Imperial History: Culture, Identity and Modernity in Britain and the Empire, 1660–1840* (Cambridge University Press, 2004) [hereafter, *New Imperial History*].

For eighteenth-century philosophical debates on identity, see: Charles Taylor, *Sources of the Self: The Making of Modernity* (Cambridge University Press, 1989); Felicity Nussbaum, *The Autobiographical Subject: Gender and Ideology in Eighteenth-Century England* (Johns Hopkins University Press, 1989); Roy Porter,

The Creation of the Modern World: The Untold Story of the British Enlightenment (Norton, 2000).

On identity in the context of colonial and imperial relations in the eighteenth century: P.J. Marshall and Glyndwr Williams, *The Great Map of Mankind: British Perceptions of the World in the Age of Enlightenment* (Dent, 1982); Nicholas Canny and Anthony Pagden, eds, *Colonial Identity in the Atlantic World* (Princeton University Press, 1987); Bernard Bailyn and Philip D. Morgan, eds, *Strangers Within the Realm: Cultural Margins of the First British Empire* (University of North Caroline Press, 1991); Nicholas Hudson, 'From "Nation" to "Race": The Origin of Racial Classification in Eighteenth-Century Thought', *Eighteenth-Century Studies*, 29 (1996); Jack P. Greene, 'Empire and Identity', in *OHBE II*; Srinivas Aravamudan, *Tropicopolitans: Colonialism and Agency, 1688–1804* (Duke University Press, 1999); Roxann Wheeler, *The Complexion of Race: Categories of Difference in Eighteenth-Century British Culture* (University of Pennsylvania Press, 2000); Laura Brown, *Fables of Modernity: Literature and Culture in the English Eighteenth Century* (Cornell University Press, 2001); Felicity Nussbaum, *The Limits of the Human: Fictions of Anomaly, Race, and Gender in the Long Eighteenth Century* (Cambridge University Press, 2003); Kathleen Wilson, *The Island Race: Englishness, Empire and Gender in the Eighteenth Century* (Routledge, 2003); Dror Wahrman, *The Making of the Modern Self: Identity and Culture in Eighteenth-Century England* (Yale University Press, 2004). See also the essays in Nussbaum, ed., *The Global Eighteenth Century* (Johns Hopkins University Press, 2003) [hereafter, *Global*], and in *New Imperial History*.

The literature on national identity is vast, but see especially: Benedict Anderson, *Imagined Communities: Reflections on the Origins and Spread of Nationalism* (Verso, 1983); Gerald Newman, *The Rise of English Nationalism: A Cultural History, 1740–1830* (Weidenfeld and Nicolson, 1987); Etienne Balibar and Immanuel Wallerstein, *Race, Nation, Class: Ambiguous Identities*, trans., Chris Turner (Verso, 1988); Raphael Samuel, ed., *Patriotism: the Making and Breaking of British National Identity*, 3 vols (Routledge, 1989); E. J. Hobsbawm, *Nations and Nationalism since 1780: Programme, Myth, Reality* (Cambridge University Press, 1990); Homi Bhabha, ed., *Nation and Narration* (Routledge, 1990); Linda Colley, *Britons: Forging the Nation, 1707–1837* (Pimlico, 1992); Tony Claydon and Ian McBride, eds, *Protestantism and National Identity: Britain and Ireland, c.1650–c.1850* (Cambridge University Press, 1998); Colin Kidd, *British Identities Before Nationalism: Ethnicity and Nationhood in the Atlantic World, 1600–1800* (Cambridge University Press, 1999); Allan Ingram and Elisabeth Détis, eds, *Borders and Boundaries: The European Spectator, vol. 5* (Paul Valéry University, 2004); see also the works of Anthony D. Smith.

The literature of postcolonial theory is equally large. Essential texts are: Frantz Fanon, *The Wretched of the Earth*, trans., Constance Farrington, introduction, Jean-Paul Sartre (Penguin, 1967); and *Black Skin, White Masks*, trans., Charles Lam Markmann (Paladin, 1970); Edward Said, *Orientalism: Western Conceptions of the Orient* (Penguin, 1978; but see 2nd edn, 1995). See also Homi Bhabha, *The Location of Culture* (Routledge, 1994), and the important essays in Henry Louis Gates, Jr., ed., *'Race', Writing, and Difference* (University of Chicago Press, 1986), and Patrick Williams and Laura Chrisman, eds, *Colonial Discourse and Post-Colonial Theory*

(Harvester Wheatsheaf, 1993). For commentaries, good starting points are: John McLeod, *Beginning Postcolonialism* (Manchester University Press, 2000); Peter Childs and Patrick Williams, *An Introduction to Postcolonial Theory* (Harvester Wheatsheaf, 1997); see also T. Minh-ha Trinh, *Woman, Native, Other: Writing Postcoloniality and Feminism* (Indiana University Press, 1995); Ania Loomba, *Colonialism / Postcolonialism* (Routledge, 1998).

RULING THE WAVES

Further Reading: John Dryden, *Don Sebastian* (1689); Thomas D'Urfey, *A Pindarick Poem on the Royal Navy* (1691); Sir Josiah Child, *A New Discourse of Trade* (1698); John Dennis, *Liberty Asserted* (1704); Henry Needler, *A Sea-Piece* (1711); Daniel Defoe, *The General History of Trade* (1713); Ambrose Philip, *The Briton* (1722); Edward Young, *The Ocean: An Ode* (1728), *Imperium Pelagi. A Naval Lyric* (also entitled *The Merchant. An Ode on the British Trade and Navigation*) (1729/1730); James Thomson, *The Seasons* (1726–30), *Liberty* (1735–36), *The Castle of Indolence* (1748); Richard Glover, *London: or, The Progress of Commerce* (1739); David Mallet, *Mustapha* (1739); John Shebearre, *Letters to the People of England* (1755–57); John Dyer, *The Fleece* (1757); Edward Gibbon, *The Decline and Fall of the Roman Empire* (1776–88).

In addition to the work of Armitage, Brown (2001), Colley (1992), Greene, Koebner, Pagden, Wilson (1995), see: John Brewer, *The Sinews of Power: War, Money and the English State, 1688–1783* (Unwin Hyman, 1989); Howard Weinbrot, *Britannia's Issue: The Rise of British Literature from Dryden to Ossian* (Cambridge University Press, 1993); Laura Brown, *The Ends of Empire: Women and Ideology in Early Eighteenth-Century English Literature* (Cornell University Press, 1993); Bridget Orr, *Empire on the English Stage, 1660–1714* (Cambridge University Press, 1994); Peter Miller, *Defining the Common Good: Empire, Religion and Philosophy in Eighteenth-Century Britain* (Cambridge University Press, 1994); Christine Gerrard, *The Patriot Opposition to Walpole: Politics, Poetry, and National Myth, 1725–1742* (Oxford University Press, 1994); Bruce McLeod, *The Geography of Empire in English Literature, 1580–1745* (Cambridge University Press, 1999); Suvir Kaul, *Poems of Nation, Anthems of Empire: English Verse in the Long Eighteenth Century* (University Press of Virginia, 2000).

ATLANTIC COLONIES

THE WEST INDIES

Further reading: Edward Ward, *A Trip to Jamaica* (1698); John Gay, *Polly* (1729, not staged until 1777 by George Colman); Charles Leslie, *New History of Jamaica* (1740); Samuel Keimer, *Caribbeana* (1741); Teresa Constantia Phillips, *An Apology for the Conduct of Mrs T. C. Phillips* (1748–49); Samuel Martin, *An Essay on Plantership* (1750); John Hill, *Adventures of Mr. George Edwards, A Creole* (1751); James Grainger, *The Sugar Cane: A Poem, In Four Books* (1764); Sarah Scott, *The History of Sir George Ellison*

(1766); Richard Cumberland, *The West-Indian* (1771); George Mackenzie, *Julie de Roubigné* (1777); George Colman, *Inkle and Yarico: An Opera* (1787); Thomas Bellamy, *The Benevolent Planters* (1789).

In addition to Wilson (2003), essays in *OHBE II, Global, New Imperial History*, see: Wylie Sypher, 'The West-Indian as a "Character" in the Eighteenth Century', *Studies in Philology*, 39 (1939); Richard S. Dunn, *Sugar and Slaves: The Rise of the Planter Class in the English West-Indies* (University of North Carolina Press, 1972); Peter Hulme, *Colonial Encounters: Europe and the Native Caribbean 1492–1797* (Methuen, 1986); Jack P. Greene, 'Changing Identity in the British Caribbean: Barbados as a Case Study', in Canny and Pagden, eds, *Colonial Identity* (1987); Michael Craton, 'Reluctant Creoles: The Planters' World in the British West Indies', in Bailyn and Morgan, eds, *Strangers* (1991).

THE AMERICAN COLONIES AND THE AMERICAN REVOLUTION

Further reading: Daniel Defoe, *Colonel Jack* (1722); George Berkeley, 'On the Prospect of Planting Arts and Learning in America' (1726); John Oldmixon, *The British Empire in America* (1741); Charlotte Lennox, *Harriet Stuart* (1751); Edward Kimber, *The History of the Life and Adventures of Mr. Anderson* (1754); Peter Williamson, *French and Indian Cruelty* (1757; but 5th edn considerably enlarged, 1762); Unca Eliza Winkfield, *The Female American* (1767); Oliver Goldsmith, *The Deserted Village* (1770); Josiah Tucker, *Four Tracts and Two Sermons on Political and Commercial Subjects* (1774); William Robertson, *History of America* (1777); Richard Price, *Observations of the Nature of Civil Liberty* (1776); Jonathan Carver, *Travels Through Interior Parts of North America* (1778–79); John Dodge, 'A Narrative of the capture and treatment of John Dodge, by the English, at Detroit', in *The Remembrancer* (1779); Samuel Jackson Pratt, *Emma Corbett; or the Miseries of Civil War* (1780). See also *The Papers of Benjamin Franklin*, ed., Leonard W. Labaree *et al.* 36 vols (Yale University Press, 1959–2001), and Martin Kallich, *British Poetry and the American Revolution: A Bibliographical Survey of Books and Pamphlets, Journals and Magazines, Newspapers, and Prints, 1755–1800*, 2 vols (Whitston, 1988).

In addition to Colley (1992 and 2002), Greene, Koebner, Marshall and Williams, Miller, Pagden, Wahrman, Wilson (1995), essays in *OHBE II*, see: Robert Bechtold Heilman, *America in English Fiction, 1760–1800: The Influences of the American Revolution* (Louisiana State University Press, 1937); Richmond P. Bond, *Queen Anne's American Kings* (Clarendon Press, 1952); Michael Zuckerman, 'Identity in British America; Unease in Eden', in Canny and Pagden, *Colonial Identity* (1987); James H. Merrell, ' "The Customs of our Country": Indians and Colonists in Early America', in Bailyn and Morgan, eds, *Strangers* (1991); Joseph Roach, *Cities of the Dead: Circum-Atlantic Performance* (Columbia University Press, 1996); Stephen Conway, *The War of American Independence* (Edward Arnold, 1995); Eliga H. Gould, *The Persistence of Empire: British Political Culture in the Age of American Revolution* (University of North Carolina Press, 2000).

LOOKING TO THE ORIENT

Further reading: Paul Rycaut, *The History of the Turks* (1700); Nicholas Rowe, *Tamerlane* (1701); Delariviere Manley, *Almyna: or, the Arabian Vow* (1707); Antoine Galland, trans., *Arabian Nights Entertainment: Consisting of One Thousand and One Stories* (1714–17); George Sale, trans., *The Koran* (1734), *Lives and Memorable Actions of many Illustrious Persons of the Eastern Nations* (1739); Anon., *The Lady's Drawing Room* (1744); John Zephaniah Holwell, *A Genuine Narrative of the Deplorable Deaths of the English Gentlemen and others, who were suffocated in the Black Hole in Fort William, Calcutta* (1758); Samuel Johnson, *Rasselas, Prince of Abyssinia* (1759); Anon. *The Nabob: Or, Asiatic Plunderers* (1773); Elizabeth Inchbald, *The Mogul Tale, Or, The Descent of the Balloon* (1784), *Such Things Are; A Play in Five Acts* (1788); William Beckford, *Vathek* (1786); Mariana Starke, *The Sword of Peace* (1788); William Thomson, *Memoirs of the Late War in Asia* (1788); Phebe Gibbes, *Hartly House, Calcutta* (1789); Eliza Fay, *Original Letters from India, 1779–1815* [unpublished until 1925]; Sake Dean Mahomet, *The Travels of Dean Mahomet, a Native of Patne in Bengal* (1794).

In addition to Aravamudan, Colley (2002), Marshall and Williams, essays in *OHBE II, Global, New Imperial History*, see: Percival Spear, *The Nabobs: A Study of the Social Life of the English in 18th Century India* (Oxford University Press, 1963); Rozina Visram, *Ayahs, Lascars and Princes: Indians in Britain, 1700–1947* (Pluto, 1986); Sara Suleri, *The Rhetoric of English India* (University of Chicago Press, 1992); Felicity Nussbaum, *Torrid Zones: Maternity, Sexuality, and Empire in Eighteenth-Century English Narratives* (Johns Hopkins University Press, 1995); Kate Teltscher, *India Inscribed: European and British Writing on India, 1600–1800* (Oxford University Press, 1995); Jyotsna G. Singh, *Colonial Narratives/Cultural Dialogues: 'Discoveries' of India in the Language of Colonialism* (Routledge, 1996); Sudipta Sen, *Empire of Free Trade: The East India Company and the Making of the Colonial Marketplace* (University of Pennsylvania Press, 1998); Robert Markely, *The Far East and the English Imagination 1600–1730* (Cambridge University Press, 2006); see also the many writings by P.J. Marshall on India in the eighteenth century.

ANOTHER NEW EDEN

Further reading: Woodes Rogers, *A Cruizing Voyage Round the World* (1712); Daniel Defoe, *A New Voyage Round the World* (1725); George Shelvocke, *A Voyage Round the World by Way of the Great South Sea* (1726); George Forster. *A Voyage Round the World, in his Britannic Majesty's Sloop, Resolution* (1777); Johann Reinhold Forster, *Observations Made During a Voyage Round the World* (1778); George Keate, *An Account of the Pelew Islands* (1788). See also, J. C. Beaglehole, ed., *The Journals of Captain Cook*, 3 vols (Cambridge University Press for the Hakluyt Society, 1955–65) [vol. I Voyage of Endeavour; vol. II Voyage of Resolution and Adventure; vol. III Voyage of Resolution and Discovery]; J. C. Beaglehole, ed., *The Journal of Joseph Banks*, 2 vols (Public Library of New South Wales, 1962).

As well as Marshall and Williams, Wilson (2003), essays in *Global, New Imperial History*, see: Michael Alexander, *Omai: Noble Savage* (Collins and Harvill, 1977);

Marshall Sahlins, *Islands Of History* (Chicago University Press, 1985); Gananath Obeyesekere, *The Apotheosis of Captain Cook: European Mythmaking in the Pacific* (Princeton University Press, 1992); 'The South Pacific in the Eighteenth Century: Narratives and Myths', eds, Jonathan Lamb, Robert P. Maccubbin, and David F. Morrill, special edition of *Eighteenth-Century Life*, 18,3 (1994); Neil Rennie, *Far-Fetched Facts: The Literature of Travel and the Idea of the South Seas* (Clarendon Press, 1995); Glyndwr Williams, *The Great South Sea: English Voyages and Encounters, 1570–1750* (Yale University Press, 1997); Jonathan Lamb, *Preserving the Self in the South Seas, 1680–1840* (Chicago University Press, 2001).

MARKERS OF DIFFERENCE

Further reading: (of course, 'difference' is not limited to the texts in this section only): William Snelgrave, *A New Account of Some Parts of Guinea, and the Slave-Trade* (1734); John Aitkins, *A Voyage to Guinea, Brasil, and the West-Indies* (1735); David Hume 'Of National Characters', *Essays: Moral, Political and Literary* (1742, and see changes by 1758 edition); John Mitchell, 'Essay on the Causes of the Different Colours of People in Different Climates', Royal Society, *Philosophical Transactions, 1744*, vol. 9 (1809); Oliver Goldsmith, 'A Comparative View of Races and Nations' (1760); Adam Ferguson, *Essay on the History of Civil Society* (1767); John Millar, *The Origin of the Distinction of Ranks* (1771; compare with changes in 3rd edn, 1781); Henry Home, Lord Kames, *Six Sketches on the History of Man* (1774); Samuel Johnson, *Journey to the Western Islands of Scotland* (1775); Georges Louis Leclerc, Comte de Buffon, *Natural History: General and Particular* (from 1749; trans., 1780–85); Thomas Clarkson, *Essay on the Slavery and Commerce of the Human Species, Particularly the African* (1786); Samuel Stanhope Smith, *Essay on the Causes of the Variety of Complexion and Figure in the Human Species* (1787).

See also: Daniel Defoe, *Robinson Crusoe* (1719); *The Farther Adventures of Robinson Crusoe* (1719); Jonathan Swift, *Gulliver's Travels* (1726); William Chetwood, *The Voyages, Travels, and Adventures of William Owen* (1736); Isaac Bickerstaff, *The Padlock* (1768); Henry Bate, *The Blackamore Wash'd White* (1776); George Colman, *Inkle and Yarico; An Opera* (1787).

See the bibliography under *Empire and Identity*, above. In addition, see: Arthur O. Lovejoy, *The Great Chain of Being: the Study of the History of an Idea* (Harvard University Press, 1936); Wylie Sypher, *Guinea's Captive Kings: British Anti-Slavery Literature of the Eighteenth Century* (Octagon, 1969); Maximilian E. Novak and Edward Dudley, eds, *The Wild Man Within* (Pittsburgh University Press, 1972); Ronald Meek, *Social Science and the Ignoble Savage* (Cambridge University Press, 1976); Hayden White, *Tropics of Discourse: Essays in Cultural Criticism* (Johns Hopkins University Press, 1978); Peter Fryer, *Staying Power: The History of Black People in Britain* (Pluto, 1984); Mary Louise Pratt, *Imperial Eyes: Travel Writing and Transculturation* (Routledge, 1992); Peter Hulme, 'Black, Yellow, and White in St. Vincent: Moreau de Jonne's Carib Ethnography' in *Global*.

THE BLACK ATLANTIC

Further reading: Francis Williams, ''Carmen, or, an Ode' in Edward Long, *A History of Jamaica* (1774); Julius Soubise, 'Ode', in anon., *Nocturnal Revels: or the History of King's Place and other Modern Nunneries*, vol.II (1779); John Marrant, *A Narrative of the Lord's Wonderful Dealings with John Marrant, a Black* (1785); Olaudah Equiano, *The Interesting Narrative of the Life of Olaudah Equiano, or Gustavus Vassa, The African* (1789). See also, Paul Edwards and David Dabydeen, eds, *Black Writers in Britain, 1760–1890* (Edinburgh University Press, 1991) and Vincent Carretta, ed., *Unchained Voices: An Anthology of Black Authors in the English-Speaking World of the Eighteenth Century* (University Press of Kentucky, 1996).

While there is a huge literature about slavery and also abolitionism (which can be traced through other bibliographies), the selection here focuses upon the writings of the 'Black Atlantic'. In addition to Aravamudan, Fryer, Nussbaum (2003), see: Folarin Shyllon, *Black People in Britain, 1555–1833* (Oxford University Press, 1977); Paul Edwards and James Walvin, *Black Personalities in the Era of the Slave Trade* (Louisiana State University Press, 1983); Henry Louise Gates, Jr., *The Signifying Monkey: A Theory of African-American Literary Criticism* (Oxford University Press, 1988); Paul Gilroy, *The Black Atlantic: Modernity and Double Consciousness* (Verso, 1993); Markman Ellis, *The Politics of Sensibility: Race, Gender and Commerce in the Sentimental Novel* (Cambridge University Press, 1996); Helena Woodard, *African-British Writings in the Eighteenth Century: The Politics of Race and Reason* (Greenwood, 1999); essays in Vincent Carretta and Philip Gould, eds, *Genius in Bondage: Literature of the Early Black Atlantic* (University Press of Kentucky, 2001); Vincent Carretta, 'Questioning the Identity of Oloadah Equiano' in *Global*.

GENDER AND SEXUALITY

Of course, these issues are imbricated within the categories above. Some texts not already mentioned: Thomas D'Urfey, *A Commonwealth of Women* (1686); Aphra Behn, *Oroonoko; or the History of the Royal Slave* (1688); Thomas Southern, *Oroonoko: A Tragedy, in Five Acts* (1695); Anon. *Bonduca, or, The British Heroine* (1696); Samuel Richardson, *Pamela, Part II* (1741); John Hawksworth, *Oroonoko, A Tragedy* (1759); 'Mrs. Crisp' [Elizabeth Marsh], *The Female Captive: A Narrative of the Facts which Happened in Barbary in the Year 1756* (1769); Anon. *An Epistle from Mr. Banks, voyager, monster-hunter, and amaroso, to Oberea, Queen of Otaheite* (1773); [Major John Scott] *An Epistle from Oberea, Queen of Otaheite, to Joseph Banks, Esq.* (1774); Richard Brinsley Sheridan, *The Camp* (1778); Elizabeth Craven, *Journey through the Crimea to Constantinople* (1789); Elizabeth Hamilton, *The Letters of a Hindoo Rajah* (1789). See also, Frank Felsenstein, ed., *English Trader, Indian Maid: Representing Gender, Race, and Slavery in the New World: An Inkle and Yarico Reader* (Johns Hopkins University Press, 1999).

As well as Brown (1993), Hulme (1986), Nussbaum (1995 and 2003), Pratt, Wilson (1995 and 2003), essays in *Global*, *New Imperial History*, see: Moira Ferguson, *Subject to Others: British Women Writers and Colonial Slavery, 1670–1834* (Routledge, 1992);

Margo Hendricks, ed., *Women, 'Race' and Writing in the Early Modern Period* (Routledge, 1994); Elizabeth Bohls, *Women Travel Writers and the Language of Aesthetics, 1716–1818* (Cambridge University Press, 1995); Michèle Cohen, *Fashioning Masculinity: National Identity and Language in the Eighteenth Century* (Routledge, 1996); Diane Dugaw, *Warrior Women and Popular Balladry* (University of Chicago Press, 1996); Nandini Bhattacharya, *Reading the Splendid Body: Gender and Consumerism in Eighteenth-Century British Writing on India* (University of Delaware Press, 1998); Stephen H. Gregg, ' "A Truly Christian Hero": Religion, Effeminacy and Nation in the Writings of the Societies for Reformation of Manners', *Eighteenth-Century Life*, 25,1 (1999).